CW00459526

On Earth as it is in Heaven
GREG RIGBY

RHAEDUS PUBLICATIONS
14 NEW STREET   ST PETER PORT   GUERNSEY

Acknowledgements

The author is very grateful to all his family, friends and colleagues who have helped him during the nine years of research. In particular Charity and Merrilye who acted as self christened donkeys on my expedition around the Cathedrals of Europe, Malcolm McFee who helped me with the computer software, Erica Smith for her constant support and Robert Seaton for getting me started.

Cover design by John Kay

Any copy of this book issued by the publisher as a paperback is sold subject to the condition that it shall not by way of trade or otherwise, be lent, resold, hired out or otherwise circulated without the publisher's prior consent in any form of binding or cover other than that in which it is published and without a similar condition including these words being imposed on a subsequent purchaser.

© 1996 Rhaedus Publications

All Rights Reserved. No part of this publication may be reproduced or transmitted in any form or by any means, electronic or mechanical, including photocopy, recording or any other information storage and retrieval system, without prior permission in writing from the publisher.

British Library Cataloguing-in-Publication Data

A catalogue record for this book is available from the British Library

ISBN 1 900706 00 8

Printed by Saunders and Williams, Belmont, Surrey

Contents

Introduction

My initial interest in the subject matter of this book was aroused when I read *The Mysteries of Chartres Cathedral* by Louis Charpentier. In this book, he claims that '. . . the Benedictine abbeys of the Caux country trace on Earth, the pattern of the Great Bear.' He also claims (on the same page) that certain cathedrals reproduce in their layout relative to one another, the constellation of Virgo. The cathedrals he claims that do this are Reims, Chartres, Amiens, Bayeaux, Evreux, Etampes, Laon and Nôtre Dame de l'Epine. (Fig 1)

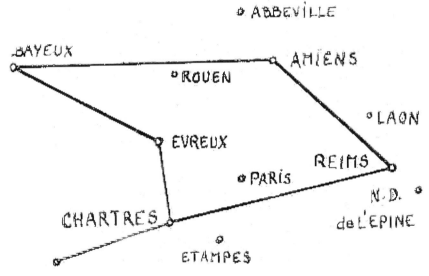

Fig 1 Louis Charpentier's Cathedral plan of Virgo

At about the same time, I read some of the fascinating books about the mysteries surrounding a small village in the South West corner of France, called Rennes-le-Château. One of the pamphlets I read, included a short essay by Siegrid Reznikov, which was entitled *'Astronomie de position et Rennes-le-Château'*. This essay suggests that those who are interested might find 'the pole star' on a map covering the region of Rennes-le-Château. (Fig 2)

This suggestion was intriguing, since I knew that the ancient Paris meridian passes several miles to the East of Rennes-le-Château.

Reading both things at the same time led me to surmise that maybe some of the cathedrals and abbeys around Paris might form the pattern of the Great Bear and if

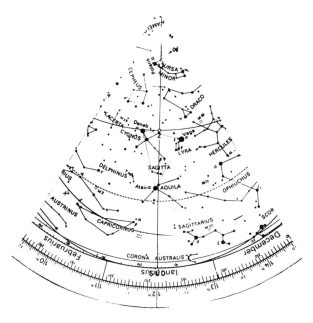

Fig 2 *Carte Céleste de 17 Janvier* as illustrated in the article by Reznikov

this were so, then a connection might exist with Rennes-le-Château through the ancient meridian which goes through the centre of Paris.

I was encouraged in this surmise by Professor Livio Stecchini, who claims that "the Egyptian charts of constellations which depict a figure of a hawk-headed man holding in his outstretched arms a line which ends against the figure of the ox leg representing the constellation of the Great Bear indicates the meridian passing through the pole of the ecliptic." (Fig 3)

Fig 3 Hawk-headed man holding a spear (pointing at the Great Bear constellation) indicates the meridian passing through the pole of the ecliptic according to Stecchini

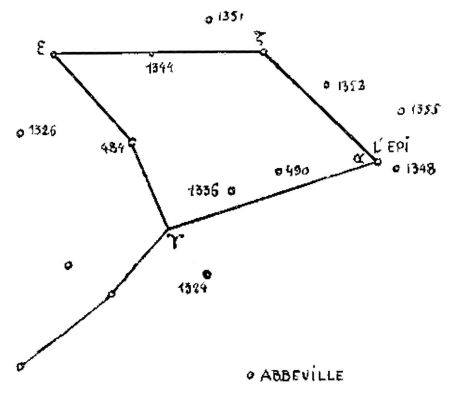

Fig 4 Charpentier's illustration of the constellation of Virgo

When I examined Charpentier's constellation of Virgo, I was frustrated by the fact that his claim is illustrated by a diagram of the constellation (Fig 4) and a plan of the cathedrals (Fig 1) which have very poor correspondence with one another. Then, when I examined the star atlas, I was somewhat surprised to find little similarity between either of these diagrams and the actual constellation of Virgo. (Fig 5)

This inaccuracy led me to do some analysis of basic maps and I discovered that other combinations of cathedrals in northern France would seem to offer a much more accurate representation of the constellation of Virgo than those listed above.

This anomaly in *The Mysteries of Chartres Cathedral* aroused my curiosity and provoked my initial research into the juxtapositions of cathedrals and abbeys in France, the vast bulk of which were built in the eleventh and twelfth centuries under the influence of the Cistercians. Edward Burman in *The Templars, Knights of God* says that "... the Cistercian Order was on the verge of failure when Bernard renounced his knightly career in the spring of 1112 and entered the monastery at Cîteaux. He arrived with 30 fellow knights and the order began to flourish immediately. In the year 1115, when the Count of Troyes gave a parcel of land to found a new house, Bernard was chosen to be superior of the abbey, which took the name Clairvaux. Within a few years the once failing organisation had become what R. W. Southern in *Western Society and the Church in the Middle Ages* described as; 'one of the masterpieces of modern planning'. Under Bernard's leadership, the Order grew from 7 abbeys in 1118 to 328 abbeys by 1152 – an addition of 321 abbeys in 34 years."

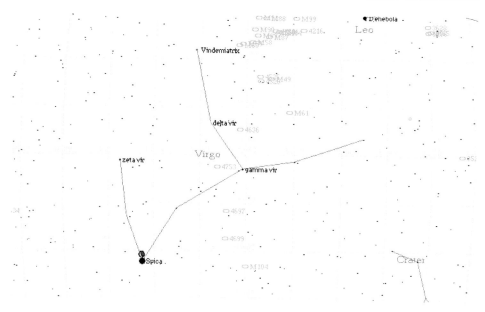

Fig 5 The constellation of Virgo

The Knights Templar, whose establishment and growth was concurrent with that of the Cistercians, was founded between 1111 and 1119. Initially under the patronage of Bernard, who later wrote the Rule, the Templars enjoyed phases of phenomenal growth and are reputed to have amassed considerable wealth before their suppression which commenced in 1307. Their connections with Rennes-le-Château were extensive in that there were a large number of Templar preceptories and other holdings in the immediate area. The strongest connection would seem to have been with the fourth Grand Master, Bertrand de Blanchefort whose ancestral home, Château de Blanchefort, was situated a few miles from the hilltop village of Rennes-le-Château.

Several current books, including the *Sword and The Grail* by Andrew Sinclair and *The Temple and The Lodge* by Michael Baigent and Richard Leigh, link the Knights Templar directly with the birth of Freemasonry.

Gothic architecture was born at Sens Cathedral when the construction of a new cathedral was started on the site of the old one in 1130. However, it is acknowledged that the magnificent new style of architecture must have taken extensive research and planning and there is conjecture that the Templars acquired some special knowledge in Jerusalem during their encampment in 'the stables of Solomon', which they brought back and which was exploited by the Cistercians. Certainly, there is tangible evidence that the architects had an in-depth awareness of Sacred Geometry which they incorporated into the design of each building. Graham Hancock in *The Sign and The Seal,* states, "I was able to confirm my earlier impression that his (St Bernard's) influence on the iconography of Gothic cathedrals had been massive, but indirect, taking the form mainly of groups of sculptures and of stained glass windows that had been inspired by his sermons and writings, often after his death. Indeed, in his lifetime, Bernard had frequently opposed the unnecessary proliferation of images and had stated 'There must be no decoration, only proportion'."

Between 1130 and 1200, in addition to the large number of "new" abbeys, 57

Gothic structures were started in France, most of which were cathedrals in the new grand style.[1] Imagine the resources in terms of planning, excavation, materials, masons, building supervision, labouring etc., which would have been required throughout the country to fulfil such an enormous undertaking. As we will see, not only were the dimensions of each construction carefully planned and executed to some grand design, but also the exact location and orientation of each edifice was precisely chosen, following some precise master plan.

This book will not attempt to provide answers – other than those which the evidence of direct observation provides. As a consequence, many new questions will need to be answered about the incredible facts which have been uncovered in the process of my research. How was the construction brought into being and to what purpose did the architects and planners set about their task? I have no doubt that others who are interested will continue my initial research and find new connections which may in the last analysis throw more light on the subject. However, the fruits of the research do offer possible solutions to some of the questions that have been raised by other writers. But I suspect that the answers, though logical, may not contain sufficient mystery to those in search of an arcane solution.

A note on the technical equipment used.

When plotting the orientation of cathedrals and abbeys, I used a heavy magnetic surveying compass manufactured by F Barker & Son Limited of Edenbridge in Kent. The compass is graduated in 1/20 units of a degree, which with the magnified reading glass allows accurate measurement to better than one minute. When measuring the orientation of any building, I took readings down each side of the building, then took an average and adjusted the average for the magnetic declination at that point to obtain the true geographic orientation for the location.[2]

The maps used in my researches were Carte Topographique and Topographische Carte 1:25000, by the Institut Géographique National, in Paris and Bruxelles and by Landesermessungsamt Rheinland-Pfalz. Where I did less accurate visual checks, I used Tactical Pilotage Charts 1:500,000 by the U S Defense Mapping Agency (the only accurate contoured maps that can be obtained at this scale)

The two computer programmes used to chart cathedrals and measure distances were 'Fastcad' and 'Mapinfo' and the location of cathedrals and abbeys were entered on to the computer utilising a digitiser and the direct entry of co-ordinates (where appropriate). The centre and reference point for each cathedral and abbey, was arbitrarily chosen as the intersection between the nave and the transept.

---

[1] Cathedrals were large churches under the direct administration of an archbishop. Basilicas were religious edifices of equal splendour without an archbishop in residence. An abbey was the church and headquarters of an abbot of a religious order.

[2] The magnetic pole does not lie in the same location as the geographic pole. For this reason it is necessary to correct compass readings in order to determine accurate orientations in relation to the geographic pole.

CHAPTER 1

Finding the pointers

My initial work was heuristic, in that I laid out my maps and marked on to them all the most prominent cathedrals and attempted to make a visual check to see if any obvious combinations formed a pattern of Ursa Major – the star constellation pattern we have come to know as The Great Bear or The Plough. It is traditional that The Plough points to Polaris, the Pole Star and that the two stars in The Plough which line up with the Pole Star are known as the pointers. (Fig 6) When searching for groupings of cathedrals which might duplicate the shape of the The Plough, I looked in particular for groupings with pointers which seemed to align with Rennes-le-Château as the position which would represent a possible Pole Star.

One possible combination of pointers I examined, was Sees and Tours which I thought might combine with Noyon and Châlons-sur-Marne to form the body of The Plough. (Fig. 7) This seemed interesting since the line through the cathedrals in Sees and Tours falls 2.5 kilometres to the east of Arques, and 12.5 kilometres to the east of Rennes-le-Château. I did not see this as a problem since the line from the pointers, Marak and Dubhe to fall one degree to the east of Polaris (looking at it), (Fig 8) and I did not know at that stage, the accuracy of any earthly duplicate. However, I rejected

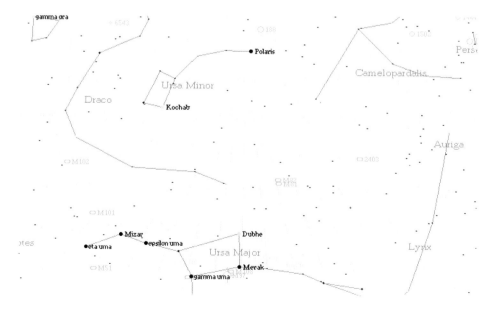

Fig 6 Marak and Dubhe, the 'pointers' which indicate the position of Polaris

this combination because the distance between Sees and Tours is 21.4% of the distance between Sees and Rennes-le-Château whereas the distance between the pointers in the constellation of Ursa Major is only 16% of the distance between the furthest pointer Marak and Polaris. Additionally, I could not find any obvious locations which would correspond to the handle of The Plough.

My second guess based on visual observation was to choose Le Mans and Caen as the pointers, linking with Abbeville and Noyon to form the body of The Plough (Fig 7). This time the line from the cathedral at Caen via the cathedral at Le Mans lay between Arques and Rennes-le-Château and appeared to go exactly through the point 3 kilometres west of Arques, where the tomb in Nicolas Poussin's painting *Les Bergers d'Arcadie – Et in Arcadia Ego* (Fig 9) was reputed to have been located. This line warranted particular examination since the tomb lay very close to the line of the ancient Paris meridian. It was obviously a coincidence that these lines were pointing towards the same place.

However, the fact that lines connecting two different sets of cathedrals crossed 500 kilometres of France ended up within a few kilometres of Rennes-le-Château, was intriguing. Despite this, the Caen – Le Mans line still suffered from the dimensional problems of the Sees – Tours line and there were even fewer locations from which I could locate a handle for my Plough. For these reasons I continued to look for other possibilities.

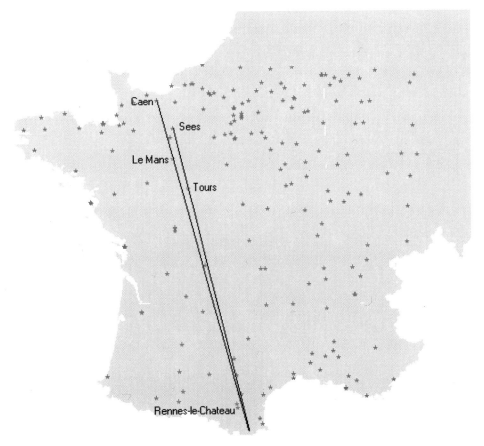

Fig 7 The first trial pointer lines

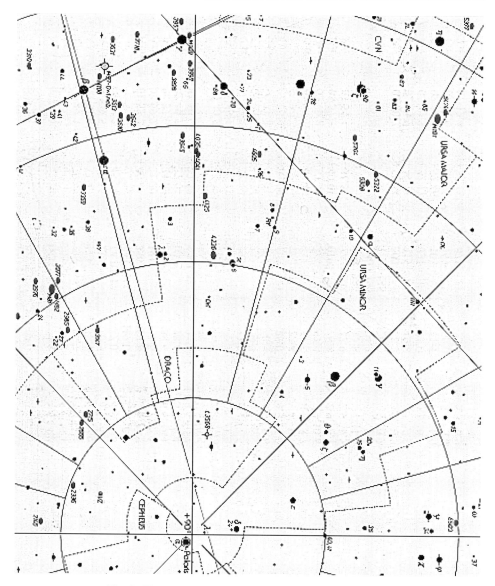

Fig 8 The line from the pointers falls 2° to the east

Amongst the combinations I examined was the line from the cathedral in Rouen via Chartres Cathedral, which appeared to end 5.6 Kilometres from the cathedral in Beziers, many miles from Rennes-le-Château. (Fig 10) This line is truer dimensionally, in that the distance between Chartres and Rouen is 16.2% of the distance from Rouen to Béziers. Additionally, the shape of the body of The Plough when Rouen and Chartres are linked to St Quentin and Epernay (as the best possible locations) gives a more accurate representation of the actual shape of the constellation. Furthermore, it seemed that if I utilised Verdun and Metz, there would be the vague possibility of a handle for The Plough.

The fact that the pointer line ended at Béziers however led me to shelve this option since I wanted to eliminate all the possible links with Rennes-le-Château before researching the other patterns.

Fig 9 The tomb near Arques which is thought to be the tomb in Poussin's *Les Bergers d'Arcadie*

During my attempts to find the perfect alignment, I examined the line from Rennes-le-Château to Chartres Cathedral. I knew that Chartres, more than any other Cathedral, incorporates the same sacred geometry which was used to construct the Great Pyramid at Cheops and that many mysteries surround the dimensions incorporated into its magnificent construction. (see *Gothic Cathedrals and Sacred Geometry* by Alec Tiranti) Additionally, Chartres Cathedral was constructed on an ancient religious site: David Jacobs in his book *Master Builders of the Middle Ages*, says, "According to Christian lore, the (original) Church of Our Lady of Chartres was built a century or more before the birth of the Virgin Mary." Nôtre Dame de Chartres as the most magnicent Gothic Cathedral in France seemed an obvious and compelling first choice for 'Dubhe', the nearest of the two pointers. Moreover, I knew that a precise line from Rennes-le-Château to Chartres Cathedral goes close to the Saint Cecile Basilica in Albi, the building which was started in 1282 after the end of the Albigensian Crusade.

The problem with this line however, was that I could not see an obvious second pointer star to the north of Chartres. You can probably imagine my excitement therefore, when, in what appeared to be close to the correct position, I located an ancient abbey, halfway between Rouen and Les Andeleys, the latter being the reported birthplace of Nicolas Poussin. The Abbey was called Abbaye de Fontaine Guérard.

During one of my Easter holidays I visited the site of the Abbaye de Fontaine Guérard and found the setting tranquil and peaceful.(Fig 11) The abbey was founded in the twelfth century and is currently owned and looked after by the Salvation Army who have an operational centre in the nearby village at Château de Radepont.

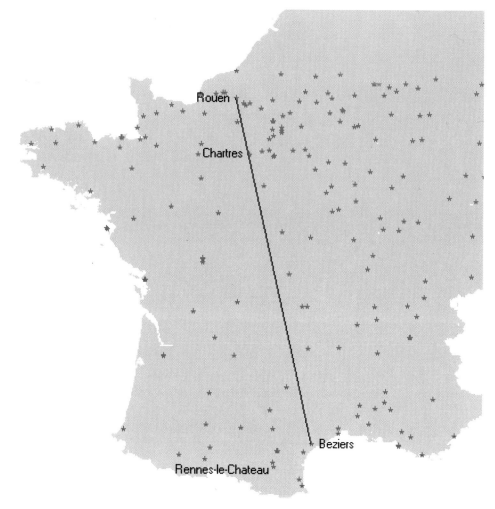

Fig 10 The line from Rouen via Chartres to Béziers

In relation to the actual date of foundation of the abbey, their guide book states; "Certain sources quote the year 1135, others point to as late as 1198. However the period between 1184 and 1190 carries the most support". The official French guide to Cistercian abbeys in France, produced by *'Caisse Nationale des Monuments Historiques et des Sites'* gives the year of foundation as 1132.

The initial construction was a simple priory and its foundation benefited from liberal gifts from Robert White Hands, who owned all the surrounding land and was also the English Earl of Leicester. It also received the support of Gautier de Coutances who was Archbishop of Rouen from 1184 to 1207. The abbey's spiritual beginnings were established by a group of like-minded women who though prayerful did not form part of any formal religious group until they joined the Cistercians in 1207. Significantly, the abbey attracted the support of a number of nationally renowned figures including five successive mediaeval kings from Philippe Auguste to Charles the Good.

Fig 11 Abbaye de Fontaine Guérard

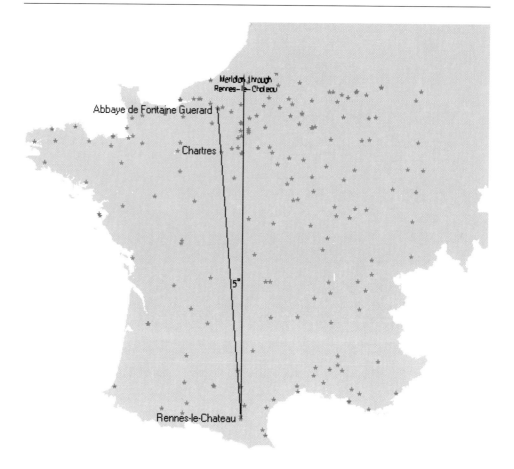

Fig 12 The Rennes-le-Château – Chartres Line lies 5° west of north

The two pieces of information which (at that stage) led me to believe that I had located Marak, the second pointer were not to be found in any of the literature:

Firstly, the guide book shows the abbey church to be lying east-west. However, when checked the actual orientation, I found that the church lies on a line 85° East of North. This was an exciting discovery at the time since it meant that if the Abbaye de Fontaine Guérard was the correct location of the second pointer, then the orientation of the body of the abbey, highlighted by a strange north-south rib in the arches over the apse, was the same as the Rennes-le-Château – Chartres line. i.e., 5° west of North. (Fig 12)

Secondly, the ceiling above the apse had been restored and the ribs in the vaulted ceiling (two of which are mentioned above) form a strange pattern (Fig 13), particularly if one regards the north-south ribs as pointers, as I did. Most of the vaulted ceilings I had seen in other churches, had ribs in some form of regular pattern around the centre. This ceiling has four ribs to the East and two to the West in addition to the north-south ribs already described. The guide book describes the effect as 'giving the illusion of a polygon'.

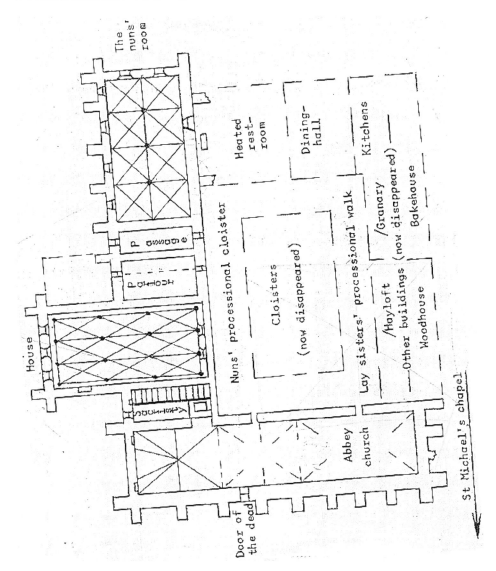

Fig 13 The axis of the abbey lying 5° from a precise east-west line

At the time, the rib pattern appeared to me to be illustrating the juxtaposition of the centre relative to the lines formed by the ribs. This caused me to get excited: I knew the Abbaye de Fontaine Guérard to be surrounded by several prominent cathedrals and abbeys in northern France and became convinced that the ribs over the apse formed a map of the connections with and between these cathedrals.

A sophisticated and accurate computer mapping programme and digitiser which I had recently purchased facilitated the transfer of data from maps on to the computer. This allowed me to plot locations exactly and to measure accurately the distances between points and lines. I was keen to return to my maps and plot the alignments between these cathedrals and (hopefully) confirm the Abbaye de Fontaine Guérard as the northern pointer.

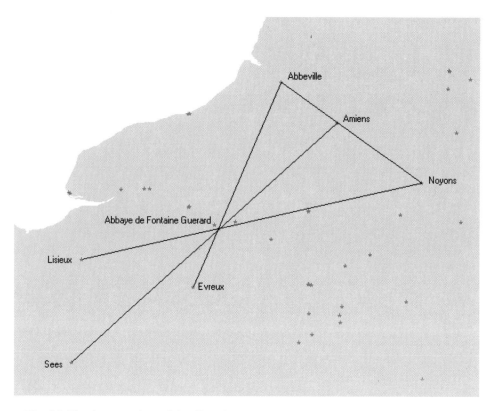

Fig 14 The intersection of the first three lines, south-east of Abbaye de Fontaine Guérard

Back at base, I studied the maps of northern France and I could see that there were possible alignments between prominent cathedrals which would produce a set of lines similar to the rib pattern I had seen at the Abbaye de Fontaine Guérard.

First, I plotted the line between the cathedrals in Evreux and Abbeville and was disappointed to find that it fell 2.985 kilometres east of the Abbaye de Fontaine Guérard at its nearest point. Next, I joined the cathedrals at Amiens and Sees and was surprised to find that this fell 3.62 kilometres south east of the abbey and intersected the first line 3.67 kilometres south east of the abbey's exact location. You can imagine my astonishment when I added the line which joins the cathedrals in Noyon and Lisieux to discover that it fell south of the abbey by 2.714 kilometres and missed the junction of the first two lines by only 770 metres. I checked and rechecked and it was definitely correct. (Fig 14). I had found three lines joining six prominent cathedrals which appeared to duplicate three of the lines in the rib pattern above the ruined Sanctuary of Abbaye de Fontaine Guérard but whose triangle of intersection fell some 3 kilometres south east of the abbey itself. As an aside, whilst plotting these positions I computed that the line from the cathedral at Amiens through the cathedral at Noyon falls within 100 metres of the centre of the cathedral at Châlons-sur-Marne.

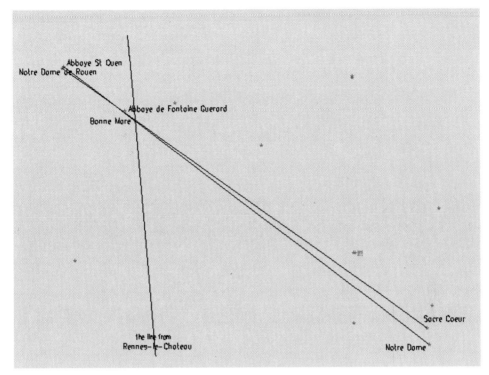

Fig 15 The connections through Rouen and Paris

Having plotted the Amiens to Châlons-sur-Marne line, I went back to the line from Rennes-le-Château via Chartres Cathedral. Incredibly, the extension of this line fell 2.558 kilometres east of the abbey and fell plumb within the triangle formed by the intersection of the other three lines. It now seemed clear that the second pointer was located in the area of these intersections and that my previous inclination towards the Abbaye de Fontaine Guérard had been based more on hope than on scientific analysis.

When I examined the local map carefully, there appeared to be no major building of any significance in the area determined by the intersection of the four lines. Tantalisingly, there is a château half a kilometre away at the south end of Bonne Mare (the nearest hamlet) but my point had been located exactly by the triangle of intersection made by the lines from the various cathedrals, and I was determined not to get sucked into further errors based on wishful thinking. I was intrigued by the name Bonne Mare however and could not help but surmise on its similarity to the Nôtre Dame title given to so many of the cathedrals. In the belief that I had established my point, I continued to search for other connections and was amazed to discover that this incredible set of coincidences did not end with these four lines.

Because Rouen is the nearest place with a magnificent Gothic cathedral, I plotted the line from Nôtre Dame cathedral in Rouen through my newly discovered northern pointer to find that it goes through the Abbaye de Fontaine Guérard and falls close to the centre of the Sacré Coeur basilica in the Montmartre district of Paris. This seemed

Fig 16 Tourbillon Castle overlooking Sion

Fig 17 The church fort at Sion Valère

strange since four of the six cathedrals that had allowed me to find the pointer are dedicated to Nôtre Dame, as is the cathedral in Rouen. I would therefore have expected any alignment through the pointer to have been with Nôtre Dame in Paris. Because of this apparent inconsistency, I carefully plotted the line from Nôtre Dame on the Ile de la Cité back through my pointer position to find that it too went through the site of the Abbaye de Fontaine Guérard but then continued and connected exactly with the magnificent abbey dedicated to St Ouen in Rouen. (Fig 15)

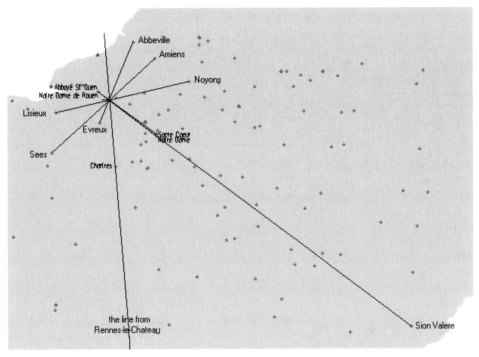

Fig 18 The first 7 lines which pinpointed the Bonne Mare position

In Rouen I had been surprised that there are two such prominent religious edifices in the centre of the city. Now I knew the reason: the abbey dedicated to St Ouen in Rouen is connected to Nôtre Dame in Paris through the point of intersection which was increasingly being confirmed as my northern pointer position.

Another interesting connection with Rouen was uncovered when it became apparent that the lines from Nôtre Dame Cathedral and the Abbaye St Ouen to Valère, the fortress church overlooking Sion in Switzerland both pass through the triangle of intersections near Bonne Mare and also go very close to Nôtre Dame in Paris. Sion is mentioned in Michael Baigent, Richard Leigh & Henry Lincoln's book, *The Messianic Legacy* as the possible location of the modern-day descendants of the Templars. It is also mentioned in a book on Rennes-le-Château by Lionel and Patricia Fanthorpe where they say "it is possible to draw a huge circle whose circumference passes through Reims, Varenne, Toul and Sion in the north-east; another Sion just north of Mont Blanc (my location), Rennes-le-Château and Montségur in the South; St Nazaire, Sion les Mines, Redons and Rennes in the north-west; and Rouen on a bearing of 345° just before the circle is completed in the north". This claim is not validated and my attempts to reproduce the circle through these points proved that it is not possible to do it with any accuracy.

The first time I visited Sion, I was stunned by the spectacular view that greeted me; I travelled 25 kilometres along a flat Alpine valley which is between two and five kilometres wide. As Sion came into view, my eye was drawn immediately to the castle known as Tourbillon rising out of the valley on a hill at the far end of the town. (Fig 16) It is everything that stories of mediaeval knights and damsels in distress bring to mind. Close by is Valère, a second hill which is just big enough to accommodate a church-fortress built in the Gothic style. (Fig 17) The guide book says "*Valère est une église-fort où la population pouvait se réfugier en cas de péril grave. Elle a rang de cathédrale et est très ancienne; certains pensent qu'elle a été construite sur les fondations d'un palais romain. La grande nef actuelle date du XIII siècle*" which translated means; 'Valère is a church-fortress where the population took refuge in situations of grave peril. It has the rank of a cathedral and is very old; some think it was built on the foundations of a Roman Palace. The existing nave dates from the 13th century'.

How was it possible that someone could have planned to link this place so precisely with Nôtre Dame in Paris through the pointer position and on to the Abbaye de St Ouen in Rouen and how were these positions established so accurately?

Not satisfied with the initial seven lines I had located which seemed to pinpoint the pointer position, (Fig 18) I went back to my maps and computer and carried out a thorough quadrant by quadrant analysis to see if I could find any other sets of cathedrals and abbeys with alignments through this same position. It was at this stage that I had to make a decision about the level of accuracy required in order to be able to claim that three buildings are in line with one another: I could not believe that the master builders of the twelfth century could consistently align three buildings within 100 metres (say) of a perfect straight line over distances in excess of 500 kilometres. For this reason, I decided that any churches with a centre point within one kilometre of the line between the centre of two other buildings could be considered to be a recordable alignment. In order to record the accuracy of these recorded alignments, I split them into three groups; those within 100 metres, those that lay between 100 and 250 metres and those between 250 metres and one kilometre. This choice of distances was arbitrary at that stage, but information which became available to me later led me to believe that I had accidentally chosen good criteria for assessing the accuracy of these alignments.

The locations entered on to my computer were the most significant cathedrals and basilicas and the founding Cistercian abbeys in France and Belgium. After a rigorous check involving these positions, I found a further 62 lines connecting locations to the 'Bonne Mare' position. In all therefore, I discovered 68 lines which aligned prominent cathedrals, basilicas and abbeys with the Bonne Mare position, 20 of which connected cathedrals and abbeys on straight lines which were accurate within 100 metres (see appendix 1 for a complete summary). You can probably imagine my incredulity – how could this be so? How could this be possible without anyone knowing about it? Could one choose any position in France and get 68 lines connecting 70 cathedrals, 22 abbeys, 34 basilicas and 4 positions of historical significance to go through that point? I did not think so and carried out an analysis of the random number of accurate alignments one could expect through a chosen point which is detailed in Chapter 5.

This incredible conjunction convinced me that I had hit on one of the most significant discoveries to be uncovered in centuries. I was certain that I had unearthed 'the seven stars' and it was only left for me to prove the other star locations and to then try to answer the most difficult question of all; why?

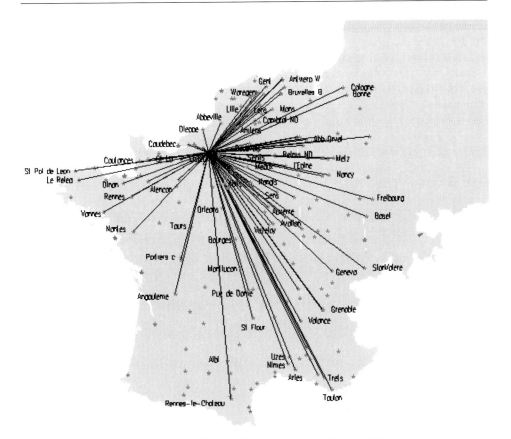

Fig 19 The 68 lines which intersect at Bonne Mare

I had 68 lines converging at the same point (Fig 19): I invite the reader to marvel at the planning and geometrical precision necessary to achieve this. How had it been done? There were no compasses, maps or theodolites to take accurate bearings. The only method available to plot positions and alignments was the one that had been used since ancient times – the stars. I was incredulous. Specific questions which puzzled me in relation to Bonne Mare were:

> Why is there nothing to the north of this point on the line from Rennes-le-Château via Nôtre Dame Cathedral in Chartres?'
> Why is there no cathedral, abbey or similarly spectacular building to mark the spot?'

The most logical answer to the first question is that the planners did not extend the line north of the 'Marak' point because they wanted it to be the northernmost point on this particular line, i.e. it is an 'end' position. This is perhaps confirmed by the fact that 36 of the 61 lines end at Bonne Mare.

The logical possibilities in relation to the second question are either that the master architects of The Plough (assuming I could accurately plot the rest of it) wanted this point and therefore the whole design to be secret, or that there used to be some edifice marking this spot which is now in ruins and hidden in the forest which surrounds the location. I resolved to do some further investigation to determine what, if anything, lies concealed where the Forêt de Bacqueville meets the Bois de Bonnemare.

In the summer of 1992, I visited Criquetuit, the farm which lies close to the Bonne Mare position. The farmer was not aware of any ruins in the woods and as far as I know has not discovered any since then. During my visit, I was interested to find that tours are conducted around Château Bonnemare, the old mansion house which lies just over one kilometre from the point where all the lines intersect. I contacted Monsieur Salmon-Legagneur Balleyguier the owner of the château, who wrote to me to say that he had no knowledge of any ruins within the proximity of the château.

I resolved to obtain and examine some aerial photographs of the area to see whether they would reveal any traces of ancient buildings. As a first stage, I ordered an aerial photograph from the Institut Géographique National but as could have been anticipated, the area in question is covered in trees. Interestingly, the trees in the bottom corner of the adjacent field appeared to form a distinct circle. (Fig 20)

Fig 20 The aerial photograph of the circle near the intersection point

Fig 21 The infra-red photograph of Bonne Mare

When I saw this I debated with myself whether the intersection point should have been 200 metres north-east of the point I had plotted, but without knowing what (if anything) was hidden in the forest, it was impossible to make any definite deductions. I had read of the use of infra-red photography in the determination of ruined sites and was increasingly confident that if any remains of old buildings did exist, that was going to be the only way of locating them. In the early part of 1994, before the spring leaves had formed on the trees I commissioned an infra-red photograph of the area. (Fig 21)

Unfortunately, the trees in the area of the intersection were all evergreens and it was not possible to deduce anything about the area of ground beneath the foliage. The photograph shows no evidence of any buildings in the area which seemed circular on the IGN aerial photograph but the circular shape is still visible. After a brief examination, I was informed by Simon Crutchley, the sitting expert on photographic interpretation at the Royal Commission in Swindon, that there is nothing of any significance in the area of the circle.

Undeterred, I was convinced that the alignments of the cathedrals must be pointing to this location and that any evidence must be hidden in the forest. I therefore resolved to continue with my quest for the seven stars.

CHAPTER 2

The Primary Pointer

During my initial attempts to locate the pointer positions, a factor which influenced my assessment of the possible locations was the relative distances between these locations and Rennes-le-Château, on the one hand, and between the pointers in the constellation of Ursa Major[1] and Polaris on the other. In assessing the likelihood of Chartres and Bonne Mare actually being the pointer positions, I measured the distance between these positions and the distance between Bonne Mare and Rennes-le-Château.

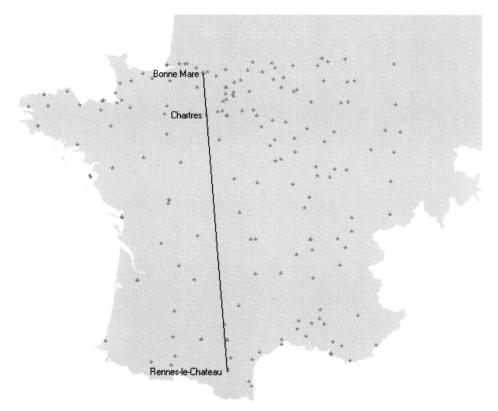

Fig 22 The line from Bonne Mare via Chartres to Rennes-le-Château

---

[1] Ursa Major is the official name of The Great Bear, which is also known as The Big Dipper and The Plough.

Bonne Mare to Rennes le Château is 715 kilometres and Bonne Mare to the centre of Nôtre Dame de Chartres is 99 kilometres – i.e. 13.85% of the total distance. This compares with 15.65% when the distance between the two pointer stars in Ursa Major is taken as a percentage of the distance between the furthest pointer and the pole star. If Chartres was to be the primary pointer, Dubhe, it meant either that the earthly designers had not stuck rigidly to the heavenly dimensions, or that I was wrong to assume that Rennes-le-Château represents the Polaris position. (Fig 22) Despite this difference in proportionality, I believed Chartres to be the location I was searching for. It seemed too important a place to be directly on the line between Rennes-le-Château and Bonne Mare and not be the primary pointer.

The current cathedral in Chartres was consecrated on 17th October 1260. It had been completely rebuilt since 1194 when a fire destroyed everything of the old cathedral except for its magnificent crypts, the newly completed western towers and the Royal Portal. This period was significant in the history of Chartres as the Chartres Cathedral School, one of the foremost scholastic institutions of mediaeval Europe was at its zenith: the school's influence on the design and construction of the new cathedral may well have been significant. Its reputation had been established by Fulbert who ran the school between 990 and 1028 and who was known as the 'Venerable Socrates of the Chartres Academy'. Amongst his successors was the neo-Platonist Bernard of Chartres (1119–1124) and Thierry, his younger brother who wrote "Philosophy has two principal instruments, the

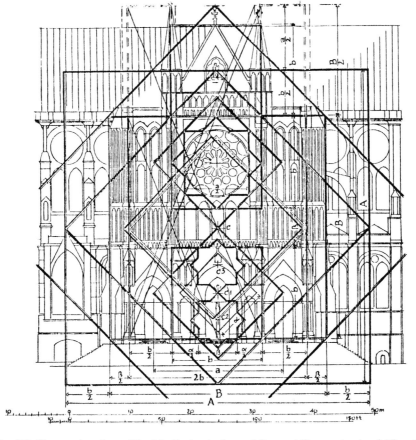

Fig 23 Illustration from 'Gothic Cathedrals and Sacred Geometry by A Tiranti

mind and its expression. The mind is enlightened by the Quadrivium (arithmetic, geometry, astronomy and music). Its expression, elegant, reasonable and ornate, is provided by the Trivium – (grammar, rhetoric and dialectic)." Several years after the death of Thierry, these seven disciplines, accompanied by those authors who best illustrated each, were sculpted on the Royal Portal of Chartres Cathedral.

The new cathedral incorporated a fundamentally new architecture which we have come to know as 'Gothic'. Lofted ceilings and arches, ribbed vaulting, flying buttresses and a harmony of design, which incorporates Sacred Geometry, produced architectural and iconographic unity. (Fig 23) It is certainly one of the foremost Gothic cathedrals in existence and has a mystery and majesty which attracts pilgrims and tourists from all over the world. (Fig 24)

Fig 24 Detail over the entrance to the Royal Portal at Chartres Cathedral

It was under Fulbert that the crypt, still the largest in France was completed. The dimensions of the current cathedral, except for the elevation and the addition of a very wide transept, were determined by the crypt and the other parts of the construction that had survived the catastrophe of 1194. This means that a large part of the geometry of the plan of the cathedral was established between 1020 and 1024 when the crypt was laid.

When I visited Chartres, I accurately computed the orientation of the nave to lie 47° east of north (magnetic) which is 44° 16′ east of north (geographic). This orientation did not seem significant and did not indicate any connection with the Rennes-le-Château to Chartres line which lies 5° west of north (geographic). Whilst there, I also noted that an excavation of Gallo-Roman ruins was in progress immediately next to the cathedral. Back with my computer, I examined the line of orientation carefully and could find no cathedral or abbey which lay along the line. I was convinced that there must be some significance to the angle and line of orientation since I could not believe that the architects, who had incorporated so many other messages into the dimensions and proportion of the cathedral would not have chosen the lie of the cathedral carefully. At this point in my reasearch I was not able to find the reason for this otherwise strange bearing of 4416′. The nearest line of any apparent significance is the Chartres – St Quentin Line which has a bearing of 41°. I examined the line through the transepts (which has a bearing of 134° 16′) in the hope that it may connect with places of significance. The nearest connections I found were the line from Chartres to Cluny which lies at 132° 30′ and the line from Glastonbury to Chartres at 138°. It was much later before the reason for this strange angle of orientation became apparent.

Fig 25 The star burst picture made by the lines

Since I had neither been able to show an exact correspondence with the pointer positions in the constellation, nor had I found any significance in the orientation of the cathedral itself, I decided that, like Bonne Mare, it would be necessary to find a series of cathedrals and abbeys which align with Nôtre Dame de Chartres to point to its position. It was at this point that I realised that the set of lines intersecting at Bonne Mare gave the stylised appearance of a star: I have strong childhood recollections of pictures of the Bethlehem Star which has rays of light shooting out from a bright centre. The lines intersecting at the pointer position were not there merely to illustrate the position, but were an extraordinary way of illustrating the position as a star. (Fig 25) To proceed, I had to determine whether it would be possible to find a similar set of accurately intersecting lines emanating from the centre of Nôtre Dame de Chartres.

Whilst attempting to locate the pointer positions visually, I had become aware of the following: when measured accurately, the line from Nôtre Dame in Rouen to St Nazaire in Béziers, misses the centre of Nôtre Dame de Chartres by 0.923 kilometres.

The next intersection was obtained by taking a line from the cathedral in Chartres through the centre of the Sacré Coeur basilica in Paris (Fig 26) (which had proved to be an important basilica when making the connections to Bonne Mare) to St Gervais and St Protais, the cathedral at Soissons.

Fig 26 The Sacré Coeur basilica in Paris

Fig 27 The star pattern on the sanctuary floor of the cathedral in Soissons

Soissons is one of the oldest Christian centres in France and is reputed to have had a bishop from about 300 AD. On the sanctuary floor is a large star pattern (Fig 27)

With my straight edge lying east – west, I plotted a series of positions on the map which I later confirmed on the computer. Even with a visual scan, I could see that there were going to be a lot of connections:

Sees – Chartres – Sens
Le Mans – Chartres – Reims
Chartres – Dourdan – Metz
Chartres – Melun – Nangis
Brest – Dinan – Chartres – Etampes
Coutances – Chartres – Bern
Caen – Chartres – Vezelay

As the many connections to Chartres unfolded, I became more and more excited. On and on I went until after lengthy and careful analysis I had located 66 lines which go through Nôtre Dame in Chartres – 13 with alignments with 100 metres and 11 with alignments between 100 and 250 metres. (see the appendix 2 for a complete list)

This time, I had found the full star burst picture with rays of varying lengths around a full 360 degrees. (Fig 28)

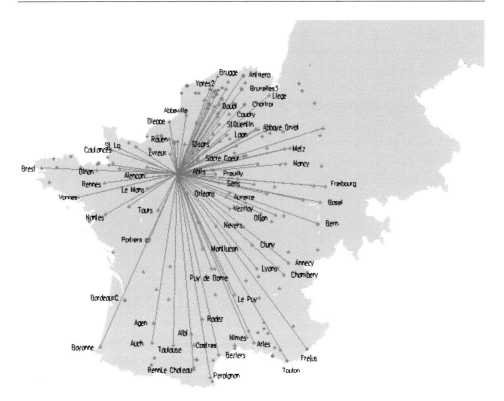

Fig 28 The pattern of lines which intersect at Nôtre Dame de Chartres

The 66 lines connect 76 cathedrals, 21 founding abbeys, 25 basilicas and 5 places of historical significance. It was a better result than I could ever have anticipated and included alignments with some of the earliest and most significant abbeys at La Ferté, Preuilly, Port Royal, Cluny, St Michel, Clairvaux, Savigny, Trois-Fontaines, Mortemer, Vaucelles and Acey.

I was on the point of discovering what must rank as the greatest construction of all time. Should it be possible to locate the other five points and thus complete the earthly constellation and establish that they too were identified by the precise positioning of such a large number of magnificent cathedrals and abbeys, the magnitude of planning endeavour and achievement would outrank any of the seven ancient wonders of the world.

From the beginning, I had toyed with the idea that Bernard de Clairvaux was central to this whole plan. He had entered the abbey at Cîteaux at the age of twenty one. At that time the whole monastery was working on sacred Hebrew texts. Four years later, Hugues de Champagne gave land in the Forest of Bar-sur-Aube to the abbey at Cîteaux. The abbot, Etienne Harding appointed the young Bernard to found the new abbey, which he duly did and which he named Clairvaux. Hugues de Champagne, together with Bernard and Hugues de Payens were central to the establishment of the Order of the Poor Knights of Christ and the Temple of Solomon (the Knights Templar). It is possible that Hugues de Champagne's quest for the Holy Grail (which may well have been a search for the Ark of the Covenant) coupled with the intellect and motivation of Bernard de Clairvaux may hold some key to this incredible construction.

In the summer of 1991 I had visited Clairvaux Abbey in le Val d'Absinthe and found that it had been converted into a prison by Napoleon in 1808. Unfortunately, the abbey church was destroyed between 1812 and 1819 so that its exact location must be pinpointed from lithographs and etchings. The first abbey was founded in 1115 by St Bernard and existed until 1135 when a second and grander abbey was constructed some 500 metres from the first location.

I realised that if the alignment of Clairvaux was important, then this displacement of the abbey location may have been significant: When plotting the lines through Nôtre Dame in Chartres, I discovered one which made my pulse quicken: the line from the abbey at Mont St Michel through Chartres to the location of the abbey church at Clairvaux. According to the computer, this line was out of alignment by 19 metres, i.e. it was so accurate that the centres of the three locations are within the limits of error set by the maps and my ability to plot the co-ordinates.

Most visitors to Normandy have taken the trip to see the abbey rising out of the sea at Mont St Michel. Like Valère at Sion, it is spectacular and breathtaking, leading one to question the imagination and force of will which led someone to sponsor such an awesome and splendid construction. (Fig 29)

I could not help but wonder whether Bernard changed the location of the new abbey at Clairvaux in order to create this exact alignment. The accuracy of this line led me to wonder whether there may be alignments from Clairvaux to one or more of the

Fig 29 Mont St Michel off the coast of Normandy

other seven stars of the earthly Plough. I decided that if I could find the positions of each of the seven stars and then find a link between some of them and the abbey at Clairvaux, that in turn might give me some clue to St Bernard's role in the entire construction.

The discovery that the second Clairvaux abbey is so accurately aligned with Mont St Michel and Chartres led me to suspect that St Bernard must have been aware of the grand construction, even if he was not the instigator. If the abbey was rebuilt in the new position, in order to create a more accurate alignment, this would prove conclusively that the person behind the displacement believed the overall plan to be of some significance. I was able to deduce that the method originally used to plot the ground position of the first abbey resulted in an error of 500 metres. In reality, St Bernard was away from Clairvaux when the planning of the second abbey was instigated. This implies that someone other than St Bernard found the error and that this other person influenced the choice of location for Clairvaux II. In turn, the broader implications of the Mont St Michel – Clairvaux line are clear: The architects of the total plan to reproduce the constellation of Ursa Major on the ground must have planned it prior to 1125 when the first abbey at Clairvaux was constructed.

On the basis of these facts, I went back to the list of alignments through Bonne Mare to see what connection I had located through Clairvaux. I found that the line from the centre of the abbey at Clairvaux to the centre of Nôtre Dame in Caudebec missed Bonne Mare by 123 metres. The basilica in Caudebec was built in 1426 and largely restored in the second world war but is a famous example of Gothic flamboyance. Caudebec-en-Caux itself is a small town which claims Roman history and which occupies a strategic position on the north bank of the Seine.

Another connection which intrigued me was the one between Nôtre Dame Cathedral in Evreux through Chartres to the Roman ruins at Puy de Dome west of Clermont-Ferrand. This was one of several accurate connections which did not appear to align with a current religious edifice and whose significance dated to a period well before the 11th & 12th centuries. Gregory of Tours in ‘*The History of the Francs’* says *“. . . he (Chroc) set fire to the Temple which was called in the Gallic language Vasso Galatae, tearing it down and completely destroying it. It had been constructed with great skill and was solidly built, for it had a double wall, the inner one made of small stones and the outer one of great squared masonry. Altogether this wall was thirty feet thick. It was decorated inside with marble and mosaics; the floor of the building was paved with marble and the roof was covered with lead.”* The footnote in Lewis Thorpe's translation says 'The site of the Gallic shrine called Vasso Galatae has been identified with that on Puy de Dome of Mercurius Dumias, a Roman God adapted from the Celtic Teutates.' (Fig 30)

Already I was making mental notes about the possible timing of this earthly 'Great Bear' and each new piece of information I uncovered led me to believe that I would need to look to a period much earlier than the 12th Century to discover those who had formulated this magnificent plan.

Despite the lack of precise correspondence with the dimensions of the constellation of Ursa Major and the lack of anything in the orientation or the design of Chartres Cathedral itself which shouts "I am Dubhe, the pointer star", I was convinced that I had identified the correct location: the line from Clairvaux together with the lines I had already plotted and the line from Rennes-le-Château meant that I had located 66 lines connecting 116 prominent cathedrals, abbeys and basilicas together with 5 locations of historical significance all of which intersected at Chartres Cathedral. This massive weight of evidence was sufficient to convince me that Nôtre Dame de Chartres

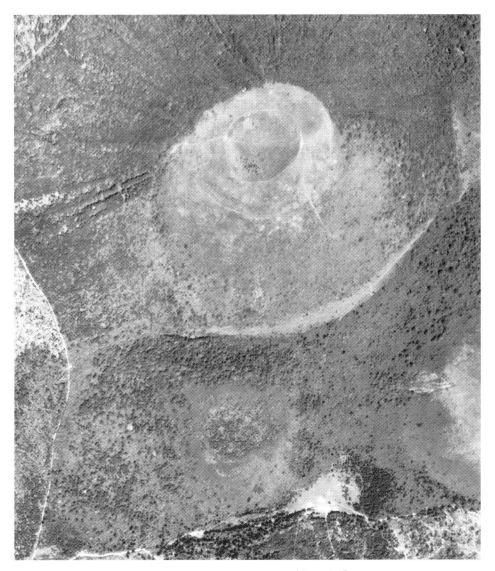

Fig 30 An aerial photograph of Puy de Dome

is the southern pointer and that the two positions I had located, form 'The Pointers' of an earthly 'Great Bear' with Rennes-le-Château in the 'Polaris' position.

Interestingly, I found nothing in the cathedral itself which tells of or even hints of a connection with the seven stars. There are pictures in the stained glass windows and a variety of carvings and statues in the porches, doorways and towers which tell many stories of religious tradition and contain a variety of hidden messages and philosophical ideas. Graham Hancock, in his book '*The Sign and The Seal*' says, "*I began to see that this vast structure was indeed a kind of 'book in stone' – an intricate and provocative opus that could be approached and understood at several different levels.*"

Given this wealth of information contained in the cathedral dimensions and ornamentation which has been the source of considerable literature, it is inconceivable that the weavers of stories and depictors of Biblical texts would not have included some-

Fig 31 Taurus from the zodiac window – early 13th century

where a reference to 'the seven stars', had they been aware of it. The only astronomical reference is in one of the many original stained glass windows which depicts the signs of the Zodiac with Christ Chronocrator at the apex of the window seated between the Greek letters Alpha and Omega.(Fig 31) If I am correct that there is no reference to Ursa Major in the design and adornments of the cathedral, then no one in Chartres Cathedral School knew of the existence of the grand plan and they were certainly not aware of the significance of any such plan in the construction of the cathedral itself. If this supposition is accurate but (as we have deduced) Bernard de Clairvaux (or someone close to him) was aware of the grand scheme, it means that knowledge of the total plan was very carefully guarded and only made known to a discreet inner circle.

It is difficult to relate the excitement I felt as these facts hit home: I was probably unravelling one of the most closely-guarded secrets to have been uncovered in many hundreds of years – there for all to see but hidden to all but those in some silent and mysterious conclave.

CHAPTER 3

Creating the body of The Plough

Having marked most of the key Gothic cathedrals and abbeys in northern France on to my maps, a simple visual observation of the possible locations made the best ground positions for Megrez and Phekda obvious. The two stars which join with Marak and Dubhe to make the body of The Plough, (Fig 32) can be chosen from St Quentin, Epernay, Reims, Châlons-sur-Marne and Nôtre Dame de l'Epine a few kilometres from Châlons-sur-Marne.(Fig 33) When choosing these locations, I had an inspiration: Nôtre Dame de l'Epine is not marked on my large scale maps nor is it mentioned in any of the available texts but I remembered that Louis Charpentier had devoted a chapter of his book 'Les Mystères Templiers' to 'Le Mystère de l'Epine' (The mystery of the bramble or thornbush). In this chapter he says, *"Nôtre Dame de l'Epine, dit Luc Benoist, offre ce double et singulier caractère d'être construite en rase campagne, relativement loine d'un grand centre, alors qu'elle est l'édifice plus remarquable de la Champagne, après Nôtre Dame de Reims bien entendu".* Translated this reads 'Nôtre Dame de l'Epine, says Luc Benoist, offers that double and at the same time singular characteristic which is designed in farming country, relatively far from a big centre, and is also the most remarkable building in Champagne, after Nôtre Dame in Reims of course.' Because

Fig 32 The Plough as illustrated in Patrick Moore's New Atlas of the Universe

of this, I had found the exact location of Nôtre Dame de l'Epine on my visit to the area, noted the longitude and latitude and transferred these to the larger maps on which all my connections were being plotted.

On the basis of the extraordinary effort that the designers had put into signposting the pointers, I could only presume that the other stars in the constellation would be equally well signposted. I therefore studied carefully all the possible combinations of cathedrals which line up with the chosen positions.

St Quentin appeared to be the only location in the correct position for the more northerly position, Phekda and I therefore concentrated on Nôtre Dame de St Quentin as the third potential star in my earthly Plough. First I examined the list of alignments through Bonne Mare to find any cathedrals or abbeys on the line through the cathedral at St Quentin. I was intrigued to discover that the line from the cathedral at Bonn in Germany to Bonne Mare misses the centre of Nôtre Dame de St Quentin by 377 metres. When I checked the alignment on the computer, I discovered that the same line misses the centre of Abbey Mortemer by 436 metres.

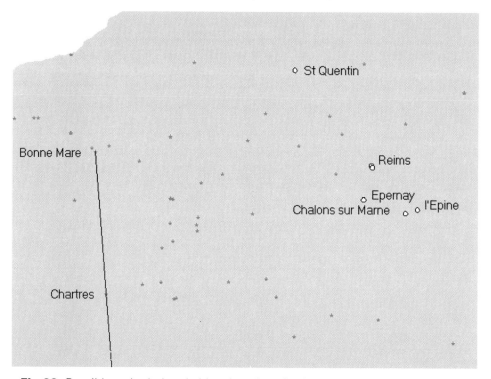

Fig 33 Possible cathedral and abbey locations for 'stars' to form the body of The Plough

Given the coincidence of names between Bonn and Bonne Mare, I investigated the origination of the name Bonn for the erstwhile German capital and discovered that it had existed as early as 30 BC when an Umbrian settlement was located at 'Bonna'. The Romans centred a military encampment at Castra Bonnensia in 16 BC.

When I examined the list of lines through the second pointer position at Chartres, I was again able to find a connection. This time the line went within 600 metres of the centre of Abbey Royaumont, north of Paris. (Fig 35)

Abbey Royaumont was founded in 1228 by Louis IX and the guide book tells us, *'Le choix du site reflète le souci de concilier les intérêts royaux et les exigences cisterciennes, et le lui repond assez bien a celles-çi. Certes, ce n'est pas une de ces forêts sauvages dont parlent certains textes décrivant les premières implantations cisterciennes; c'est tout de même une terre boisée, marécageuse et, à l'époque, à l'écart du monde,'* which translated means, 'The choice of the site reflects the need to reconcile the royal interests and the demands of the Cistercians, and it satisfied both of these very well. Certainly, this is not one of those wild forests mentioned in certain texts which describe the first Cistercian establishments; all the same, it is wooded swamp land, and at the same time, distanced from the world.'

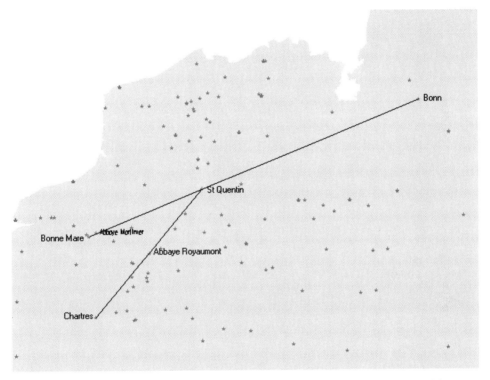

Fig 34 The lines joining Nôtre Dame St Quentin to the two 'pointer' positions

Louis IX was a very religious king and is described in the guide book as 'Saint Louis'. The records tell us that the choice of this site for a new and magnificent abbey was based on discussions between 'St Louis' and the Cistercians. In 1228, Louis IX was forty years old and had not met St Bernard (1090–1153). However, the influence of the Cistercians in the early part of the 13th century must have been pervasive and it may well be that a 'Holy King' would have been party to secrets which were previously kept from others. The guide book tells us that the abbey was completely financed by Louis and that he visited the site more than twenty-five times during its construction. He is even reputed to have rolled up his sleeves and joined in with the work on the site. It is small wonder that it was called 'Mons Regalis', then 'Mont Royal' and eventually 'Royaumont'. (Fig 35)

Fig 35 The cloister at Royaumont Abbey

Having established connections through Bonne Mare and Chartres, the next obvious set of points to try were the cathedrals of Abbeville, Amiens and Noyon which lie in a straight line and which had helped me find and plot the Marak pointer at Bonne Mare. I found connections to Abbeville and Amiens on my maps and was then able to enter them on to the computer to confirm the accuracy:

* The line from St Wulfran in Abbeville to the centre of the basilica at Stenay, misses the centre of Nôtre Dame St Quentin by 486 metres.
* The line from the centre of Nôtre Dame Cathedral in Amiens to the centre of the cathedral in Arlon misses the centre of Nôtre Dame de St Quentin by 132 metres.

When I lay my straight edge on to the map to plot the line through the cathedrals in St Quentin and Noyon, it appeared to be very fruitful and indicated possible connections at Mons, Compiègne, Senlis, Versailles, Ablis and Tours. I plotted these points on to the computer and I was able to separate the connections through St Quentin into two lines:

* The line from the centre of the cathedral at Mons in Belgium to the centre of the St Jaques Basilica in Compiègne which misses Nôtre Dame St Quentin by 210 metres and Nôtre Dame Noyon by 117 metres.
* The line from the centre of Nôtre Dame St Quentin to the centre of St Gatien in Tours which misses the centres of Nôtre Dame Noyon by 466 metres, St Jaques Compiègne by 1068 metres, Nôtre Dame Senlis by 296 metres, the cathedral at Versailles by 279 metres and the basilica at Ablis by 349 metres. In fact, the line directly from the centre of Nôtre Dame St Quentin to the centre of the basilica in Ablis goes exactly through the centre of the cathedral in Versailles.

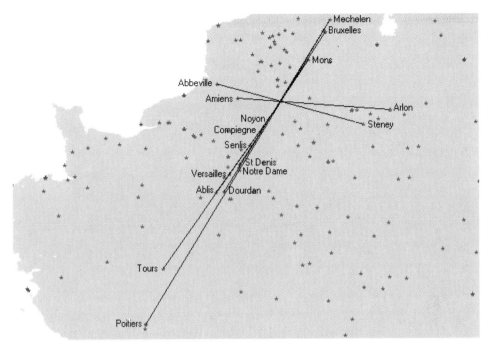

Fig 36 The lines joing St Quentin to Abbeville, Amiens & Noyon and to the three main basilicas in Paris at Nôtre Dame, Sacré Coeur & St Denis

Next I turned to Paris and found connections through all three of the main cathedrals and basilicas:

* Brussels – Mons – St Quentin – Noyons – **St Denis**
* Dourdan – **Sacré Coeur** – St Quentin – Mechelen
* Mechelen – Brussels – St Quentin – **Nôtre Dame** – Poitiers

These connections were all confirmed when they were entered on to the computer 'map info' system . (Fig 36) A further line which provided validated connections and which included a point which had been significant in the plotting of alignments through Bonne Mare was **Sion** – Nôtre Dame en Vaux – St Etienne, Châlons-sur-Marne – Vauclair – Laon – St Quentin – Calais

A complete 360 degree sweep was completed and each possible line was confirmed on the computer. When completed, I had located 66 lines with alignments through the centre of Nôtre Dame St Quentin, 9 with alignments within 100 metres and 19 with alignments between 100 and 250 metres. These lines connect 72 cathedrals, 33 basilicas and 18 abbeys and once again form the stylised picture of a star. (See appendix 3 for the complete details) It seemed that I had chosen the correct position at the first attempt and by now I felt convinced that my theory of 'the seven stars' was correct. (Fig 37)

Two of the lines that I had plotted went through Mont St Michel and Clairvaux, the locations which connected so accurately with Nôtre Dame de Chartres:

* The line from the centre of the abbey at Clairvaux to the centre of St Vaast, the basilica in Béthune misses the centre of Nôtre Dame St Quentin by 594 metres to the south-west. This means that the movement of the second abbey at Clairvaux in a north-easterly direction would have brought the Clairvaux – Béthune line closer to

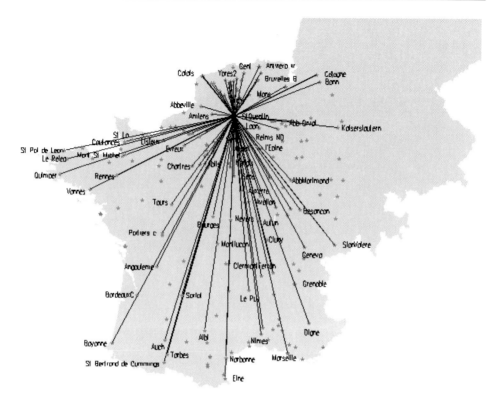

Fig 37 The 66 lines connecting Nôtre Dame St Quentin with cathedrals, abbeys and basilicas in France, Germany, Belgium and Switzerland

the centre of the cathedral at St Quentin. The hypothesis that St Bernard (or someone involved in the positioning of the first Cistercian abbeys) had deliberately chosen the new position of the second abbey at Clairvaux in order to ensure a more accurate correspondence with the locations of at least three of the seven stars, remained credible.
* The line from Nôtre Dame St Quentin to Abbaye St Michel, misses the centre of the basilica in Avranches by 730 metres.

When I visited St Quentin, I discovered a series of coincidences which gave interesting but unscientific corroboration to the theory that St Quentin is Phekda in a grand and earthly representation of Ursa Major.

The first Christian chapel was created on the site by Eusebie in 342. It was expanded by St Eloi in 640 after the discovery of the relics of St Quentin. The first stone of the forerunner to the current magnificent Gothic edifice was laid between 1113 and 1119 and the building was not completed until some time in the 15th century. The particular aspects of the basilica which I found interesting were:

* The pentagram contained in the northern transept window (Fig 38)
* A labyrinth installed in 1495, 11.6 metres in diameter which duplicates the concept established in Nôtre Dame de Chartres (Fig 39)
* Stars decorating the basilica floor: A 7 pointed star at the entrance, two 8 pointed stars in the centre of the nave and a 6 pointed star behind the sanctuary.(Figs 40 & 41)
* An 8 pointed star in the passageway under the apse, south of the altar.

Fig 38 The pentagram contained in the window above the northern transept

Fig 39 The labyrinth in the floor of Nôtre Dame St Quentin

Fig 40 The 6-pointed star behind the sanctuary

Fig 41 The 7-pointed star at the entrance to the cathedral

The orientation of the basilica was 72°E (true geographic) and at the time of writing, I have found no significance in this angle of orientation. The line from Nôtre Dame St Quentin to Bonne Mare has a bearing of 67°E and the line from St Quentin to Chartres, a bearing of 41°E. On the assumption that Nôtre Dame, St Quentin was the correct location of the third star Phekda of our earthly Plough, I proceeded to examine the positions of the cathedrals which could combine with my first three locations to give me the fourth star, Megrez. (Fig 36) I carefully studied the angles and dimensions of the constellation from the photograph contained in the Mitchell Beazley New Atlas of the Universe written by Patrick Moore. As near as I could judge, the distance between the pointers is 82.8% of the distance between Phekda and Megrez. On the ground, the distance between Chartres and Bonne Mare is 98.8 kilometres. On this basis, if the dimensions of the earthly Plough are to be similar to those in Ursa Major, the point which represents Megrez would need to be 81.8 kilometres from the centre of Nôtre Dame St Quentin.

From the basilicas chosen as possible locations, the one which best fits this dimensional requirement, is Nôtre Dame Cathedral in Reims, which lies 85.3 kilometres from Nôtre Dame St Quentin. If this was to be the correct location, I decided that an error of 4.3% would be acceptable given the methods which must have been used to determine each position. Interestingly, if St Quentin was moved 3.5 kilometres nearer to Reims, its bearing from Chartres at 42° would lie 1° closer to the line of orientation of Chartres – 44° 16' and the new bearing of the Bonne Mare – St Quentin line would then be 69° and would have moved 2° closer to the orientation of Nôtre Dame St Quentin (72° 29'). I was intrigued and wondered if the cathedral in St Quentin had been sited in the wrong position.

When the alignments through Nôtre Dame in Reims were plotted 74 lines were located connecting Reims with 65 cathedrals, 38 basilicas, 22 founding abbeys and 5 places of historical interest. (see Appendix 4 for complete list) (Fig 42) Alignments which were of particular interest are:-
*   The line from the centre of Nôtre Dame Le Mans to the centre of Nôtre Dame Reims which misses the centre of Nôtre Dame Chartres by 147 metres.
*   The line from the centre of Nôtre Dame Reims to Clairvaux Abbey which misses the centre of Abbey St Remy in Reims by 28 metres.
The first of these lines accurately links three of the most prominent cathedrals in France and gives a link to the primary pointer. The second appears to confirm the precise siting of the second abbey at Clairvaux and with it, the hypothesis that St Bernard (or someone close to him) was aware of the overall construction. At this stage, there appeared to be no connection with Bonne Mare, but later on it became clear that there is in fact one very significant connection which does much to confirm the overall design.

Reims Cathedral is oriented 58° East (true geographic) and I was able to find no reason for this angle of orientation. The Reims – St Quentin line is 140° E, the Reims – Bonne Mare line is 93.5° E and the Reims – Chartres line is 65° E. There did not appear to be any connections close to the 58° line. What was clear from these angles was that there appeared to be a pattern, the first clue to which was the isosceles triangle made when the Reims – St Quentin line is projected on to the north-south line through Chartres (Fig 43)

In attempting to confirm Reims as Megrez in the earthly reproduction of The Great Bear , I measured the angles in the constellation and compared them with the angles on the ground. As near as could be determined, the angle between the Marak – Dubhe

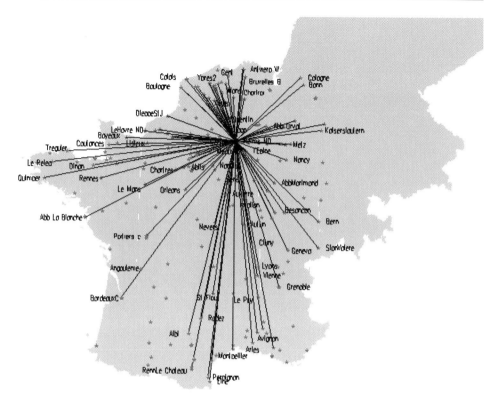

Fig 42 The 74 lines which intersect at Nôtre Dame Reims

line and the Dubhe – Phekda line is 101 degrees and the angle between the Dubhe – Phekda line and the Phekda – Megrez line is 106 degrees. When I measured the angles between the lines joining the earthly positions, I was amazed: the angle between the Chartres – Bonne Mare line and the Bonne Mare – St Quentin line is the same as the angle between the Bonne Mare – St Quentin and the St Quentin – Reims lines. They are both 108 degrees – the interior angle of a regular pentagon.[1] (Fig 44)

Was this why the planners had chosen to displace the location of Nôtre Dame St Quentin? Did they want the four stars which form the body of The Plough to hold the shape of a regular pentagon?

These extraordinary circumstances confirmed to me that I had uncovered one of the most incredible feats of planning of all time and gave me my first real clue to the reasons which motivated its existence.

I extended the Bonne Mare to Chartres and the St Quentin to Reims lines so that they were both equal in distance to the Bonne Mare to St Quentin line. I then drew arcs of equal distance from the two new end points so that their point of intersection located the fifth point of the pentagon. The shape which emerged was the five pointed star of a pentagram[2] with one of the key diagonals going very close to the centre of Nôtre Dame, Paris. (Fig 45)

---

[1] The regular pentagon is a five sided shape, with each side the same length and five interior angles of 108°.
[2] The pentagram is the five pointed star obtained by joining the corners of a regular pentagon – ★.

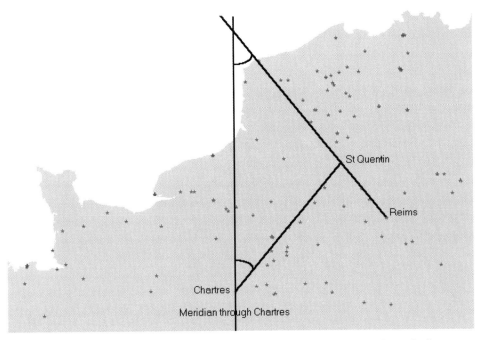

Fig 43 The isosceles triangle formed by projecting the Reims – St Quentin line onto the meridian through Chartres

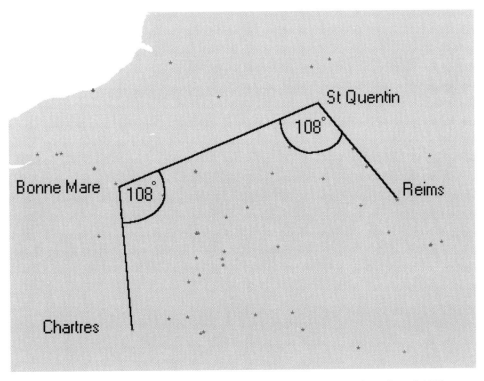

Fig 44 The body of The Plough which contains two equal angles of 108°

The framing of a pentagram within the body of The Great Bear amazed and intrigued me. The figure has been associated with occultists, the Ancient Mysteries and more recently with Jesus Christ. Pythagoreans were aware of its link to the golden section ($\varphi = 1.618033989 \ldots$), which has been described as a 'geometer's hymn'. This proportion, often referred to in the context of sacred geometry, was much used in the construction of the Gothic cathedrals. John Michell in *The Dimensions of Paradise* tells us: "An example of its (the golden section's) wonderful properties is that a rectangle with sides in proportion $1:\varphi$ can be divided into two parts, one of them a square and the other a rectangle with the same properties. (Fig 46) The spiral which it creates occurs in many natural forms and patterns of plant growth, giving support to the tenet of traditional philosophy that number preceded creation and determined its development. Christian mystics made the pentagram an emblem of Jesus, who fed five thousand with five loaves and two fishes and who represents the archetypal man (with five senses and five fingers on each hand). Its esoteric connection with the crucified man is given further point by the fact that the square on the height of the five pointed star, contained in a pentagon with each side measuring one unit, is equal to 2.368 square units, 2368 being the number of Jesus Christ[1]."

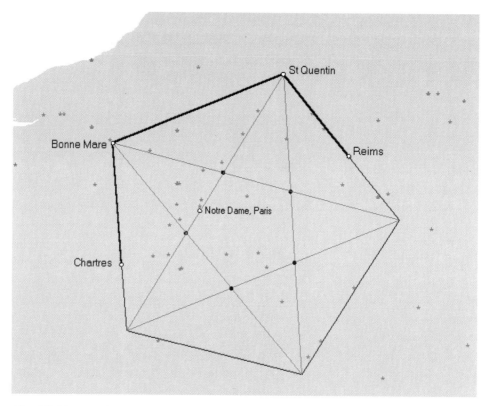

Fig 45 The regular pentagon and the pentagram it prescribes, contained within the body of The Plough

---

[1] This number related to the number of Jesus Christ using Gematria which is described in Chapter 6.

This was not the first time I had seen The Great Bear linked with a sign representing Virgo and I can do no better than to quote the appropriate paragraph from *The Holy Blood and the Holy Grail*: "In 1188 the Ordre de Sion is also said to have modified its name, adopting the one which has allegedly obtained to the present – the Prieuré de Sion. And, as a kind of subtitle, it is said to have adopted the curious name 'Ormus'. This subtitle was supposedly used until 1306 – a year before the arrest of the French Templars. The device for Ormus was ♍ and involves a kind of acrostic or anagram with the letters 'o', 'u', 'r' and 's' contained inside the 'M' and which combines a number of key words and symbols. *'Ours'* means bear in French – 'Ursus' in Latin, an echo, as subsequently became apparent, of Dagobert II and the Merovingian dynasty. 'Orme' is French for 'elm', 'Or' of course is 'gold'. And the 'M' which forms the frame enclosing the other letters is not only an 'M' but also the astrological sign for Virgo – connoting, in the language of mediæval iconography, Nôtre Dame."

I wondered what Henry Lincoln and his co-authors would say when they saw the pentagram held inside the body of 'The Great Bear'. When I recovered from my surprise and I examined the pentagon in relation to the bearing of the three cathedrals, my first suspicion was that I had discovered the reason for the orientation of Nôtre Dame Reims (58° E) and I was disappointed when I plotted the line from Nôtre Dame Reims to the corner of the pentagram south of Chartres and Bonne Mare, and found that it lies 52° East – exactly 6 degrees less than the directional lie of the cathedral. (Fig 47)

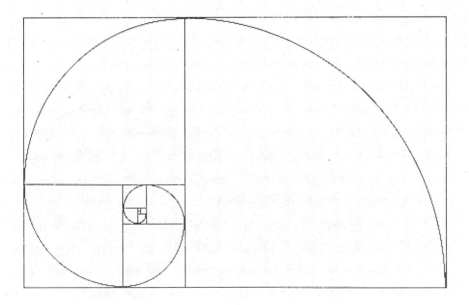

Fig 46 The spiral contained by the golden section rectangle

The first Bishop to take up residence in Reims was Saint Sixtus in the middle of the 3rd Century. The first Christian buildings stood south of the existing cathedral and close to the current location of Abbey St Remi. The original cathedral, called The Church of the Sacred Apostles and later renamed Saint Symphorien, preceded them and lay about 300 metres east of the present building. In the early 5th century, Bishop

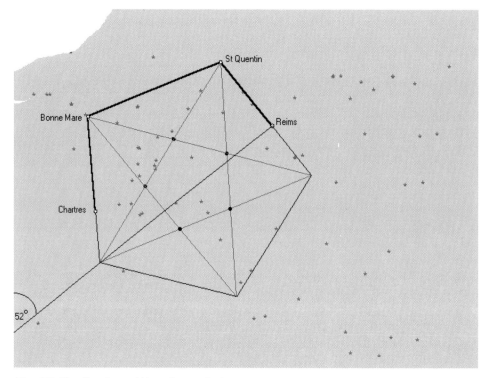

Fig 47 The line from Nôtre Dame Reims to the bottom corner of the pentagram has a bearing of 52°

St Nicasius chose the current site and constructed a basilica dedicated to the Virgin. The official cathedral guide book tells us: *'This patronage, prior to the Council of Ephesus (431) which spread the worship of the Saviour's mother to the West, proves the eastern origin of the Bishop and makes Our Lady of Reims one of the most ancient marian churches in France.'*

The present cathedral was commenced in 1211 and retains the exact orientation of the original 5th century basilica. When first constructed, like St Quentin and Chartres, it had a maze set into the stone floor of the nave and was designed to have seven spires; a spire over the cross and six smaller ones standing on the towers of the facade and the transepts. (Fig 48)

In 498 King Clovis was baptised by Saint Remi and this established the link between the monarchy and Reims. In 816, Louis chose the town of Reims for his coronation and from the time of Henry 1 (1027) to Charles X (1825) all royal coronations except two, have taken place in the existing cathedral.

The idea that selected cathedrals in northern France might form the pattern of The Plough had first occurred to me in 1985. In the early years I worked with maps and visited the cathedrals and other sites which I knew to be involved. It was not until 1993, when I had the benefit of a powerful computer, that I discovered all the inter-related facts which led me to the conclusion that a complex geometric shape, incorporating a representation of the constellation Ursa Major had been constructed in northern France.

The principal facts that convinced me I was correct to believe that an incredible representation of The Great Bear existed and that I had located the four points which form the body of the construction were:

* All four locations I had located have a large number of precise and accurate alignments with prominent cathedrals, basilicas and abbeys.
* Two of the cathedrals, Chartres and Reims are two of the three most prominent cathedral locations in France.
* The shape made by the four locations which form the body of The Plough, contain equal angles of 108°, indicating that they hold a regular pentagon which in turn holds a pentagram.
* The location of the abbey at Clairvaux was moved to give very accurate alignment to Chartres and Reims through two of the most prestigious abbeys in France.
* The orientation of Chartres and St Quentin Cathedrals are close to the dimensionally correct location for Phekda. The actual location of St Quentin Cathedral ensures the validity of the two angles of 108 degrees.

Fig 48 Nôtre Dame Cathedral in Reims

* The transepts of Reims Cathedral point exactly to Langres Cathedral and Abbey Vaucelles.
* The lower corner of the pentagram on the Bonne Mare – Rennes-le-Château line can be connected by a line joining Nôtre Dame in Paris to Nôtre Dame St Quentin.
* The two locations which represent The Pointers, accurately point towards Rennes-le-Château.

It was when I attempted to confirm the correspondence of Rennes-le-Château with the position that would be taken up by the point representing Polaris, that I discovered, incredibly, that **the ancient Paris meridian,** which falls 6 kilometres east of Rennes-le-Château and 1 kilometre west of Nôtre Dame in Paris, **exactly bisects the Bonne Mare to Nôtre Dame St Quentin line** – the base line of the earthly representation of the Plough. (fig 49)

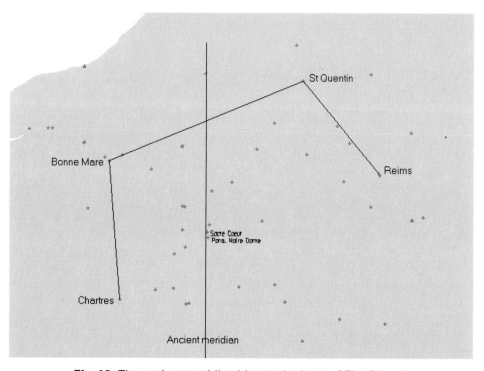

Fig 49 The ancient meridian bisects the base of The Plough

The name Paris which is known to have existed at the time of the Roman conquest of Gaul has two parts: 'par', meaning equal in Latin and 'is' meaning equal in Greek. In other words the name Paris probably means 'equal-equal', which could well be another way of describing the place that is cut into two equal parts by the meridian. The fact that this same line cuts the base of The Plough into two equal parts indicates the precision with which this massive construction was planned and executed. It also implies certain ancient beliefs about the meridian and the seven stars which are expanded when I come to examine the reasons for this incredible achievement.

Convinced of the efficacy of my original theory, I needed only to identify the final three locations, which make the handle of the Plough, in order to prove the existence of the complete plan.

CHAPTER 4

Putting a handle on The Plough

In the constellation of Ursa Major the first star in the three star extension from the main body is called Alioth and on a line projected from Dubhe, lies 2° from the the straight line between Marak and Megrez. (Fig 50) Given this geometrical information, to locate the point I was looking for, I plotted a line from Bonne Mare through Nôtre Dame in Reims and then drew an arc south east of Reims with the radius calculated by referring to the proportional distances between the stars in the constellation of Ursa Major. The place which appeared to be in the correct position is the small town of Etain east-north-east of Verdun.

The town has two churches. However, when I tried to align either church with cathedrals and abbeys, the only direct and accurate line I obtained was the one from the cathedral in Strasbourg through to the cathedral in St Quentin. There are no other discernible lines and no connections to either of the pointers.

The only cathedral of any significance in the area is Nôtre Dame Verdun. However, I discovered that this cathedral does not fit the plan, if the dimensions are to accurately conform to the dimensions of the constellation of Ursa Major: Verdun is 4.84 kilometres too close to Reims and is on the wrong side of the extended Bonne Mare – Reims line. However, on the basis that I had accepted St Quentin in the wrong place and for what in the end turned out to be very good reasons, I decided to look more carefully at Nôtre Dame Verdun and its location, to see if I could establish the position as the first of the three missing stars. The orientation of Nôtre Dame Verdun was 67° 15′ E (magnetic) in the summer of 1992 which is a geographic orientation of 65° 17′ E. Incredibly, when I projected this line of orientation on to my charts, I discovered that it precisely intersects the corner of the regular pentagon south of Chartres. Because of what I had previously discovered about this corner, that meant that the tip of the pentagram could be located by a junction of the Bonne Mare – Rennes-le-Château line, the extended line from Nôtre Dame St Quentin through Nôtre Dame Paris and an extended line through Nôtre Dame Verdun which back tracks the orientation of the cathedral. (Fig 51)

It could not just be a coincidence that the projected line along the axis of the cathedral so accurately meets the corner of the pentagram. This discovery, convinced me that Verdun is part of the pattern, and that it is probably the location which represents Alioth in our earthly Plough.

(a)

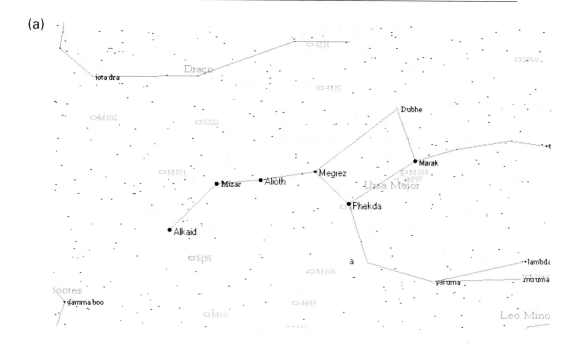

(b)

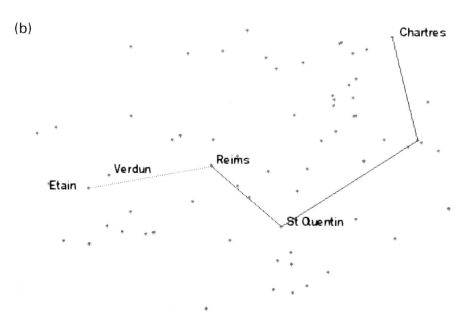

Fig 50 The seven stars of Ursa Major and the locations of Verdun and Etain relative to the four locations which form the body of the earthly plough

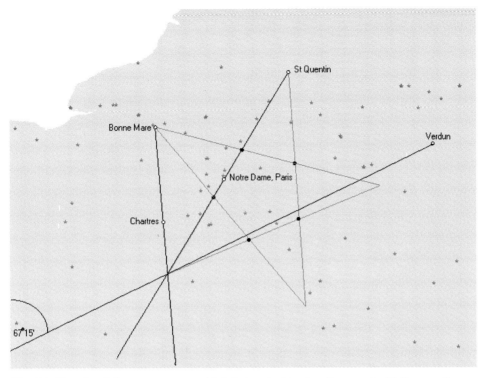

Fig 51 The tip of the pentagram which is located by the Rennes-le-Château – Bonne Mare line, the line from St Quentin through Nôtre Dame in Paris and the line which tracks the orientation of Nôtre Dame de Verdun

When I plotted connections with other cathedrals, basilicas and abbeys, I located the following:

* The line from the centre of Nôtre Dame Verdun to the centre of Nôtre Dame **Chartres**, misses the centre of the basilica at Ablis by 209 metres.
* The line from the centre of St Etienne, the cathedral in Metz to **Bonne Mare,** misses the centre of Nôtre Dame Verdun by 990 metres.
* The line from the centre of Nôtre Dame Verdun to the centre of Cathedral St Flour misses the centre of the abbey site at **Clairvaux** by 195 metres. This line lies NW of the current abbey site and therefore the movement of the abbey location would have done little to alter the lie of the abbey relative to the Verdun – St Flour line.
* Altogether, 61 lines aligning 56 cathedrals, 39 basilicas, 17 founding abbeys and 4 places of historical interest pass through the centre of Nôtre Dame, Verdun. (see appendix 5, for the complete list) (Fig 52)

"The cathedral in Verdun is one of the oldest constructions in Lorraine. (Fig 53) The current cathedral is on the same location of the first cathedral, built in 450 AD in the heart of the Gallo-Roman castrum. Since the fifth century, it has been dedicated to the Virgin Mary and was probably the first to be so dedicated, in France."[1]

---

[1] L Brunner, M Mortitz, J-C Brossard: La Cathédrale de Verdun 990-1990;A C C V 1989.

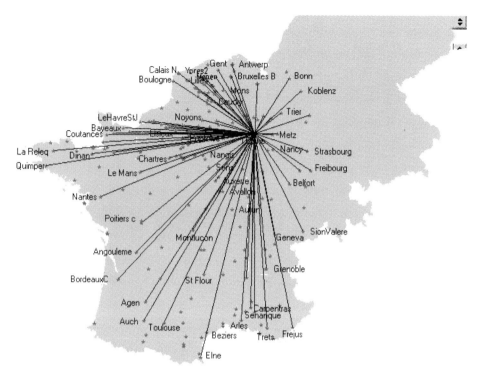

Fig 52 The 61 lines which intersect at Nôtre Dame Verdun

The alignments through Verdun and the orientation of the cathedral which links it to the pentagram, were sufficient to convince me that I had located the fifth star, Alioth of the earthly Plough. The location of the cathedral in St Quentin which had the effect of creating the two angles of 108° had convinced me that the positions of the cathedrals had been chosen carefully as part of a grand master plan. Because of this, I could see that there must be some logical reason why Nôtre Dame Verdun had been moved in a south-westerly direction (from the position dictated by the shape of the actual constellation). Despite this rationale, I was totally unprepared for the significance of the movement, which I discovered when tracking the line to Chartres through the pentagram.

The line from Nôtre Dame Verdun to Nôtre Dame Chartres goes precisely through the centre point of the pentagram. (Fig 54) The architects of this massive construction had moved the Alioth position southwards in order to point out the centre of the pentagram and had carefully chosen the orientation of its position on the ground to point to the south-west corner of the regular pentagon and thus, one of the points of the pentagram it contains. These incredible facts were sufficient to show beyond doubt that Nôtre Dame in Verdun is the location of the fifth point in the earthly Plough.

The sixth star 'Mizar' proved to be the most difficult to locate. My initial suspicion was that it might be located at Metz. However, an examination of the constellation showed that there is a straight line between the northern pointer Marak, the fourth star Megrez and the sixth star Mizar and I knew from my attempts to plot alignments through Reims, that whilst close, Metz and Reims are not in exact align-

Fig 53 The nave of Nôtre Dame Verdun — the canopy over the altar is a copy of the canopy at St Peter's in Rome

ment with Bonne Mare. (Fig 55) The second reservation I had about the cathedral at Metz being the sixth star, was that it was not located in a position which duplicated the dimensional relationships of the constellation: the distance between the cathedral at Metz and the cathedral at Verdun is only 57% of the distance between the cathedral in Verdun and the cathedral in Reims whereas the distance between Mizar and Alioth is 80% of the distance between Alioth and Megrez. Additionally, I could find no other cathedrals which are positioned to give direct and accurate straight line connections with the cathedral in Metz other than the ones through Chartres and Verdun and no connections to Bonne Mare. At the same time, I could find no cathedral or abbey in the vicinity which might be better located: I seemed to have come to a dead end.

I was determined not to be halted by this difficulty: At this point in my research, I was convinced that the incredible number of exact alignments from a relatively small number of Gothic cathedrals, basilicas and abbeys could not have occurred by chance and that there is in fact a man-made construction which duplicates the seven stars of The Plough in northern France. My conviction was not affected by the lack of an obvious position for the sixth star and I decided to do a full exploration of the area to see if I could find something which was not obvious when studying the maps.

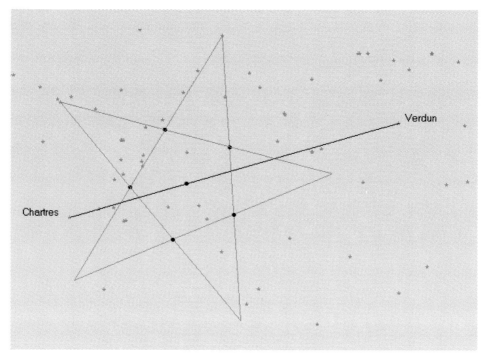

Fig 54 The line from Nôtre Dame Verdun to Nôtre Dame Chartres goes precisely through the centre of the pentagram

The search took me first to the ancient abbey at Villers Bettnach, north-east of Metz, now used as a convalescent home. However, I could find no alignments of any significance through this location.

Next, I visited Courcelles-Chaussy, east of Metz. The ordinance survey map shows a church in the town and next to the church on the map is the word temple. When I looked in my Harraps French-English dictionary, it says "nm,temple; (Protestant) church, chapel; Hist **les chevaliers du** T.,the Knights Templar(s)". Again, despite hours of intensive research, I was unable to find alignments which connected the temple to any major cathedrals or abbeys. Three kilometres to the north-east of Courcelles-Chaussey on the outskirts of the village of Varize the map says 'Le Château', but when I went to look there was no sign of any château or anything else of any significance. It was another blind alley.

It was at this stage, scrutinising the map millimetre by millimetre, that I came across the location of some ruins. According to the map these ruins are in the middle of a wood (Forêt Domaniale de Landonvillers) two kilometres north-east of Courcelles-Chaussy. Since I had no other possibilities, I decide to visit them.

They were quite difficult to locate since many of the tracks through the wood have faded with poor usage. When I did find the site, I discovered that there was almost nothing left to be seen. Healthy undergrowth covers the area and there are no signs of any buildings above ground level. (Fig 56)

The only indication that a building had once occupied the site are the remains of what must have been an underground exit for the water system, and a single stone block which incorporates an inscription that has been defaced. (Fig 57)

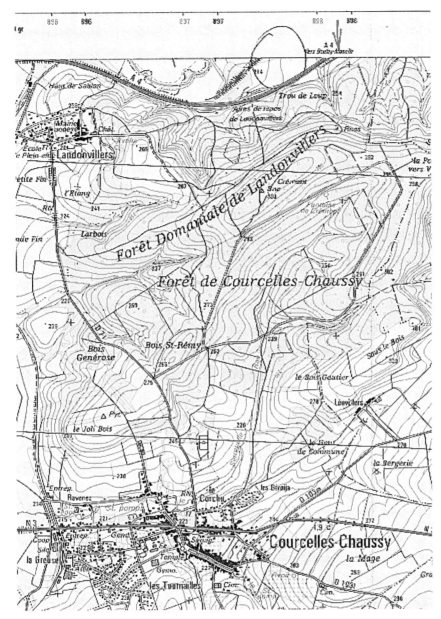

Fig 55 The IGN map of the area north of Courcelles-Chaussy with the ruins in the Forêt de Landonvillers indicated by a red arrow

When this location was plotted on to the computer, I discovered that there is a very accurate dimensional fit, in that the distance between the ruins and Nôtre Dame Verdun is 80% of the distance between Nôtre Dame Verdun and Nôtre Dame Reims.

A careful analysis of the connections with the locations of major religious buildings that had been previously recorded, showed 60 alignments through the position of the ruins with prominent cathedrals, basilicas and abbeys in France and Belgium. (Fig 58) (The complete list is detailed in appendix 6.)

Fig 56 The entrance to the underground water system at the site of the ruins in the forest of Landonvillers

The alignments worthy of note (Fig 59) include:

* The line from the ruins to **Bonne Mare** which misses the centre of **Nôtre Dame Reims** by 16 metres. This means that, within the limits of accuracy that I had available to me, **Bonne Mare, Nôtre Dame Reims and the ruins near Courcelles-Chaussy lie in an exactly straight line.**
* The line from the ruins to Vannes which misses the centre of Nôtre Dame, **Chartres** by 560 metres.
* The line from the ruins to Cluny, the first Benedictine abbey which misses Cîteaux, the first Cistercian abbey by 73 metres.
* The line from the ruins to the centre of the cathedral in Limoges which misses **Clairvaux** Abbey by 744 metres to the north-west.

Another interesting fact that I discovered, was that the distance from the ruins to the centre of Nôtre Dame Chartres is only 364 metres longer than the distance from the ruins to Bonne Mare. These coincidences seemed to be pointing inevitably to the position of the sixth star Mizar.

Despite the alignments and dimensional correctness of the position, there were several facts about the location which presented me with doubts:

* Mizar has a companion star, Alcor and is therefore a double star.
* The number of alignments through this point is significantly less than the number located through the previous five points.

Fig 57 The defaced stone block located at the ruins

*   What literature I could find, mentions the existence of the ruins of Roman villas in the Forests of Landonvillers and Courcelles-Chaussy but makes no mention of any edifice which might have had religious connotations.

In view of these doubts, I ordered an aerial photograph of the area from IGN (the French equivalent of Ordnance Survey) to see if it might provide any better evidence in favour of this location. I was not prepared for what the photograph shows: 825 metres north-east of the ruins, sheltered between the forest and the motorway is a circle, 100 metres in diameter with lines of trees radiating from the centre. It is an exact replica of any circle drawn around one of the star positions, with lines of alignment intersecting the centre. (Fig 60)

When I questioned local historians and local government officials about this circle, I was told that it had occurred in the recent past when the motorway had been constructed. Apparently, the area of the circle was an area of forest, which had been cleared by the motorway construction company as a temporary storage area. When they had vacated the site it was empty of vegetation and the growth of the trees in the remarkable pattern, which can be seen in the photograph occurred naturally. I could not help being reminded Dr Joseph Raftery's remarks in *The Celts* where he says about the druids: "The absence of formal buildings for religious purposes struck the classical world as peculiar, as did the setting of the *locus consecratus* away from the village or *oppidum*, rather than within its bounds. Instead the sanctuary was a lonely forest clearing, perhaps delimited by an earthwork or palisade enclosure; a *nemeton*." I could not help but wonder what force of nature had encouraged such a strange pattern.

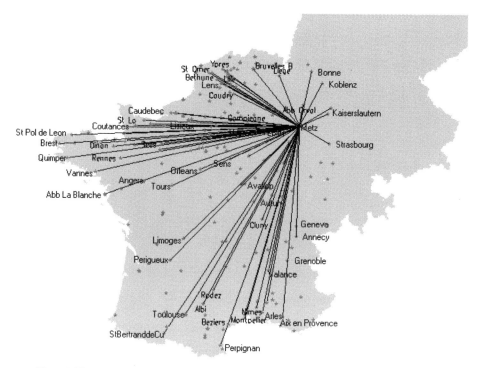

Fig 58 The alignments through the ruins, north-east of Courcelles Chaussy

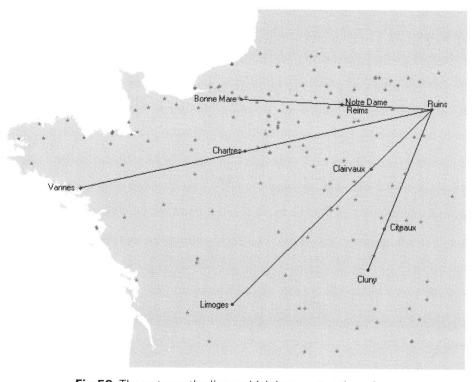

Fig 59 The noteworthy lines which intersect at the ruins

Fig 60 The strange pattern made by the trees in the forest of Landonvillers

On the ground it was very difficult to discern the pattern that I had seen in the aerial photograph and I was reminded of the phrase; 'you cannot see the wood for the trees'. Adjacent to the circle is a small lake, which seems dead and unfriendly (Fig 61)

Despite my doubts, I decided to proceed on the basis that the sixth star of our earthly Plough, the double star, Mizar, is located in the Forêt Domaniale de Landonvillers, 3.5 kilometres north of Courcelles-Chaussy.

In the early part of 1995, I received a copy of an article by P. MARQUE, from 'Cahiers Lorrains – April 1970 No 2. Which said; *"La situation à l'aboutissement d'un chemin ancien montant tout droit est un signe d'antiquité. Le plan en ellipse exclut un travail de l'époque gallo-romaine. C'est donc un travail barbare ou celtique."*

Having found and confirmed the position and its origin, it was only left for me to locate and verify the seventh point in the pattern in order to validate the entire construction. First I measured the distances between the stars in the constellation and found that the distance between the seventh star, Alkaid, and the sixth star Mizar is 34% of the distance between Marak and Mizar and that the angle between the two lines is 35° 30′.

On the ground, the distance between Bonne Mare and the ruins near Courcelles-Chaussy is 369 kilometres. Accordingly, I drew an arc 125.5 kilometres from the ruins at Courcelles-Chaussy and was disappointed to find that no major towns are located within 20 kilometres of the arc. The nearest town of any significance is Kaiserslautern which is 103.4 kilometres from the ruins and the nearest Cistercian abbey is at Otterberg, north of Kaiserslautern and 107.4 kilometres from the ruins.

On the large scale tactical pilotage charts, there is a steeple or tower marked close to the required location and I decided that the best course of action would be to carry out a thorough field investigation. You can probably imagine my disappointment therefore, when I first saw the hill to the east of Rockenhausen and realised that the tower marked on the tactical pilotage chart is a very tall radio mast (Fig 62).

Fig 61 The lake which is next to the enchanting circle

Fig 62 The radio mast on the hill at Donnersberg

The 'Topographische Karte 1:25000' for the area gives the name of the hill as 'Donners Berg', the literal translation of which is 'Thunder Mountain'. The map also shows the location of a second tower on top of the hill and the outline of an almost oblong construction, 2 kilometres by 1.5 kilometres, marked 'Keltischer Ringwall' which translated, means Celtish Outer Wall. Intrigued, I continued to the top of the hill and discovered a historic site containing a tower, some 30 metres high, which was called Ludwigsturm. (Fig 63) Additionally, marker boards surrounded the top of the hill and indicated the location of the ancient Celtic fortifications which, once they had been pointed out, were easy to identify. (Fig 64) The library at Kaiserslautern had a wealth of material on the fortifications and the surrounding area, which enabled me to uncover a series of telling facts . . .

Fig 63 Ludwig's Tower

* The Celtic wall corresponded to the style of fortification described by Caesar as a "Gallic Wall". It encloses an area of 240 hectares and is 20 metres broad at the base, with a top wide enough to allow a vehicle to drive along it. The wall is a Celtic mountain fortification from the last century before Christ. Inside the ringwall a series of other fascinating areas have been excavated:

  An oval cinder wall, 200 metres by 90 metres, made of vitrified stone which indicates the existence of high temperatures (1000–1100°C) for which no satisfactory explanation has been found.

  – A relatively large number of finds from the Urnfeld culture of the late Bronze Age (1200–800 BC).

  – Some fragments from the late Neolithic/Bronze Age.

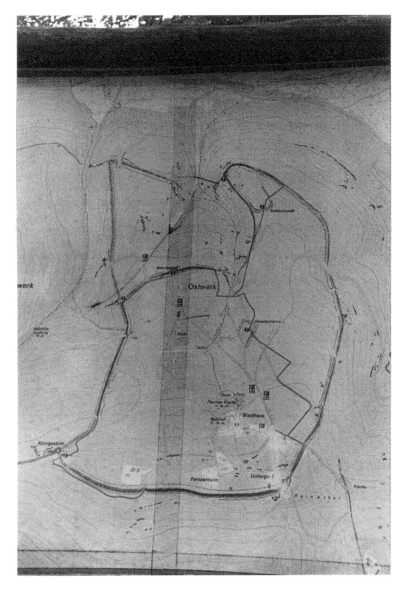

Fig 64 The marker board at the entrance to the Celtic site at Donnersberg

— The 'square earthwork' of a Celtic ritual enclosure. This is a U-shaped structure consisting of a wall and boundary ditch with sides unequal in length. It has traditionally been known as the 'Pagan Cemetery'. The characteristic ritual shaft of up to 40 metres in depth which was used for sacrifices has not been found on the Donnersberg site.
* There are no traces of any Roman activity on the site and no Roman or Merovingian historical records about the area.
* There was no clear mention of Donnersberg in a list of fiefs from the reign of Werner II around 1195
* In 1335, Philip of Sponheim and Loretha, widow of Otto 1 gave the hermit's chapel St

Jacob on Donnersberg to the priest Heinrich von Speyer, who was probably a member of the Monastery of the Holy Sepulchre, to found the 'True order of the Hermits of St Paul, the first hermit'. A monastery was in fact founded in 1370 when Heinrich II von Sponnheim gave to the order, 'the chapel of St Jacob, the house, the farmyards and the surrounding fields and woods as far as the old boundary ditch.' The first reference to the territory being owned by the house of Bolanden was made in 1335 but it is assumed that they came into possession of Donnersberg prior to 1220 since it was the castles on Donnersberg that gave the different branches of the family their names.

* Ludwig's Tower was constructed in 1842

Given the weight of historical evidence which pointed towards Donnersberg as a site of some special significance, I was becoming more and more convinced that I had happened upon the position of the seventh star. First however, I needed to resolve the small dimensional anomaly: I had arbitrarily chosen the tower, known as Ludwigsturm, as the reference point and the distance to Ludwigsturm from the ruins near Courcelles-Chaussy, measured 122 kilometres when it should have been 125.5 kilometres if the relative dimensions were to be the same as those in the constellation of Ursa Major. Additionally, the angle between the Bonne Mare – Ruins line and the line from the Ruins to Donnersberg is 32° instead of the 35° 30′ angle contained in the Great Bear. Like St Quentin, the site appeared to be 3.5 kilometres south west of its designated position relative to Bonne Mare and Reims. I knew however, that if Donnersberg was to be the position of the seventh star, as with Nôtre Dame St Quentin and Nôtre Dame Verdun, there would need to be some significant reason for the actual sited position. When I analysed the situation of Donnersberg relative to the other six positions I had located and to the pentagram, I discovered a remarkable coincidence:

> The line from Donnersberg through Nôtre Dame St Quentin is oriented 92° 20′ E and the line from Bonne Mare through the centre of Nôtre Dame Reims to the Ruins north of Courcelles-Chaussy is oriented 92° 40′ E: a difference of only 20 minutes which could perhaps be eliminated by relatively small adjustments to the locations of the three positions that were not designated by a cathedral construction. From the evidence that confronted me, I was convinced that the planners of this extraordinary geometric construction had intended these two lines to be parallel to one another (Fig 65)

The connections between Donnersberg and prominent cathedrals, basilicas and abbeys produced 57 alignments which are detailed in appendix 7. (Fig 66) The most noteworthy of these connections are:

* The series of accurate connections from Donnersberg, through the basilicas in Virton and Rethel, through **Bonne Mare** and on through the centre of St Etienne, L'Abbaye aux Hommes in **Caen** to the centre of Nôtre Dame Cathedral in **St Lo**.
* The accurate line from Donnersberg which misses the centre of Nôtre Dame **Verdun** by 246 metres, misses the centre of Nôtre Dame de **l'Epine** by 371 metres, goes through the centre of Nôtre Dame en Vaux, misses the centre of St Etienne, the cathedral in **Châlons-sur-Marne** by 113 metres, and ends at the centre of Nôtre Dame **Le Mans**. (Fig 65)
* The line from Donnersberg to Mont St Michel, which falls 531 metres from the centre of Abbey Royaumont.
* The line from Donnersberg to the centre of St Peter & St Paul Cathedral in Troyes, which misses the **Ruins** near Courcelles-Chaussy by 497 metres to the south-east.

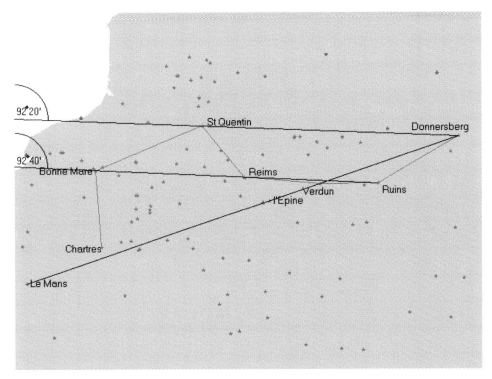

Fig 65 the almost parallel lines which connect 5 of the 7 points of The Plough and the line from Donnersberg to Le Mans which misses the centre of Nôtre Dame Verdun by 246 metres

* The connection with **Chartres** through Ablis and the link to Quimper through **Reims**.
* The line from Donnersberg to **Rennes-le-Château**, which misses the centre of Nôtre Dame Le Puy by 232 metres.

The only connection I could find with the Abbey at **Clairvaux**, is the line which goes from Donnersberg to St Pierre, the cathedral in Angoulême and which misses the Abbey by 731 metres to the north-west.

When I examined these connections again, I had an inspiration. Because of the precise straight line alignment between the cathedrals in Le Mans, Chartres and Reims, I wondered whether the same accurate alignment was meant to exist between Le Mans, Verdun and Donnersberg. To check this hypothesis, I extended the line from Nôtre Dame Le Mans through the centre of Nôtre Dame Verdun and noted that this line fell 363 metres from Konigs Tower on Donnersberg.

I then introduced a new point south of Konigs Tower and exactly on the extended Le Mans – Verdun line. This completed I plotted the line from the new point on Donnersberg through Nôtre Dame St Quentin and as I anticipated, it was 10 minutes nearer the 92° 40′ of the Ruins – Bonne Mare line. (Fig 67) This convinced me that the exact location of the Alkaid, the seventh star of the earthly plough is on the hill at Donnersberg and several hundred metres south of Konigs Tower and that the other line (Bonne Mare to the ruins near Courcelles-Chaussy) should be adjusted slightly by moving the positions of Bonne Mare and the site in the Forêt de Landonvillers by just over 100 metres each.

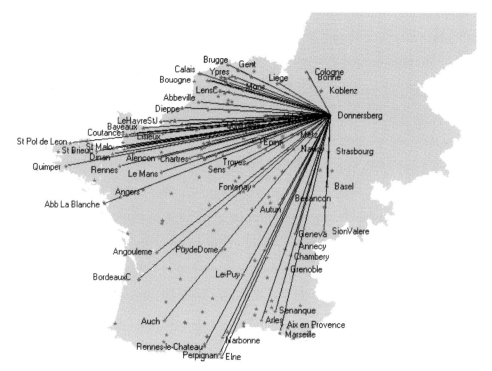

Fig 66 The 57 alignments through the centre of the Celtic fortress at Donnersberg

This being done, all seven points had been located and the earthly representation of the constellation Ursa Major, known variously as The Great Bear, The Plough, The Big Dipper or simply the Seven Stars, was now visible (Fig 68). Its proportions overwhelmed me and I knew that it represented the most magnificent construction ever conceived by man. It covers a little over three hundred miles from Chartres in the West to Donnersberg in the east, and incorporates a precision over such long distances that it is difficult to comprehend the methods that were used by the original surveyors.

Who had conceived this masterpiece of design and what methods had these architects used to superimpose their perfect design on to the landscape of northern Europe? Those questions burned into my mind and yet at the same time I knew that this could not have been constructed without some record of the task having been preserved for posterity.

The design was secret and hidden, particularly at Bonne Mare and Landonvillers. Despite this, I knew that the overall result could not have been achieved without some magnificent purpose. For that reason, I was convinced that somewhere in history and inherited myth, the story of this master plan was to be located and unravelled. Some record must have been left to tell the world why this extraordinary duplication of the constellation of Ursa Major had been undertaken. At the stage that I had uncovered the seven points and identified the pentagon and pentagram contained within the body of the shape, I was not aware how justified my suspicions would be. In the chapters that follow I will present the findings of my research into how, why, and by whom. At the same time, a weight of circumstantial evidence will be presented to link the complete design with the most exciting and enduring legends of our time.

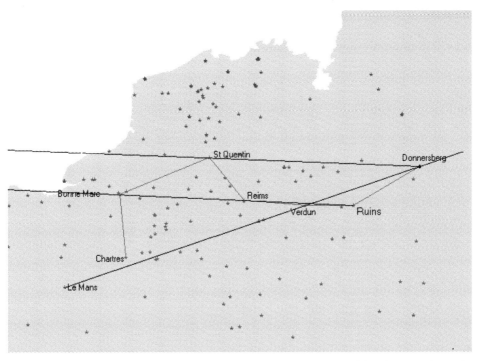

Fig 67 The amended parallel lines when the Donnersberg position is moved south from from Ludwig's Tower by 363 metres on to the extended Le Mans-Verdun line

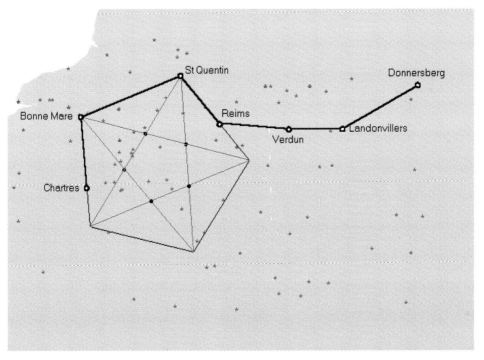

Fig 68 The seven points of the earthly Plough and the regular pentagram which it holds

CHAPTER 5
The Pole Star

In the introduction, I explained how I started my research by looking for seven stars which would put Rennes-le-Château in the Polaris position. In fact, as we have seen, the line from Bonne Mare through Chartres goes directly to the centre of Rennes-le-Château. (Fig 69) It is traditional that the two stars known as the pointers signpost the Pole Star and assuming that Rennes-le-Château can be confirmed as the intended location for Polaris, our analysis will then need to consider the possibility that the entire construction exists solely to point to Rennes-le-Château. Dimensionally, Polaris does not link to the pointers in Ursa Major in the same way that Rennes-le-Château relates to the earthly construction:-

* Rennes-le-Château is directly in line with Chartres and Bonne Mare whereas Polaris is almost 2° from the extended pointer line. If this were duplicated on the ground, the position of the point representing Polaris would be 20 kilometres east of Rennes-le-Château.

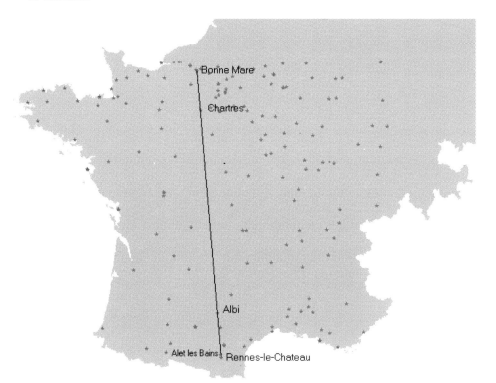

Fig 69 The line linking Bonne Mare and Chartres to Rennes-le-Château

* In the constellation, the distance between the pointers is 15.6% of the distance between the furthest pointer Marak and Polaris. In the earthly construction, the distance between Bonne Mare and Chartres is 13.73% of the distance between Bonne Mare and Rennes-le-Château.

Unfortunately, the discrepancy cannot be explained by the fact that the position of Polaris continually changes in relation to the pole of the ecliptic and to the positions of the stars in Ursa Major. Over a period of many thousands of years different stars take the position of the Pole Star, but interestingly, we are currently in a phase when Polaris is nearer to the pole of the ecliptic than it has ever been and when the line from the pointers to Polaris is only 2° from being a straight line. To be able to make an assessment of the current ground positions therefore, we must assume that when the ground plan was designed, the designers were attempting to duplicate the tradition of alignment rather than the actual geometry that they saw represented in the heavens. The only other alternatives were that (a) they they were attempting to predict a time in the future when they believed the alignment and dimensions would be similar to the picture they had created on the ground, or (b) The seven stars and the geometry they contain was all that was important to the architects and the close alignment with Albi and Rennes-le-Château was just another extraordinary coincidence.

When I measured the distance between the pointers and related it to the distance from the furthest pointer to Polaris, it never fell below 15.6% and never exceeded 16.1%. Copies of the star charts for the years 2500 BC, 1500 BC, 500 BC, 100 AD , 1100 AD, 2000 AD and 2500 AD are included as appendixes 9–15. A search for other possible contenders for the Pole Star position, showed that St Cecile, the cathedral at Albi (Fig 70) lies on the extended line from the pointers. When I measured the distance between Bonne Mare and Chartres and compared it with the distance between Bonne Mare and Albi I discovered that the smaller distance is 16.3% of the total. This closer dimensional fit with the constellation meant that I had to examine the possibility that the St Cecile position was designed to be the Pole Star in the grand earthly plan .

The archaeologists tell us that the first signs of civilisation in the town of Albi date from between 200,000 and 80,000 BC and that the Ruthenes and then the Celts were established on the site of Castelviel close to the cathedral. The Romans arrived about 100 BC and established a thriving commercial centre. By the third century, a Christian community was known to have been established and St Cecile, daughter of a noble Roman family, is reputed to have been martyred here in 220 AD, along with her husband and brother. The first known bishop was Diogenien in 405AD and St Salvi led the Church between 574 and 584. In the 9th Century, Albi was granted an earldom by Charlemagne.

In the Middle Ages, Albi developed a reputation as the centre of the Cathar religion which became known within the church as the Albigensian heresy. With the election of Pope Innocent III in 1198 the persecution of the Cathars took on a new dimension. A bloody crusade against them was led by Simon de Montfort and in the process, the entire populations of towns such as Béziers and Carcassonne were massacred. The 'crusade' lasted until 1229 when the treaty of Paris was signed which linked Languedoc to the French Crown. Despite the treaty, the authorities found it necessary to persecute their orthodoxy until 1244 when the last stronghold of the Cathars at Montségur (Fig 71) was besieged for 10 months. The strength of feeling can be measured by the actions of these last devotees: Rather than capitulate or surrender, the 200 'heretics' left the fortress and committed suicide by climbing, whilst singing, on to an enormous pyre.

Fig 70 – St Cecile at Albi

The Cathar religion itself had several essential characteristics which separated it from Christianity:

* It recognised two Gods, one of good and light, 'Ahura Mazda', and one of evil and darkness, 'Arhiman'.
* Disciples believed that individuals were able to communicate directly with God without the intervention of the church and the sacraments.
* It believed in reincarnation, which took man little by little to perfection and eternal life.
* It promoted the feminine aspect of the Godhead.

Fig 71 The mountain fortress of Montségur

The official Albi guidebook with text by Didier Poux claims that the origins of the Cathar beliefs are to be found with Zoroaster in the 6th Century BC and with the Manichaean world religion in the 3rd Century AD. This claim is interesting in view of the links between these early religious movements and the growth of Gnosticism. The discovery of the Nag Hammadi scrolls has thrown considerable light on Gnostic beliefs and their links with early Christianity. The apparent suppression of the scrolls and their translations by the church since their discovery in December 1945 indicates that the Church may still fear the essential truths that they contain. In a later chapter, I will attempt to trace the architects of the construction that I have uncovered and I will analyse their likely motivation. In so doing, I will briefly examine the links with Gnosticism and Hellenism and the rift between the Gnostics and the orthodox Church.

If the Cathars were the protectors of Gnosticism and it could be shown that the Gnostics were the driving force behind the duplication of the Seven Stars, it would be a possibility that Albi holds the position of the Pole Star, which would explain the choice of Albi as the centre of the Cathar religion. There are no facts on which such speculation can be based however and the likelihood of the 1st and 2nd century Gnostics being the instigators of the earthly design, are remote, since they never owned or built anything and only occupied buildings at the discretion of others.

When I carried out a computer analysis to check for alignments through Albi, I discovered 23 lines connecting Albi to prominent cathedrals, basilicas and founding abbeys (excluding connections to the seven star locations). This was a considerably smaller number of alignments than had been plotted through any of the seven locations of The Plough and is close to the number of alignments which would be expected for any random point within France. To confirm this, and to ensure that the number of alignments found through each of the seven points of The Plough is significant, I plotted alignments through a series of cathedral locations and found that the number of alignments within 1 kilometre, connecting cathedrals, founding abbeys and basilicas, is normally less than thirty.

Cathedral location	Number of connecting lines with cathedrals Basilicas & abbeys	Number of alignments when lines to the seven 'stars' are excluded
Auxerre	34	30
Châlons-sur-Marne	34	28
Nôtre Dame, Paris	34	28
Troyes	48	42
Bourges	28	27
Albi	26	23
Metz	43	36

Four of these cathedrals (Auxerre, Châlons-sur-Marne, Nôtre Dame Paris and Troyes) lie within the regular pentagon which holds the pentagram contained by the body of The Plough. When the connections to the seven points of The Plough are excluded, all but one have thirty six or fewer alignments with other cathedrals, basilicas or founding abbeys. The significant exception is Troyes and it was not until later during my research that I discovered why the location of this cathedral had been specially highlighted.

The orientation of St Cecile Cathedral is 93° 40' East, (magnetic) which corrects to 90° 50' East, (true geographic). This is only 50' from a precise east-west lie and I was not surprised to discover that the constructors of this cathedral, which commenced 53 years after the treaty of Paris was signed, chose to be both conventional and orthodox.

Given a lack of alignments signposting the position, the only clue pointing to Albi as the location of the Pole Star was the fact that the location of Albi Cathedral is very close to the location designated by the distances between Polaris and the Great Bear. At the same time, I know that there exists a weight of evidence pointing to the fact that there is something very special about Rennes-le-Château. It was when I was confronted with this dilemma, that I recalled that there is a difference between the heavenly locations of the Pole Star and the pole of the ecliptic. Unfortunately, when I examined the star altas, I discovered that the pole of the ecliptic, which is the point around which the Heavens appear to rotate, is nearer to Ursa Major than is Polaris.

There is one small star in Cepheus which lies in the dimensionally correct position (Fig 72) but we would probably have to get involved in the realms of science fiction in order to find any significance in this positional relationship.

When I examined the position of Rennes-le-Château and attempted to find alignments with cathedrals, abbeys and basilicas I located 54 lines. (Fig 73) (Full details are

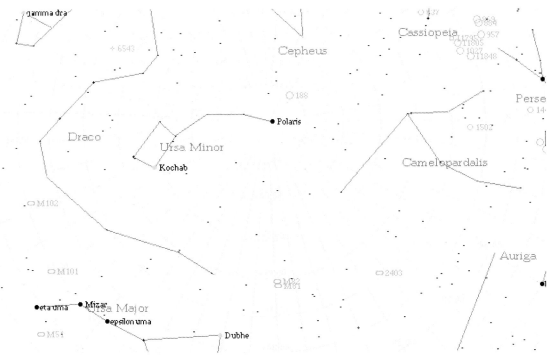

Fig 72 The star in Cepheus which aligns with the pointers

set out in appendix number 8) The most significant of these connections other than the line to Bonne Mare were

Rennes-le-Château – Metz – Trier

Rennes-le-Château – Auxerre – Eperney – Nôtre Dame, Reims

Rennes-le-Château – Le Puy – Donnersberg

Rennes-le-Château – Nôtre Dame, Paris – Sacré Coeur.

Rennes-le Château – Fonteney – Trois Fontaines

Rennes-le-Château is a small village nestling in the foothills of the Pyrenees (Fig 74). The museum adjacent to the church tells us that it had Celtic origins with the Tectosages between 500 and 100 BC and that there is evidence of occupation back to prehistoric times. It assumed significance as a fortified royal city under Alaric and the Visigoths in the early 5th century AD when it was called Rhedae (which means travelling chariots)

Between the 12th and 14th centuries it was attacked, sacked, besieged and eventually destroyed by successive predators. Alphonse II, Count of Barcelona and King of Aragon made his claim in 1170 followed by 'the buzzard', Simon de Montfort in 1210. This was followed by the Routiers in 1360 and the Spanish Count of Trastamarre in 1362.

From 1422, Rennes-le-Château was owned by the house of Hautpoul whose masters took the title Lord of Blanchefort, the name of the family who provided two Grand Masters of the Knights Templar during the 12th century. In 1781, Marie de Nègre, (the last in the Hautpoul line) died. Before her death she is reputed to have passed on a secret which had been handed down from generation to generation, which had been coded and incorporated into some 'important' documents which included;

– A genealogy of the Counts of Rhedae who were the descendants of the Merovingian kings, from Mérovée the first king up until 1244.

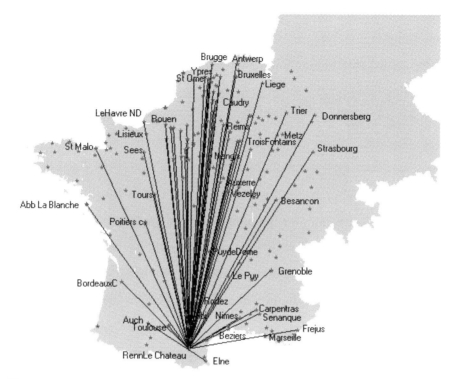

Fig 73 The 54 lines which connect Rennes-le-Château to cathedrals and abbeys in Belgium and France

Fig 74 The village of Rennes-le-Château viewed from the north

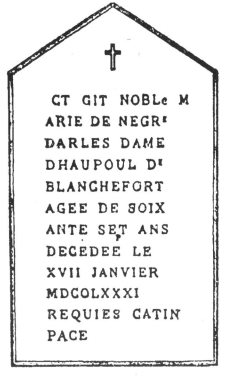

Fig 75 The Marie de Nègre tombstone

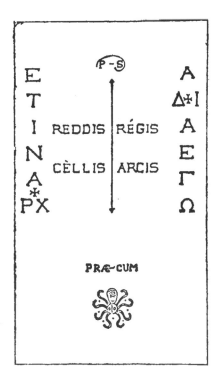

Fig 77 The 'Et in Arcadia Ego' inscription.

– The will of François-Pierre d'Hautpoul, drawn up on 23rd November 1644 which includes the names of the descendants of the above genealogy from 1244 to 1644

– Henri d'Hautpoul's will dated 24th April 1695 including a Latin invocation in 64 letters to five saints.

The recipient, Antoine Bigou, Curé of Rennes-le-Château decided to hide the documents inside the hollow altar pillar in the church and to engrave a tombstone (Fig 75) and a stone slab (which was placed on the grave of Marie de Nègre) with the secret. The documents and slab are reputed to have been found by Abbé Bérenger Saunière in 1891 and he is known to have exploited the knowledge in such a way that he accumulated and spent a fortune, prior to his death on 17th January 1917.

A considerable number of books have been written in recent years which attempt to decode the various messages. The most prominent of these are *The Holy Blood and the Holy Grail* by Baigent, Leigh and Lincoln, which claims a bloodline from Christ and *Genisis* and *Geneset*, the first by David Wood and the second by David Wood & Ian Campbell, which link the messages to precise geometric patterns locked into the geography of the area. The most recent of these books *(Geneset)* illustrates exact mathematical relationships between the ancient meridian, a circle of churches (which includes the church at Rennes-le-Château), an irregular 36° pentagram which has one of its points lying outside the circle and one of its points at Rennes-le-Château, the peaks of various local hills, (Fig 76) the square of the circle, and the rectangle that con-

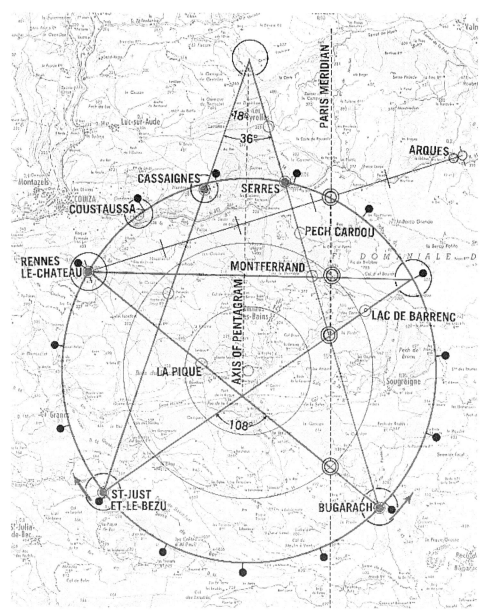

Fig 76 The circle of churches and the irregular pentagram discovered by David Wood

tains all the other figures.(Fig 4) Their mathematics is impeccable but I am not convinced by the sleight of hand that links the mathematics to the 'ET IN ARCADIA EGO' inscription (Fig 77), which was engraved on the slab that covered the grave of Marie de Nègre d'Hautpoul and which was brought to prominence by its inclusion in the Nicolas Poussin painting, Les Bergers d'Arcadie. This inscription has been the Blanchefort family motto since the thirteenth century and is claimed by many to hold the key to the secret of Rennes-le-Château.

Fig 78 The devil's font

Fig 79 The statue of Mary Magdalen with the skull at her feet

The church in Rennes-le-Château, dedicated to St Mary Magdalen and reconstructed by Bérenger Saunière, incorporates many strange features in its decoration, which again are supposed to be clues to the secret:

— The Latin inscription over the door, *Terribilis est locus iste* – This place is terrible.
— The devil who holds the holy water font on his shoulders. (Fig 78)
— The many signs of the rose+cross which are incorporated into the confessional and signs of the cross.
— The statue of St Anthony the Hermit whose feast day is 17th January – the same date engraved on the tombstone of Marie de Nègre d'Hautpoul and the date of Saunière's death.
— A picture under the altar of Mary Magdalen kneeling in a cave with an open book and a skull at her feet, identical to the one that was painted by Giovanni Francesco Barbieri (Guercino) in 1622 above the motto of 'ET IN ARCADIA EGO'. This picture is enhanced by a statue of Mary Magdalen, also with a skull at her feet. (Fig 79)
— Stations of the cross which (it is claimed[1]) incorporate a guide to the terrestrial zodiac in the area and a map to the location of the treasure.

---

[1] This claim ios made in Elizabeth Van Buren's book; Refuge of the Apocalypse.

The sight of a permanent and steady stream of visitors to the village and the church is an indication that the literature that exists has kindled the curiosity of people from all over the world. In some instances, they come believing that they have solved the mystery and they can be seen with maps, theodolites, picks and shovels prowling the fields and pathways that surround the region. Unfortunately, some of the less principled visitors vandalise the artifacts and the surrounding terrain as ego and greed blind them to the fact that they are guests in the area.

Since both David Wood and Henry Lincoln had mentioned 'connections' locally (i.e. in the area of Rennes-le-Château) I went back to my maps to see if I could spot any obvious alignments through the church or the château. It was not difficult to spot what seemed like connections to the various castles, forts and towers that populate this south-west corner of France. Encouraged, I purchased the 100 1:25000 topographical maps that cover the region and entered the sites of these mostly ruined castles and forts on to my computer. Where I came across a fortified or fortress town I entered the location of the church and to complete the picture, I entered the sites of remote hermitages, abbeys and cathedrals. When all the sites were on the computer, I tracked any alignments through Rennes-le-Château and was staggered to find 96 lines connecting some 300 medieval castles, forts, towers, hermitages, abbeys and cathedrals. (Fig 80) (The full list of these connections is included in Appendix 16).

To test the significance of these connections, it would be necessary to choose several random points in the region and track the connections through those points.

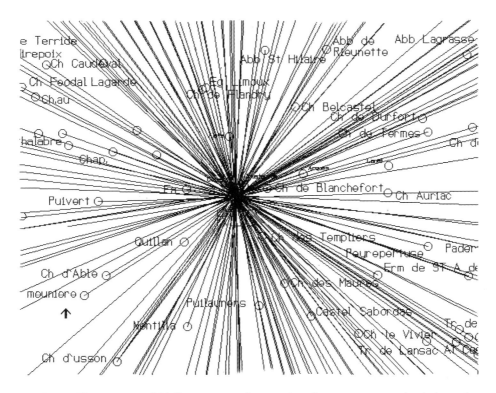

Fig 80 The pattern of 96 lines connecting castles, forts, towers, cathedrals and remote hermitages and chapels to Rennes-le-Château

Certainly, there are sufficient castles, towers and forts in Languedoc Roussillon to ensure that a number of direct alignments would be made, no matter where the points were chosen. Whether there would be as many, or the pattern so comprehensive, I doubt! The only sure thing, is that Rennes-le-Château is a place of mystery. If, in the past, it was believed to be a place of special significance, it may indeed be the location of The Pole Star and may even be the reason for the construction of The Plough. If there is no connection between the two, as with the rest of the 'discoveries', it would be necessary to believe that it is simply a giant coincidence!

CHAPTER 6

The new connections

During one of my Christmas breaks I had visited the ruins at Ephesus in Turkey. Unlike any other place I had ever seen, the streets, houses, temples and amphitheatre of the ancient town were all still present so that I was able to get a real sense of what it must have been like to live there. (Fig 81)

Below the town on the marshy plain caused by the silting of the river Cayster is the site of the temple of Diana (Artemis), one of the seven ancient wonders of the world. (Fig 82) In its glory, the temple was raised and surrounded by marble steps on all four sides. The raised platform measured 255 ft by 131 ft and was surrounded by fluted marble columns which were 60 ft high and it is thought to have been constructed about 600 BC. The temple was initially destroyed by the Goths in 262 AD but was partly rebuilt. In 401 AD it was completely destroyed by St John Chrysostom. (Fig 83)

Fig 81 The streets of the ancient town of Ephesus

Fig 82 The site of the Temple of Diana – one of the seven ancient wonders of the world

A few kilometres away from the ancient town of Ephesus in a secluded hillside location is a small chapel which (it is claimed) is the location of the house where Mary spent the last of her days, after Jesus' death. By contrast, the battlements of a well preserved mediaeval stone fortress dominate the north eastern skyline. (Fig 84) The stone blocks and mid– European architecture take nothing away from the lasting grace and 2500 year old marble and granite blocks that have protected the historical integrity of the ancient town. Close to the castle and abreast the same hill are ruins of the church of St John. The church was built in the 6th century and is reputed to be on the site of the burial place of St John the Evangelist.

Fig 83 The 13th century French manuscript which shows St John destroying the Temple of Diana

Fig 84 The fortress ruins that dominate the north-eastern skyline

When originally constructed, it was a huge building (400ft x 130ft) and contained columns taken from ancient Ephesus. In 1330 AD it was converted into a huge mosque; it was sacked 70 years later and was eventually destroyed by an earthquake. Attached to a wall, in the middle of the ruins, is a large plaque which (it says) was presented by 'The Christian Beacon Plaque fund of 1977'. (Fig 85) The plaque quotes the Book of the Apocalypse, Chapter 2, verses 1–7:
"UNTO THE ANGEL OF THE CHURCH OF EPHESUS WRITE: THESE THINGS SAITH HE THAT HOLDETH **THE SEVEN STARS** IN HIS RIGHT HAND WHO WALKETH IN THE MIDST OF THE SEVEN GOLDEN CANDLESTICKS.
2 I KNOW THY WORKS AND THY LABOUR AND THY PATIENCE, AND HOW THOU CANST NOT BEAR THEM WHICH ARE EVIL; AND THOU HAST TRIED THEM WHICH SAY THEY ARE APOSTLES, AND ARE NOT, AND HAST FOUND THEM LIARS.
3 AND HAST BORNE, AND HAST PATIENCE AND FOR MY NAMES SAKE HAST LABOURED, AND HAST NOT FAINTED.
4 NEVERTHELESS I HAVE SOMETHING AGAINST THEE, BECAUSE THOU HAST LEFT THY FIRST LOVE.
5 REMEMBER THEREFORE FROM WHENCE THOU ART FALLEN, AND REPENT, AND DO THE FIRST WORKS OR ELSE I WILL COME UNTO THEE QUICKLY, AND WILL REMOVE THY CANDLESTICK OUT OF HIS PLACE EXCEPT THOU REPENT.
6 BUT THIS THOU HAST, THAT THOU HATEST THE DEEDS OF THE NÏC-Ō-LÄ-Í-TÄNS WHICH I ALSO HATE.
7 HE THAT HATH AN EAR, LET HIM HEAR WHAT THE SPIRIT SAITH UNTO THE CHURCHES: TO HIM THAT OVERCOMETH WILL I GIVE TO EAT OF THE TREE OF LIFE, WHICH IS IN THE MIDST OF THE PARADISE OF GOD."

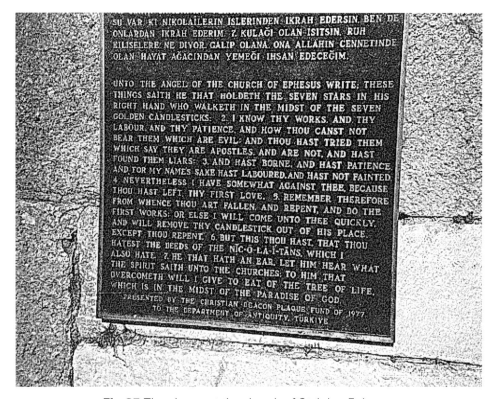

Fig 85 The plaque at the church of St John, Ephesus

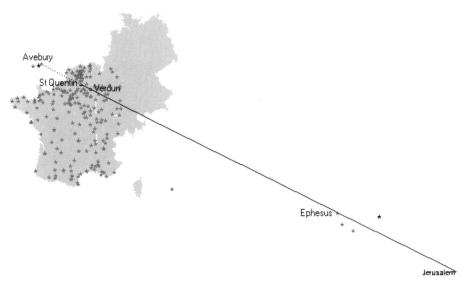

Fig 86 The line joining Nôtre Dame St Quentin, Nôtre Dame Verdun, Ephesus and Jerusalem

(a)

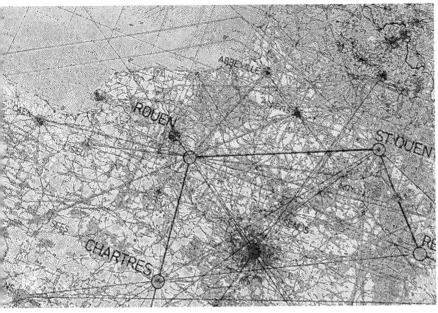

(b)

Fig 87 The line from Rouen via Bonne Mare and
Nôtre Dame Paris to the Temple of Isis at Philae

This reference to the seven stars made me wonder whether there might be some connection between the seven stars that I had located in northern France and Ephesus, the place of one of the seven ancient wonders of the world and the reputed home of Mary, the mother of Jesus. Back at base, I tracked a line through Ephesus back to The Plough over a series of tactical pilotage charts that I had carefully joined together. Once I had established a connection, I entered the latitudes and longitudes on to my 'map info' computer system and then changed the projection to UTM 31 Northern. The computer confirmed what the maps had told me:

There is an exact straight line between Nôtre Dame St Quentin – Nôtre Dame Verdun – Ephesus and Jerusalem. (Fig 86). Remarkably, in the other direction the same line goes through the Celtic stone circle at Avebury.

I could not and do not believe that this is simply a coincidence. It would have been understandable if the cathedrals in St Quentin and Verdun were oriented towards Jerusalem in reverence of Christ, which they are not. To have the line which joined the two of them orientated accurately towards Jerusalem made me think once more about the methods that had been used to fix the locations of these cathedrals. Who had designed this master plan, who had ensured its execution and, more importantly, why? I do not have high resolution maps of either Ephesus or Jerusalem and it will be necessary for me to return to these places with hand held survey equipment, which will allow me to identify the correct co-ordinates of all the key ground positions (using the survey satellite).

When this is done I will know the exact sites, in Jerusalem and Ephesus, which lie on the St Quentin – Verdun line. (To track the initial alignment, I used 31° 47'N, 35°13'E as the Jerusalem co-ordinates and 37°55'N 27°19' E as the Ephesus co-ordinates). In view of the link between St Quentin, Verdun and the Middle East, I looked carefully at each of the seven stars of The Plough to see if any other alignments existed. What I found was in some ways even more extraordinary than the extended St Quentin – Verdun line: The line from Abbaye St Ouen in Rouen which I already knew went through the centres of Bonne Mare and Nôtre Dame in Paris, when projected onwards, goes directly to the Temple of Isis at Philae in southern Egypt: **St Ouen, Rouen – Bonne Mare – Nôtre Dame, Paris – Temple of Isis, Philae** (Fig 87)

The Temple of Isis sits on an island between the old and new dams at Aswan. When the Nile was dammed in 1902 only part of it was closed, but the level of the river was raised and the Island of Philae flooded. The flooding of 'the pearl of Egypt' caused great distress and sparked considerable protest. With the advent of the high dam which was to be located behind the British dam, a UNESCO sponsored rescue mission was mounted for the Nubian temples south of the new dam. The rescue of Philae, the remarkable and beautiful island temple dedicated to Isis, was at the heart of this operation and all the temples on the island were moved stone by stone to the island of Algilkia some 300 metres away. The engineers who undertook the project were careful to ensure that all the buildings retained their same relative positions and orientations on the new island, which was unlikely ever to get flooded.

This Temple, which dates to the late Ptolemaic and early Roman periods must represent one of the best preserved historic monuments in the world and is awe inspiring in its construction. (Fig 88) Small holes set into walls 10 feet thick allow the sun's rays to cast their light on to a particular part of the painted hieroglyphics which cover the walls of the otherwise unlit rooms, thereby telling a different story at each of the different times of the year. (Fig 89)

Recently, another island close to Aswan has been given prominence by Graham Hancock in his book *The Sign and the Seal*. The book diaries his attempts to plot the movement and current location of the Ark of the Covenant and proposes that Elephantine island had a Jewish Temple between 650 and 410 BC, when it was destroyed. Apparently, this Jewish Temple had the same dimensions as the Temple of Solomon in Jerusalem and had housed the Ark for some two hundred years.

When I examined the location of Philae relative to Ephesus and Jerusalem the series of remarkable geometric coincidences continued: (Fig 90)

* The line from Philae to the location of Solomon's temple in Jerusalem lies 17° East of the longitude line through Philae and goes through Hebron and Bethlehem on its way.
* The line from Philae to the location of the Temple of Diana at Ephesus lies 17° W of the longitude line through Philae and passes close to the locations of three other ancient wonders of the world: The Pharos lighthouse at Alexandria, the Colossus at Rhodes and the Mausoleum at Halicarnassus.

In ancient Egypt, the name Isis probably meant 'seat' or 'throne'. She was of special significance for the king, being regarded as his symbolic mother. Isis was worshipped as 'the great goddess of magic' who had protected her son Horus from snakes, preda-

Fig 88 The Temple of Isis at Philae on the Upper Nile

Fig 89 The beam of light on a section of hieroglyphics

tors and other dangers; thus she would protect mortal children also. She was queen to Osiris (her brother) and greatly revered. Nowhere in the pyramid texts is there any record of her death and in recent time she has become a cult figure as 'the mother goddess' associated with fertility and the protection of the earth and its environment within many organisations who claim some affiliation to 'the ancient knowledge'.

The Secret Teaching of the Ages by Manly P Hall tells us that, "The world virgin is sometimes shown standing between two great pillars – the Jachin and Boaz of Freemasonry – symbolising the fact that Nature attains productivity by means of polarity. As wisdom personified, Isis stands between the pillars of opposites, demonstrating that understanding is always found at the point of equilibrium and that truth is often crucified between the two thieves of apparent contradiction." . . . "During the Middle Ages the troubadours of Central Europe preserved in song the legends of the Egyptian goddess. They composed sonnets to the most beautiful woman in the world. Though few ever discovered her identity, she was Sophia, the Virgin of Wisdom whom all the philosophers of the world have wooed. Isis represents the mystery of motherhood, which the ancients recognised as the most apparent proof of Nature's omniscient wisdom and God's overshadowing power. To the modern seeker she is the optime of the Great Unknown, and only those who unveil her will be able to solve the mysteries of life, death, generation and regeneration." On the basis of this, and the fact that Isis, like Paris, means equal-equal, it may be possible to consider the meridian as a representation of Isis. This possibility provoked me to examine the St Ouen – Philae line to see where it crossed the ancient meridian through Paris.

When I examined these two lines, I was surprised to find that their point of intersec-

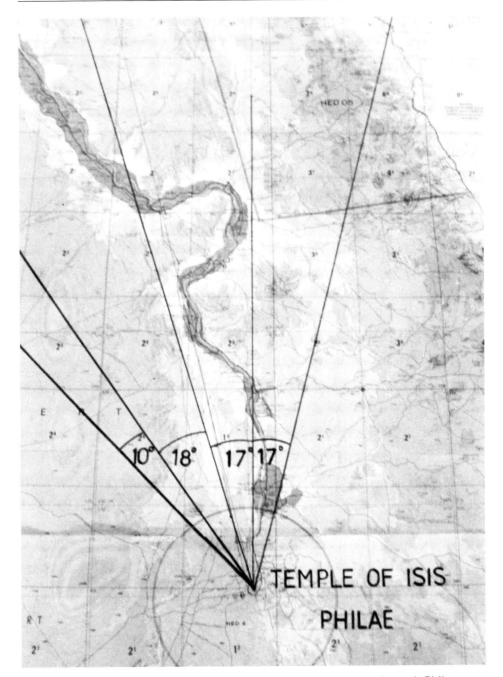

Fig 90 The 17° lines on either side of the line of longitude through Philae

tion occurs in the 'Palais du Louvre'. The Louvre's construction was started by Philippe Auguste in 1200 and was rebuilt in 1546. This was followed in 1564 by the Palais des Tuileries which was destroyed in 1871. For those interested in similarities, it is amazing how the plan of the Louvre and the Tuileries gardens down to the Egyptian obelisk at La Place de la Concorde are similar in layout to the Egyptian temples. The photographs below compare the Louvre with the complex at Luxor. (Fig 91)

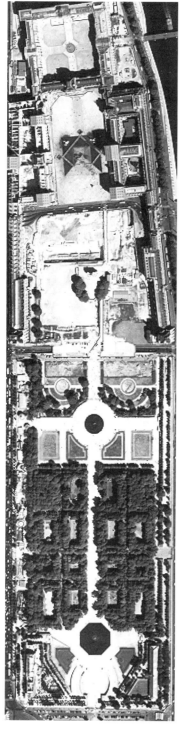 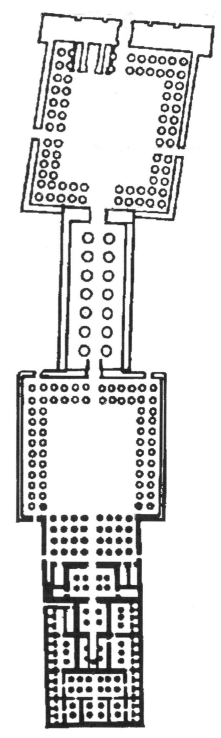

Fig 91
Left – the aerial photograph of the Palace of the Louvre
Right – The layout of the Egyptian Temple at Luxor

Given the link between Isis and Paris[1] , and the ancient Paris meridian[2] which falls so close to Rennes-le-Château, some readers may be interested in the coincidental significance contained in the opening lines of a phonetic interpretation of the Marie de Nègre tombstone at Rennes-le-Château, (Fig 75) which reads:

Cette gitane obéit à le meridien agé, le rai d'or
Elle est la dame d'haut
Pour elle, des belles ans, sèche et forte
Mages et eux des haut indices
le démontez et assemblerez la réponse raide
même à cette idée . . .

This gypsy follows the old meridian, the golden line
She is the mother of Heaven
For her, beautiful years dry and strong
Wise men and those with high IQ's
will take it apart and will put together the unbending answer
even to this idea . . .

This inscription could well be attempting to link Isis with the Paris meridian and may indicate that the secret held for many years within the Blanchefort family, was linked to hidden design that had been carved into the principal cathedral towns of France.

The line from Philae has obvious links with the earthly representation of the Plough and I therefore I looked carefully at the important points on the line, other than Bonne Mare, Rouen and Paris . . .

* Rouen: Abbaye St Ouen (Fig 92) is located where a church existed in the late 4th century but there is uncertainty about the exact date of the first church. St Victrice, the eighth Bishop of Rouen established many religious buildings at this time and it is because of this, that Dom Toussaint Duplessis wrote in 1740 that the first church was probably constructed close to 399 AD. The current building was prefixed by a magnificent edifice which was constructed between 1046 and 1126 but was destroyed in a fire in 1136. In 1318 the existing abbey was constructed on the same site and is larger and more magnificent than many of France's cathedrals. An interesting feature (in view of the pattern that I have uncovered) is the pentagram in the rose window at the end of the north-east facing transept, which duplicates the pentagram in the equivalent window of Nôtre Dame, the other cathedral on the same line (Fig 93).

  Abbaye St Ouen, (like the cathedral of Nôtre Dame in Rouen) is orientated at 113º East (true geographic) which is 14º less than the bearing of the line to Philae (127º) but very close to the bearing of the line from Abbey St Ouen to Jerusalem.

* Paris: The cathedral in Paris is reputed to have been located on the site of an ancient Roman Temple. In 1710 carved blocks of stone were excavated during work enlarging the archbishop's burial vaults. The blocks are believed to have been part of an altar and the following message is engraved in Latin into one of them;

  In the reign of Tiberius Caesar Augustus the nautes of the Parisii raised this monument to very great and very good Jupiter at their own expense.

---

[1] The names mean the same thing. Isis means equal equal in Greek and Paris equal equal from a mixture of Latin and Greek

[2] The Paris meridian goes through the centre of Paris and (as we know) cuts the base of the earthly plough into two exactly equal parts.

It is believed that the 'pillar of nautes', as it is called, (Fig 94) was erected around 20 – 30 AD and it indicated that the Celts were willing to honour and pay reverence to the Roman Gods.

Since Roman times the Ile de la Cité has been the home of three churches. The first of these was the old cathedral dedicated to St Etienne. This large building, constructed in the 5th or 6th century, occupied part of what is now the nave and a large part of the square in front of what is now the present cathedral. The first church dedicated to Nôtre Dame was constructed in the 7th century and rebuilt in the 9th after the Normans had

Fig 92 Abbaye St Ouen, Rouen

been and gone   it covered part of the current nave. After this came the ancient round church, Saint Jean de la Ronde, used as a baptistry. This was continually rebuilt up to the eighteenth century and was situated to the left of the current facade.

Nôtre Dame, the cathedral you see today, was commenced in 1163 and is thought to be the first complete Gothic cathedral to be designed and built in France. (Fig 95) It is a magnificent example of Gothic architecture, which (these days) is difficult to appreciate as a place of religious contemplation and worship, for the almost permanent multitude of camera flashing tourists that babble around its inner sanctum. The cathedral is oriented at 114° E which is the precise bearing of the line to Jerusalem from the cathedral's centre.

In one of the windows of the north-east transept I again found the regular pentagram (Fig 93) and I could not help but speculate why the only two significant religious edifices I had visited that had a pentagram as part of their right hand transept decoration (looking down from the altar) were both on a line joining Bonne Mare (one of the two pointer stars in the earthly Plough and one of the five points of the pentagram it contains) and the Temple of Isis at Philae in Egypt. Back at my desk, I looked again at the Book of Revelations and was intrigued when I read verses 12 – 20 of Chapter 1:

12 And I turned to see the voice that spoke to me. And being turned, I saw seven golden candlesticks:

13 And in the midst of the seven golden candlesticks, one like the Son of man, clothed with a garment down to his feet, and girt about the paps with a golden girdle.

14 And his head and his hairs were white, as white wool, and as snow, and his eyes were as a flame of fire.

15 And his feet like unto fine brass, as in a burning furnace. And his voice the sound of many waters.

16 And he had in his right hand seven stars. And from his mouth came out a sharp two edged sword: and his face was as the sun shineth in his power.

17 And when I had seen him, I fell at his feet as dead. And he laid his right hand upon me saying: Fear not I am not the first and the last.

18 And alive, and was dead, and behold I am living forever and ever, and have the keys of death and of hell.

19 Write therefore the things which thou hast seen, and which are, and which must be done hereafter.

20 The mystery of the seven stars which thou sawest in my right hand; and the seven golden candlesticks, **the seven stars are the angels of the seven churches**. And the seven candlesticks are the seven churches.

Since reading the plaque on the walls of the ruined church of St John, I had wondered whether the construction of the earthly Plough – the seven stars, had been carried out by early Christians to celebrate the words contained within the Apocalypse. If it had, then I surmised that there might also be a representation of the seven golden candlesticks amongst the cathedrals. The only two pictures of the seven branched candlestick of the Temple of Jerusalem (which may not be what is referred to in the book of Revelations) are the carving on the Arch of Titus in Rome depicting the spoils of Jerusalem and the painting of *The Destruction of the Temple of Jerusalem* by Nicolas Poussin. (Figs 96, 97) I did not find any pattern, which I could justify as an accurate representation of the seven branched candlesticks. The nearest I got were the shapes in figure 98.

In *The Dimensions of Paradise*, John Michell offers an interesting and succinct analysis of the way ancient texts were related to numbers: "Ancient science was based, like that of today, on number, but whereas number is now used in the quantitative sense

Fig 93 upper – the pentagram at Abbey St Ouen **lower** – the pentagram at Nôtre Dame in Paris

Fig 94 The Gallic God Esus on the piller of Nautes

for secular purposes, the ancients regarded numbers as symbols of the universe, finding parallels between the inherent structure of number and all types of form and motion. Theirs was a very different view of the world from that which now obtains. They inhabited a living universe, a creature of divine fabrication, designed in accordance with reason and thus to some extent comprehensible by the human mind." In relation to the number seven, he writes, "Seven is a unique decad because, as Pythagoras said,

Fig 95 Nôtre Dame Cathedral in Paris

Fig 96 Reconstruction of the 7-branched candlestick on the arch of Titus by Leon Yardley

'it neither generates nor is generated', meaning that it cannot be multiplied to produce another number within the first ten, nor is it a product of other numbers. For that reason the heptad was called the Virgin and was a symbol of eternal things rather than created things. It was particularly related to the measurement of time, the seven ages of man, the seven days of the week or quadrant of the lunar month. It is thus connected with the perfect number 28 which governs the periods of the moon and the female, and is also the cause of 28 being a triangular number, for 1+2+3+4+5+6+7 = 28."

The ancient science of writing text so that the number value of each word and phrase was interrelated and meaningful was called 'gematria'. This science is claimed to have been established by Pythagoras and although for 2500 years, philosophers of all nations have attempted unsuccessfully to unravel the Pythagorean skein, it is safe to say that with the death of Pythagoras, the key to this science was lost. The table containing the numerical values of letters which was included in Godfrey Higgins' *Celtic Druids* is shown below (Fig 99). Manly Hall's *The Secret Teachings of All Ages* tells us; "The first step in obtaining the numerical value of a word is to take it back to its original tongue. Only words of Hebrew and Greek derivation can be successfully analysed using this method and all words must be spelled in their most ancient and complete forms. Old Testament words and names must be translated back into early Hebrew characters and New Testament words into the original Greek. An example is the mysterious Gnostic pantheus *Abraxus*. For this name the Greek table is used.

Abraxus in Greek is Αβραξασ: Α=1, β=2, ρ=100, α=1, ξ=60, α=1, σ=200. The sum of these is 365, the number of days in the year.

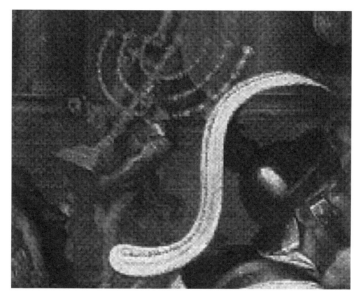

Fig 97 Detail of the destruction of the Temple at Jerusalem by Poussin

In *The Dimensions of Paradise*, John Michell presents the dimensions of the new Jerusalem as interpreted from Revelations 21 and shows how the dimensions of the wall of New Jerusalem form a plan of the earth. His illustration of the use of gematria provoked me to wonder whether other parts of the book of Revelations might not be subject to the same rules and analysis. Because of this I have included a comprehensive breakdown of the appropriate sections of chapters 1 and 2 of the book of Revelations;

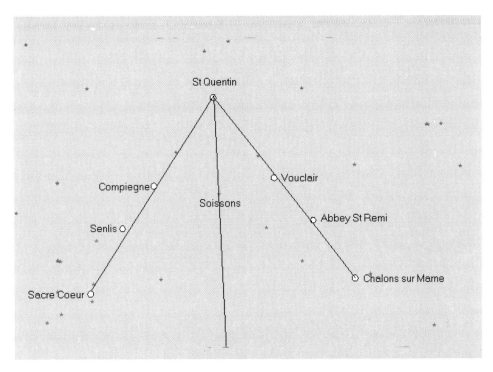

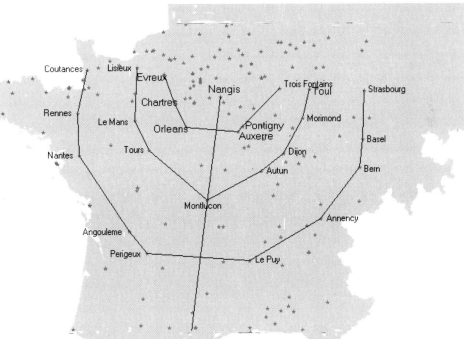

Fig 98 Two (different shaped) attempts to trace patterns of a 7-branched candlestick amongst the cathedrals and abbeys of France – both of which have their central candle holder at St Quentin and thus lie within the seven stars

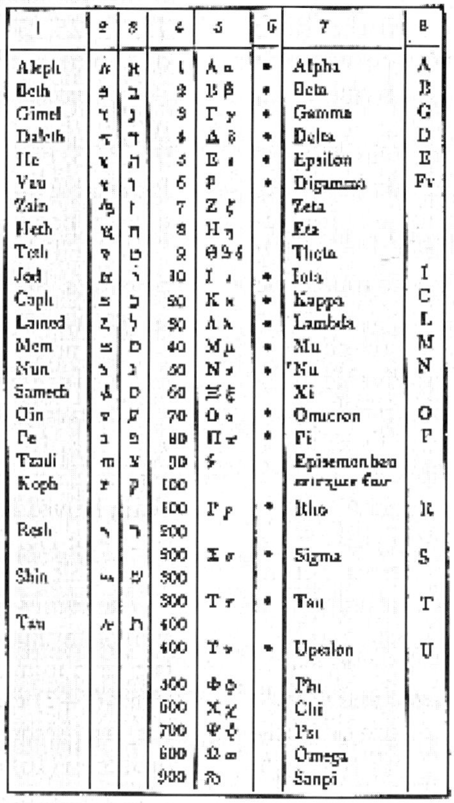

1	2	3	4	5	6	7	8
Aleph	ࠀ	א	1	Α α	•	Alpha	A
Beth	ࠁ	ב	2	Β β	•	Beta	B
Gimel	ࠂ	ג	3	Γ γ	•	Gamma	G
Daleth	ࠃ	ד	4	Δ δ	•	Delta	D
He	ࠄ	ה	5	Ε ε	•	Epsilon	E
Vau	ࠅ	ו	6	Ϝ	•	Digamma	Fv
Zain	ࠆ	ז	7	Ζ ζ		Zeta	
Heth	ࠇ	ח	8	Η η		Eta	
Teth	ࠈ	ט	9	Θ θ ϑ		Theta	
Jod	ࠉ	י	10	Ι ι	•	Iota	I
Caph	ࠊ	כ	20	Κ κ	•	Kappa	C
Lamed	ࠋ	ל	30	Λ λ	•	Lambda	L
Mem	ࠌ	מ	40	Μ μ	•	Mu	M
Nun	ࠍ	נ	50	Ν ν	•	Nu	N
Samech	ࠎ	ס	60	Ξ ξ		Xi	
Oin	ࠏ	ע	70	Ο ο	•	Omicron	O
Pe	ࠐ	פ	80	Π π	•	Pi	P
Tzadi	ࠑ	צ	90	ϛ		Episemon bau	
Koph	ࠒ	ק	100			επισημον βαυ	
			100	Ρ ρ	•	Rho	R
Resh	ࠓ	ר	200				
			200	Σ σ	•	Sigma	S
Shin	ࠔ	ש	300				
			300	Τ τ	•	Tau	T
Tau	ࠕ	ת	400				
			400	Υ υ	•	Upsilon	U
			500	Φ φ		Phi	
			600	Χ χ		Chi	
			700	Ψ ψ		Psi	
			800	Ω ω		Omega	
			900	ϡ		Sanpi	

Fig 99 The numerical values of the Hebrew, Greek and Sumerian alphabets as illustrated in Higgins' Celtic Druids

The gematria of Revelations1,12-20 and 2,1

	31	1396	182	355	1408	518	81	345	515
12	Και	επεστρεφα	βλεπειν	την	φωνην	ητις	ελαλει	μετ	εμου
	And	I turned	to see	the	voice	which	spoke	with	me

31	1601	139	386	1291	1501
και	επιστρεφας	ειδον	επτα	λυχνιας	χρυσας
and	having turned	I saw	seven	lampstands	golden

	31	55	1045	1150	1940	310	530	1510	683	270
13	και	εν	μεσω	των	λυχνιων	ομοιον	υιον	ανθρπουω	ενδεδυμενον	ποδηρη
	and	in	(the)midst	of the	lampstands	(one) like	a son	of man	*having been* clothed	to the feet

31	1422	450	580	821	915	1351
και	πριεζωσμενον	προς	τοις	μαστοις	ζωνην	χρυσαν
And	*having been* girdled round	at	the	breasts	girdle (with) a	golden

	8	9	564	1171	31	11	1215	466	1000	235
14	η	δε	κεφαλη	αυτου	και	αι	τριχες	λευκαι	ως	εριον
	the	and	head	of him	and	the	hairs	white	as	wool

575	1000	1460	31	80	730	1171	1000	660	850
λευκον	ως	χιων	και	οι	οφθαλμοι	αυτου	ως	φλοξ	πυρος,
white	as	snow	and	the	eyes	of him	as	a flame	of fire

	31	80	359	1171	270	1614	1000	55	921	1768
15	και	οι	ποδες	αυτου	ομοιοι	χαλκολιβανω	ως	εν	καμινω	πεπυρωμενης
	and	the	feet	of him	like	*to* burnished brass	as	in	a furnace	having been fired

31	8	1358	1171	1000	1358	1555	1060
και	η	φωνη	αυτου	ως	φωνη	υδατων	πολλων
and	the	voice	of him	as	a sound	waters	of many

16

31	1455	55	308	80	725	1171	807	386	31	25	770	1181
και	εχων	εν	τη	δεξια	χειρα	αυτου	αστερας	επτα	και	εκ	του	στοματος
and	having	in	the	right	hand	of him	stars	seven	and	out of	the	mouth

1171	722	894	146	853	31	8	980	1171	1000	70
αυτου	ρομφαια	διστομος	οξεια	εκπορευομενη	και	η	οφις	αυτου	ως	ο
of him	sword	two mouthed (edged)	a sharp	proceeding	and	the	face	of him	as	the

310	576	55	308	510	1171
ηλιος	φαινει	εν	τη	δυναμει	αυτου
sun	shines	in	the	power	of it

17

31	375	139	826	291	450	970	355	1171	1000	445	31
Και	οτε	ειδον	αυτου	επεσα	προς	τους	ποδας	αυτου	ως	νεκρος	και
And	when	I saw	him	I fell	at	the	feet	of him	as	dead	and

97	358	130	1171	85	50	888	48	1042	808	65	70
εθηκεν	την	δεξιαν	αυτου	επ	εμε	λεγων	μη	φοβου	εγω	ειμι	ο
he placed	the	right (hand)	of him	on	me	saying	fear	not	I	am	the

1550	31	70	1376
πρωτος	και	ο	εσχατος
first	and	the	last

18

31	70	857	31	231	445	31	484	857	65	215	970
και	ο	ζων	και	εγενομην	νεκρος	και	ιδου	ζων	ειμι	εις	τους
and	the	living (one)	and	I became	dead	and	behold	living	I am	unto	the

1062	1150	1711	31	1405	501	265	770	831	31	770	475
αιωνας	των	αιωνων	και	εχω	τας	κλεις	του	θανατου	και	του	αδου
ages	of the	ages	and	I have	the	keys		of death	and		of hades

19

924	520	1	224	31	1	275	31
γραφον	ουν	α	ειδες	και	α	εισιν	και
Write thou	therefore	(the) things which	thou sawest	and	the) things which	are	and

1	120	283	346	1002
α	μελλει	γενεσθαι	μετα	ταυτα
(the) things which	(is) are *about*	to occur	after	these things

20

370	1178	1150	386	1456	678	224	95	508	280	510	31
το	μυστηριον	των	επτα	αστερων	ους	ειδες	επι	της	δεξιας	μου	και
The	mystery	of the	seven	stars	which	thou sawest	on	the	right (hand)	of me	and

501	386	1291	501	1501	80	386	811	122	1150	386	1143
τας	επτα	λυχνιας	τας	χρυσας	οι	επια	αστερες	αγγελοι	των	επτα	εκκλησιν
the	seven	lampstands	the	golden	the	seven	stars	messengers	of the	seven	churches

275	31	11	1101	11	386	386	304	275
εσιν	και	αι	λυχνιαι	αι	επτα	επτα	εκκλησιαι	εισιν
are	and	the	lampstands	the	seven	seven	churches	are.

2.1

1100	842	508	55	1510	494	924	310	53	70	1271
Τω	αγγελω	της	εν	Εφεσω	εκκλησιας	γραψον	Ταδε	λεγει	ο	κρατων
To	the messenger	of the	in	Ephesus	church	write thou	These things	says	the (one)	holding

970	386	807	55	308	80	1171	70	1426	55	1045
τους	επτα	αστερας	εν	τη	δεξια	αυτου	ο	περιπατων	εν	μεσω
the	seven	stars	in	the	right (hand)	of him	the (one)	walking	in	(the)midst

1150	386	1940	1150	2150¹
των	επτα	λυχνιων	των	χρυσων
of the	seven	lampstands		golden

---

¹ The gematria of the first two chapters of Revelations was supplied by Bonnie Gaunt of Michigan,,U S A

Readers who have a mathematical bent will enjoy breaking down the numbers to find interesting combinations: The two phrases, 'in the midst of the lampstands one like the son of man' and 'having been clothed to the feet and having been girdled round at the breasts with a golden girdle and the' add up to 6540

This number equals 6000 (the number representing the creation of the Universe) + 540 (the total of the angles of the regular pentagon)

According to John Michell, some of the key numbers in gematria are:

1008	=	The twelve Gods; the diameter of the circle with a circumference of 3168
1080	=	The Holy Spirit; The earth spirit; the virgin Goddess of earth
12	=	The basic building block of the new Jerusalem
1224	=	The Lord God; God's creation; divine circle; the divine circle (Paradise)
1480	=	Christ; Son of the Cosmos; holiness; master and lord
1728	=	Reed like a rod
1746	=	Jerusalem, the city of God; the universal spirit; grain of mustard seed; son of Virgin Mary
2368	=	Jesus Christ
3168	=	Lord Jesus Christ
5040	=	Plato's number
666	=	'the heart, mind understanding, reason'; divine wrath; weapons of God
864	=	an altar; Jerusalem (as a world centre)
888	=	Jesus

In verse 1.20 (above) of the book of Revelations, the phrase, '**the mystery of the seven stars**' has a number of **4540. This equals 540 + 540 + 1480 + 1980.**

Incredibly, these numbers are the numbers of the two pentagons (the inner and the outer) + Christ (the pentagram) + 1981 (the number of Kallisto, the constellation of the Great Bear). This means that **the number of 'the mystery of the seven stars' corresponds with the numbers of the pattern which has been identified on the ground.** Does this imply that the book of Revelations uses via gematria some ancient knowledge of the ground pattern in northern France or do both the ground pattern and the book of Revelations refer to some more ancient beliefs that the authors of both these permanent records attempted to pass down to us? Either way, to ascertain how the bible and other ancient literature are linked to ancient mystical tradition through gematria may require further study.

The alternative of course is that this correspondence is simply an interesting coincidence and that we can make something of everything if we just look hard enough! Another interesting set of numbers which add up to 4540 are:

864	=	the corner of the earth on which the angel stood – Revelation 7.1, Jerusalem, Pythagarous, the throne of Abraxus.
504	=	the building block of the new Jerusalem
1080	=	the Holy Spirit, the Earth Spirit, fountain of wisdom.
1480	=	Son of the Cosmos, throne of wisdom, Master and Lord, Christ
612	=	Zeus, the Good Shepherd
4540		

The book of Revelations (1.20) tells us that 'the seven stars are the messengers of the seven churches'. If there is truly a link between Revelations and the pattern on the ground, the gematria of the phrase 'the seven stars are the messengers of the seven churches' should in some way link to the geometry of the figure on the ground.

The gematria of the phrase 'messengers of the seven churches' is 2801 which translates to the number 2800. The number 28 is significant in sacred geometry where a circle with the circumference of 31680 (Lord Jesus Christ) divides into 28 equal parts of 360. 28 (as we know) also gives the number of days in the lunar month and in the female cycle. More significantly (from our point of view) it is the sum of the first seven numbers (1+2+3+4+5+6+7

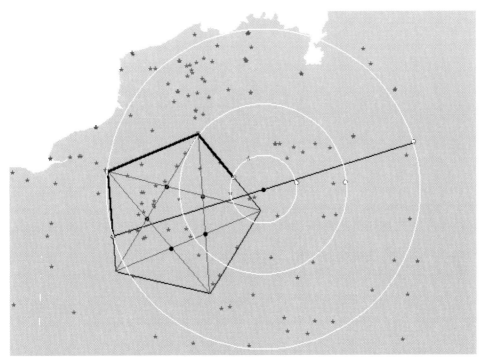

Fig 99a The Plough, two pentagons and the pentagram together with the three circles, centred on the same point, which go through the seven stars

= 28). Because of the relationship between 28 and a circle of circumference of 31680, I examined the ground plan carefully and made a series of incredible discoveries:

* The centre of the circle connecting Chartres, Bonne Mare and Donnersberg lies midway between Chartres and Donnersberg.
* The same point is the centre of a circle connecting Reims and Verdun and a wider circle connecting St Quentin and Landonvillers.
* The distance between the centre of Nôtre Dame Chartres and the Donnersberg position is exactly 1596670 feet. This equals 3168 (Lord Jesus Christ) x 5040 (Plato's number and the building block of the new Jerusalem).
* The line connecting Donnersberg and Chartres goes through the centre of the pentagram.

On the basis that the circumference (2r) of 31680 = 28 x 360, it is possible to calculate the unit of measure that was used when constructing these circles.

$$1596670\pi = 28 \times 72 \times 792 = 31680n = 28 \times 360\pi \times n$$
$$1596670 = 28 \times 360 \times n$$

n = 158.4 which according to John Michell is one of the sacred numbers of the canon

The diameter of the circle containing all seven points (1596670 ft) equals the following units of measurement:

1640622.9	Roman feet	
1093748.629	Roman cubits	
4166.667	Roman furlongs	
328.125	Roman miles	
1574998.027	Greek feet	(1574500)
1049998.684	Greek cubits	(1050000)
2519.9968	Greek furlongs	(2520) – The diameter of Plato's world soul
314.9996	Greek miles	(315)
1385998.3	Egyptian feet	(1386000)
923998.8	Egyptian cubits	(924000)

If we assume that the diameter of the circle is 2520 Greek furlongs which is equal to the diameter of Plato's world soul we are presented with an interesting and additional numerical connection. In gematria, as we have seen, the number of The Plough (Kallisto) is 1980 and the number of the pentagon is 540. The sum of these two is 2520. Which means that the plough plus the pentagon it contains is equal to the number which corresponds the diameter of the construction in Greek furlongs.

The number 2520 also has the unique quality that it is the product of all the numbers that have been central to the higher mysteries – 12, 7, 5, 3, 2.

Another interesting combination of numbers which can be obtained from the construction is the sum of the numbers of the two pentagons: 540 + 540 = 1080 which is the number (in Gematria) of The Holy Spirit. In other words, the outer pentagon and its reflection created by the pentagram (Christ) it contains, brings us to the number of the Holy Spirit. This analysis would seem to correspond accurately with the conventional Christian explanation of this mysterious element of the Godhead.

Could it be that an in depth analysis of the mathematics and geometry of this incredible construction would give us answers the mysteries of so called Sacred Geometry?

The list of numbers above would seem to indicate that the original construction was conceived using Greek or Egyptian measure, that the basic building block (n) was 1/4 of a Greek furlong 2520/(28x360) and that the circumference of the outer circle can be split into 28 equal parts of 90π Greek furlongs or 49500π Egyptian feet. The fact that the diameter of the outer circle corresponds to the diameter of Plato's world soul as calculated by John Michell, draws us inevitably to the Greek furlong as the fundamental unit of measure used in the construction. This would support the hypothesis that the construction was planned and executed by those adhering to an ancient philosophy and represents a meeting ground between Egyptian, Greek and Anglo Saxon measures. These Greek and Egyptian measures are the first real clue to the origins of the construction and make it easier to substantiate a link between the Hellenic tradition as practised by the Gnostics, the Druidic tradition and the links with Christianity as formulated by the authors of Revelations. One can only wonder at the precision with which this plan was constructed and the techniques used to measure distances and angles so accurately. Perhaps we will never know whether this was meant to be a magnificent and yet secret monument, a construction in reverence to Polaris and the seven stars, a giant talisman or a message destined to be uncovered at some time in the future.

The last remaining ground shape that remained for me to identify (if only for my own peace of mind) was the representation of the constellation of Virgo by the cathedrals and abbeys of northern France. Charpentier's poor representation of this constellation (Fig 1) had been largely responsible for my initial research into the patterns formed by the French cathedrals and I felt obliged (if only to you, the reader) to show that my claim in the introduction (that cathedrals other than those selected by Charpentier form a much better representation of Virgo) was justified. After much trial and error, my selected group of points is presented in Figure 100 and joins Vannes, Alençon, Melun, Vezelay, St Etienne, Epernay, Virton, Cologne, Donnersberg and Freiberg. This should be compared with the picture of the constellation of Venus that adjoins it. The only point which is included in both the earthly representations of 'Ursa Major' and 'Virgo' is Donnersberg.

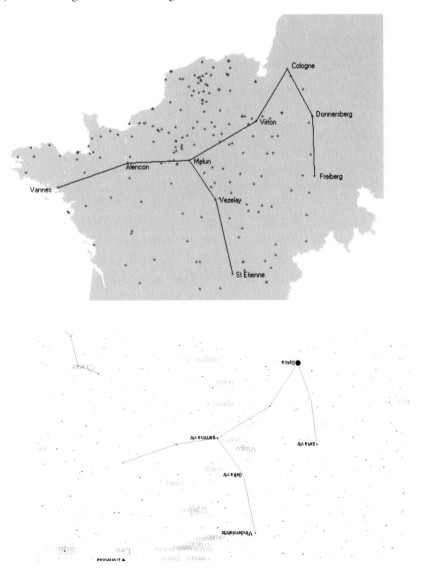

Fig 100 The ground plan of Virgo (top) The constellation of Virgo (bottom) as viewed from the south

CHAPTER 7
When was The Plough designed and constructed ?

I decided that the simplest way to carry out this intriguing piece of detective work was to concentrate on the timing of the construction: once I knew when it had been conceived, it would be easier to determine the identity of the architects.

When I looked at all the alternatives, it was self-evident that five periods and consequently, five distinct groups of architects were possible:-

* The Druids, during the time when the Celtic tribes were the dominant force in Gaul, prior to Roman occupation.
* The Romans, between the conquest of Gaul by Julius Ceasar which was completed in 51 BC and the Christianisation of Gaul in the fourth century AD
* The early Christians, between 150 AD and 500 AD
* The Visigoths, in the fifth century AD
* The Christians, in the Middle Ages between 1035 AD and 1300 AD

To narrow this down, I looked carefully at the historical information I had gathered for each of the seven locations and selected the facts that might lead to an informed conclusion.

Chartres: The official history of La Cité des Carnutes et du Pays Chartain (Chartres) written by Michel-Jean-François Ozeray in 1834 talks of the Gallic (Celtic) army led by the king of the Bituriges (a Celtic tribe), which included Carnutes, in 600 BC. At the end of an inter tribal war, this army pushed into Germany, Hungary, Italy and even as far as Greece.

One of the earliest documented records about the Carnutes themselves (the people who lived in the region of Chartres) was made in Julius Caesar's *Gallic Wars* where he describes "annual meetings of a Druid assembly in a sacred place (*in loco consecrato*) in the tribal territory of the Carnutes, believed to be the centre of all Gaul." Claudius Ptolemy's *Geography* written in 150 AD tells us that the towns of the *Carnutae* were Autricum and Cenabum – Chartres and Orleans. This linking of Chartres to the Druids is fascinating, not least because of the Druidic tradition of a pre-Christian virgin-mother cult. André Blondel in his book *Chartres*, says; "*Les environs de Chartres abritaient les sanctuaires des Druides et leurs écoles: là était le centre réligieux de la Gaul, la terre sacrée où la culte celtique enseignait ses doctrines et procédait à ses mystérieuses cérémonies. Aujourd'hui encore, les monuments que l'on est convenu d'appeler druidiques, dolmens et menhirs, autels ou tombeaux, se rencontrent fréquemment autour de Chartres.*"
– "Chartres sheltered the sanctuaries of the Druids and their schools: it was the religious centre of Gaul, sacred earth where the Celtic cult taught its doctrines and carried out its mysterious ceremonies. Today, the monuments we call *druidic*, dolmens and menhirs, altars or tombs, are frequently found around Chartres."

He goes on to say: "*Il est possible qu'ainsi que le veut la légende, un des principaux autels de la religion druidique se trouvât à la place ou s'élève aujourd'hui la cathédrale."* – "It is possible, as it says in the legend, that one of the principal altars of the Druidic religion was to be found in the place where the cathedral stands today."

Little is known of Chartres under the Roman administration other than that the city was controlled from Lyons until the middle of the third century when Lyonnaise was partitioned. From then on it was controlled from Sens. Archaeological remains of an amphitheatre and two aqueducts show that the city was a centre of some significance.

When the Visigoths crossed the Rhine in 406 AD they destroyed everything in their path until they reached Spain. However, *The History of Chartres* by Chevard tells us that 'Toulouse and Chartres stayed intact and in business.' Specific information concerning this period is not available.

The evangelization of Chartres by the first Christians is not recorded. Amongst the first Bishops was St Adventius who lived in the mid-4th century and a St Martin. They were followed later by Solemnis who, according to the chronicle, De vita Sancti Deodati, helped Clovis 1 in the Christian faith in the late 5th century. Solemnis's successor, Bishop Adventus attended the first council of Orleans in 511. The existence of these Bishops points to an early cathedral in Chartres but the first reference was to its destruction by Hunald, Duke of Aquitaine in 743. A few years later, one of Charles Martel's sons, Pépin the short (751-768), in a royal decree mentions gifts to the 'Church of St Mary' at Chartres, which is evidence that cathedrals at Chartres had been dedicated to Mary at least since the 8th century.

Charles Martel was the grandfather of Charlemagne and his son Pépin deposed Childeric III and thus the Carolingians displaced the Merovignian dynasty on the throne of France.

Fulbert, 'The Venerable Socrates of the Chartres Academy', arrived at Chartres Cathedral School in the 980's and before his death in 1028, established the school as one of the foremost scholastic institutions in mediaeval Europe. He was enthroned Bishop in 1006 and the Carolingian cathedral, which he inherited was destroyed by fire in 1020. Fulbert raised funds from royalty throughout the Christian world for a new cathedral. A small martyrium known as Lubin's crypt was retained when the new cathedral was built. Around it was constructed a new crypt, which even today is the largest in France and is the only part of Fulbert's cathedral that remains intact. The cathedral was severely damaged by fire in 1134 and its replacement, which is the current cathedral was built rapidly and eventually consecrated in 1260.

Fulbert's successors as principals of the Chartres Cathedral School, Ivo of Chartres (1040 – 1117), Bernard of Chartres (1119 – 1124) and Gilbert de la Porée (1124 – 1141) were all known for their neo-Platonist views and Gilbert is famous for his dispute with St Bernard de Clairvaux about the application of Platonic metaphysical doctrines to the theology of the Trinity. We can only assume that they (and the Cathedral School) owed their Platonic orientation to initial work carried out by Fulbert.

On the basis of this historical evidence, the existing cathedral is probably placed on the site of the first Christian church and, if legend is to be believed, may occupy a location, which was the site of one of the most important Druid altars in Gaul. Given the limited evidence, we must therefore limit our choice of those who selected the location for the current cathedral to the Druids or the early Christians. The orientation of the current cathedral is the same as that chosen by Fulbert in 1020, which may retain the orientation of the building that preceded it.

Bonne Mare: We know nothing of the area of forest close to the Bonne Mare Château and in the last analysis this lack of evidence will probably be the most important factor in the construction of any conclusions. Three kilometres north of the Bonne Mare position is the village of Radepont, which was the ancient Roman city of Ritumagus. This city was mentioned by Claudius Ptolemy as the town of the *Veneliocasi* tribe but nothing remains today of its illustrious Roman past.

In the 11th and 12th centuries, the area was once again a centre of activity. In 1011, the area of land which became home to the Abbaye de Fontaine Guérard was given by a Norwegian earl to the Abbey St Ouen in Rouen. Some time later, in 1090, the Earls of Breteuil built a castle close to the Roman Bridge – *Château de pont-St-Pierre* and it was in this period that the Abbaye de Fontaine Guérard was founded. In 1136 the castle was besieged, without success, by Thibaut the Earl of Chartres. A few years later, Richard the Lionheart, who wished to resist Philippe-Auguste's efforts to unify Normandy with France, built a magnificent fortress at Les Andelys and started the construction of subsidiary fortresses at Radepont, Orival and Moulineaux. The fortress at Radepont was finished after Richard's death in 1199. Since those days the fortress and the abbey have gradually fallen into ruins so that all there is left of the fortress today is debris.

The fact that there are no Roman or Christian ruins at our point of intersection, forces the conclusion that if this was a place of significance it was more likely to have been an ancient Druidic site than any of the other possibilities. The name Bonne Mare conjures a past that points us towards the worship of the Celtic Mother Goddess and it is easy to imagine a Druidic religious site in the 'forest of the good mother'.

St Quentin: The oldest history of St Quentin, written by Quentin la Tou in the 18th Century, says: "St Quentin, capital of the *Vermandois*, was founded by the Romans between 27 and 12 BC. Auguste, nephew of Julius Caesar gave it his first name Augusta, to which he joined the name of the most notable and ancient Celtic people in Belgian Gaul: the *Veromandues, Augusta Veromanduorum.*

Several notes in *Les éclaircissements sur Vermand, capitale des Veromandui*, by M J Rijollot & Fils states that Augusta Veromanduorum was the ancient Gallic town of Samarobriva, or Sambrobriva. This town is mentioned in Ptolemy's *Geography* as the town of the *Ambiani* and is recorded as north west of Augusta Viromandeum of the *Viromandues*. Ptolemy's co-ordinates were inaccurate, but it is unlikely that Samorobriva, which he shows as west of Paris could have been St Quentin. The disagreement amongst historians only illustrates that little definitive information exists.

The first Christian record of a church was when the reverend Eusébie erected a chapel in 342 to celebrate a miracle he is said to have witnessed with his own eyes. By the 7th century, the records talk of a church, established by St Rémy, Bishop of Reims. In 640, this church was enlarged by St Eloi, Bishop of Vermandois after he discovered the relics of St Quentin. A series of churches were built and destroyed by fire until, somewhere between 1113 and 1119, Count Mathieu laid the first stone of an imposing new church which lasted until the 12th century. The church we know today was started in the 12th century and the work continued until 1495 when the labyrinth was installed in the nave. In 1257 St Louis assisted in the consecration of the choir. The history of the basilica implies that successive buildings ocupied the same site but nowhere is this fact stated or claimed.

The dearth of information about St Quentin means that the location could have been chosen at any of the five points in time, specified at the begining of the chapter:

pre-51 BC by the druids, post 51 BC by the Romans, the time of the early Christians, the time of the Visigoths or the Christians during the Middle Ages.

Reims: The origins of Reims are wrapped up in legends, the most popular of which is that the people of Reims descended from the soldiers of Remus, brother of Romulus and founder of Rome who came to live in Gaul after the death of their leader and 750 years before the birth of Christ. A second story, claims that at the time of Priam of Troy, a prince named Remus who descended from Hercules of Libya, reigned in Gaul and founded the city of Reims in Champagne. This story is echoed by many French writers who cite as their source, a passage from *Manéthon*, where it says that *"le quatriesme prince d'Egypt, nommé Aménéphus, tint le sceptre 27 ans; à la quatriesme année dequel Rémus commença à régner sur les Galois, de qui les Rémois ont esté dénommés."* – "the fourth prince of Egypt named Amenephus held the sceptre 27 years; to the fourth year from which Remus commenced to rule the Gauls after whom the Remois are named."

A history of Reims written by R P Dom Guillaume Marlot in 1863 tells how the pre-Roman history of Reims was Druidic. He explains that the Druids were very advanced in geometry and mathematics and says that the Druids taught the doctrines and philosophies later propounded by Pythagoras and Plato and were probably the source that the Greeks drew from.

Another history written by Georges Boussines & Gustave Laurent explained that; *"Il y a donc tout lieu de supposer que les Rêmes avaient un culte tout spécial pour la triple incarnation de 'Cerunnos-Balar'."* – "There is therefore good cause to suppose that the 'Rêmes' had a particular cult for the triple incarnation of 'Cerunnos-Balar'." Cerunnus, was one of the greatest Celtic Gods and was widely revered throughout the whole of Gaul; he was both the son and the consort of the Mother God at different phases of the yearly cycle. He was also the Hunter God, sometimes known as Cernunnus. He was normally depicted as horned and was represented by the stag. (Fig 101). In Celtic myth, Balar was King of the Fomorians (those worshipping the giant forces of nature) and Lord of chaos and could kill a host of men with his glance. His existence indicates that the Celts in Gaul did contemplate the wondrous and the mystical and were not simply barbaric tribes led by prestigious witch doctors.

When the Romans arrived, they gave the name Durocottorum to the town and Caesar wrote that the Rémois were highest (relative to the other tribes) in dignity and virtue and that their town was abundant with men, houses and riches. As in other places, they introduced Roman gods and Boussines and Laurent say that; "the gods lived together without combining and on the same altar one found, side by side, statues of both Gallic and Roman gods."

Christianity arrived in the middle of the 3rd century with the mission of St Sixte and St Senice who fixed their religious centre (church) in the high part of the town. One of their successors, Betause (Inbetausius) transferred his cathedral to the heart of the city in the church of the Apostles which later was dedicated to St Synphorium. St Nicaise dedicated the first cathedral to the Blessed Virgin, Mother of Christ in 401 AD and in 496 AD, Clovis, the first Christian King of France, was baptised there by Archbishop St Remi. This was replaced by another cathedral in the same location in 852 AD.

In 816 Louis chose the town of Reims for his coronation and from the time of Henry 1 (1027) to Charles X (1825) all coronations except two have taken place there. The present cathedral was commenced in 1211 and celebrated the coronation of King St Louis in 1226. It was not in fact completed until the end of the century.

Fig 101 The image of Cerunnus, 'the horned one' from Paris

The only two of the five time periods eliminated by this short history are the Visigoths in the 5th century and the Christians from 1035 to 1300. It is possible that the early Christians wanted to establish their first church in the city centre and were restricted from so doing. In this scenario, they simply moved into their preferred location at the first feasible opportunity. Given such circumstances, the location of the current cathedral might have been chosen by the first Christians. Alternatively, the information which eventually designated the cathedral's location may not have been known until Betause's arrival, which still falls within the time frame I originally specified.

Of course, when the Christians moved into the city centre they could well have chosen a location which had already been used for religious ceremonies by Druids and/or Romans, which would mean that the position was designated by the Druids or the Romans.

Verdun: According to Claudius Ptolemy, the Gauls that occupied the land from Reims to Metz were the *Mediomatrices* – people of the good country. Verdun itself is not mentioned by Ptolemy and historians have needed to speculate regarding the pre-Roman origins of the town. The etymology of the name 'Verdun' gives us a Celtic or Gallic origin and meant, large or special place on a hill.

Caesar laid siege to Verdun which he called Uxellodunum and in the years that followed it became a thriving Roman fortress with its own coinage. The Druidic and Roman gods lived side by side as is shown by a statue found in the forests of the Ardennes with the inscription *Deanæ Arduinæ,* Diana being the mother goddess of the Romans and Arduina being the mother goddess of the Celts. *The Holy Blood and the*

Holy Grail tells us that "Like the ancient Arcadians they worshipped the bear in the form of Artemis (Isis) or, more specifically, the form of her Gallic equivalent, Arduina, patron goddess of the Ardennes."

There is some confusion concerning the beginnings of Christianity in Verdun. St Saintin is known to have been the first person to preach the gospel there and it is believed that he came from Paris and was a disciple of St Denis. The problem arises over the timing of St Denis's mission, claimed by some to have been in the 1st century but said by Gregory of Tours, the earliest writer on the history of the church in France, to have been in the year 250 AD.

The local legend of St Saintin, as reported in the *History of Verdun* by M. l'Abbé Clouët who says, "St Saintin travelled with a friend and assistant, named Antonin. St Denis sent him first to Chartres, then he entrusted him with the church in Meaux where he converted many pagans. At this time, Domitian, faithful imitator of Nero commenced a major persecution (of the Christians) and St Denis was arrested by the 'lectors' of the court of Paris. Understanding that his hour of martyrdom was near, he hastily commissioned Saintin and Antonin to write down the story of his death and to take it to the Pope so that he could nominate a successor. The two faithful disciples left to obey his orders but on the route, the angels who protect the town of Verdun, appeared to them, like angels appeared several times to St Paul in Macedonia, and asked them to divert from their path a little to pass by the land of the 'Verdunois'. Not believing that they could disobey a message from the heavens they made their way immediately towards Verdun. From the first moment St Saintin saw the town from the top of the hillock which looks over the west he knelt down and prayed to God to bless his work: then three doves flew into some trees that the Pagans had consecrated to fauns and satyrs. Encouraged by this sign, the two missionaries crossed this grove full of idols and entered the town, where, with the Lord's blessing to help them they soon had numerous converts. When their holy victory was complete, they established in the same pagan grove, a church in honour of St Peter and St Paul. This church was dedicated in 98 AD which was the thirteenth year of the rule of Domitian."

During the ensuing years, the inhabitants of Verdun, who became known as the *Claves*, established their own identity to such an extent that, at the council of Cologne in 346 AD, the Verdun representative was recorded as 'the Bishop of the Claves'. This may be significant if 'Clave' originated from the Latin *clavis* meaning key.

The cathedral in Verdun which has been dedicated to the Virgin Mary since the 5th century, underwent a succession of fires and lootings until, between 990 and 1024, a new grand cathedral was constructed. It was built in the place of the existing cathedral and retained only the Carolingian choir. This building was enhanced between 1040 and 1089 when the high windows of the nave were rebuilt and decorative lozenges set between them. After damage to the Carolingian choir, a new chancel with a large crypt was built between 1136 and 1160 and the cathedral was consecrated by Pope Eugene III in November 1147. Due to a fire, major repairs were undertaken to the high parts of the cathedral (towers and framework) in 1755 and, after the first world war bombardments, the nave vaults and cloister galleries needed extensive rebuilding work. Despite these repairs however, the building is essentially the same one that was constructed at the end of the 10th century.

The cathedral in Verdun would appear to be in the exact same place as the original cathedral and if the legend of St Saintin is to be believed, then the location (and possibly the orientation) of this cathedral could well have been established by the position (and layout) of an ancient Druid site. If the legend is not to be believed (even in part) we are still left with the possibility that the first cathedral was situated on a previously Druid or Roman religious site and therefore that the site of the existing cathedral dates to the Druid, Roman or early Christian periods. The location and orientation of Notre Dame Verdun is key to the position of the pentagram contained within the body of The Plough and I am inclined to believe that the 3rd and 4th century designation of the people of Verdun as 'the people of the key' may well relate to this. This being so, then the timing of the construction would definitely be limited to the Druid or early Christian eras.

Ruins north of Courcelles Chaussy: Unless the ruins in the forest of Landonvillers are shown to be those of a Roman Temple or Christian Church (which is unlikely), we are left with little positive information about the origins of this particular site. Since we know that the Druids and Celts chose forest groves for their religious sites we are forced to assume that, if anything, this site must have been Druidic.

Donnersberg: In chapter 4, I gave some information, which indicated that Donnersberg was an ancient Celtic site. To discover whether or not there are historical connections which might place the origination of The Plough in some other time period, I will summarise what is known about the area:

A series of stone axes strongly suggest a stone age settlement. These were joined by shards of pottery from the late Neolithic/Bronze age and a large number of finds from the Urmfeld culture (1200 – 800 BC), which indicate that the site was occupied prior to the construction of the ringwall by the Celts in the late La Tène period (from 200 BC to the birth of Christ). A large number of finds from this late La Tène period show that the site was continually occupied during this time.

The origins and purpose of an oval wall, 200 metres long and 90 metres wide, consisting of vitrified ryolite which must have required temperatures of up to 1400°C, continues to elude archaeologists and historians. The fact that pieces of this vitrified stone exist in the outer ringwall indicates that this oval 'cinder wall' was probably constructed before the outer wall.

In the centre of the 240 hectare area encircled by the Celtic ringwall is a U-shaped structure (approximately 92 metres long by 33 metres wide). This consists of a wall (height 1 metre and base width 7–8 metres) and boundary ditch with sides of unequal length and has traditionally been known as the Pagan Cemetery. Archaeological research has identified this structure as one of a group of Celtic ritual sites, the so-called "square earthworks". Finds inside the "square earthwork" date it to 300–200 BC, but the lack of direct evidence leaves only the comparison with other "square earthworks" to signify its use.

Archaeologists claim that a few finds of Roman pottery provide insight into the trading practices of the Celts. Coins with Pallus-Minerva on the front (Rome) and a Gallic horse on the back are thought to be from the *Nemetes,* a tribe of Celts, which were said by Ptolemy to occupy the land between the Rhine and the Mosel. He named their towns as Neomagus (Trier) and Rufiniana.

In 893 AD documented claims were made that an ancient vineyard had existed on the Donnersberg. Historians indicated that the vine-dresser's knife found there and the method of binding the vines eight times, point to a Greek rather than Roman origin. They presume that the Greek influence came up the Rhone and the Rhine and was subsequently followed from the Greek colony in Marseilles, which was established in about 600 BC.

The Romans constructed a road from Mainz to Kaiserslautern, which passed only 4 kilometres from the peak at Donnersberg and extensive renovations of Roman structures from 1st to 4th century have been excavated in Falkensa and Rockenhausen, 9 kilometres west of Donnersberg. Despite these signs of Roman activity in the area, there are no signs of any Roman occupancy of Donnersberg itself.

This may be conclusive since Dr Friedrich Sprater in *Die Pflaz unter den Römern*, tells us that, "Particular attention is drawn to the fact that Temples of Mercury are often found on mountain tops; there are two inscriptions to Mercury to be found on the summit of Roßberg near Becherbach Gangloff and a Temple to Mercury was excavated on the Lemberg in Duchroth".

Donnersberg appears to have been unoccupied during the period of early Christian evangelisation and it was not until the 7th century when a church is known to have existed at Kirchheimbolanden (3.5 kilometres east of Donnersberg) that we have any proof of Christian influence. In 835 AD, it was recorded that Ludwig gave Albisheim and the surrounding land on the Donnersberg to the monastery at Prum on the Eifel. Land at Weierhof (Donnersberg and the lands to the east) is mentioned in the *Golden Book*, (a list of monastery lands) in 893 AD. Following that date, the lands were settled by the Mennonite community.

Pope Lucius III (1181-85) confirmed the gift by Werber II of Bolanden and his wife Gulda of the estate at Weierhof and a chapel to the monastery of Hane near Bolanden; it is however unknown how the Emperor's advisor, von Bolanden, came to give the estate at Weierhof to the monastery founded by his father in 1129. Even the records at Prum Abbey offer no reason for the transfer of ownership of the estate. Most remarkable is that Lucius makes reference only to an estate at "Wilre" (which is only a small part of Weierhof); apparently the large Weierhof estate had fallen victim to the nearby developing villages such as Mannheim-Neu-Bolanden, of whose expansion Neu-Bolanden Castle forms part, and its population had fallen dramatically. Shortly after the fall of the Hohenstaufen dynasty the end came for the powerful von Bolanden family who held the hereditary office of the King's seneschal. Their power quickly disintegrated after the death of Werner V (1220 – 1296).

In 1335 a pilgrim's chapel dedicated to the Apostle Jacob stood high up on the Donnersberg and other buildings around it were occupied by a hermit. The precise date of its foundation is not known. Andreæ quotes a notice purporting to be from the book of souls from St Jacob's monastery (though it is missing from the copy of the book prepared in 1790) according to which, Brother Conrad of Dreis, the first hermit died in 1323. Research has attempted to derive the date of the foundation of the chapel from this mention of the first hermit, Conrad and to place it around 1300. However, 13th century pottery found in the area of the hermit's dwelling, points to a somewhat earlier date.

In this same year (1335) Philip of Sponheim and Loretha, widow of Otto 1st, gave the hermit's chapel of St Jacob to the priest Heinrich von Speyer to found the "True Order of the Hermits of St Paul, the first hermit". A monastery was in fact only founded in 1370 when Heinrich II von Sponheim gave to the order; ". . . the chapel of St Jacob, the house, farmyards and the surroundings fields and wood as far as the old boundary ditch shall determine the length and breadth thereof."

In summary, whilst there is some evidence of pre-Celtic activity and a connection with The Church in the Middle Ages, the history of this hill would appear to point conclusively to the pre-Christian period and offers concrete evidence of Celtic/Druidic origins.

The locations of the four cathedrals at Chartres, St Quentin, Reims and Verdun were all chosen by the early Christians and there is a possibility that their choice was independent of any existing Druid or Roman influences in the towns. Although he ruled much later, (6th century) the words of Gregory the Great as reported in the history of St Bede give us some clue to the early Christian thinking concerning the Druids, Romans and their Temples: *Do not after all pull down the temples. Destroy the idols, purify the buildings with holy water, set relics there and let them become temples of the true god. So the people will have no need to change their places of concourse, and whereof they were wont to sacrifice cattle to demons, thither let them come on the day of the saint to whom the church is dedicated, and slay the beasts no longer as a sacrifice but for a social meal in honour of Him whom they now worship.*

My own view is that the four basilicas most likely stand on locations which were once Druid religious sites. *Celtic Gods, Celtic Goddesses* by R J Stewart says; 'The early church did not destroy pagan shrines, but booted out the residents and replaced them, admittedly with frequent failure and backsliding, with the unified new religion.'

The absence of Roman or Christian constructions at three of the seven points of The Plough, together with the evidence at Donnersberg and the strong Druidic tradition at Chartres, Reims and Verdun all point overwhelmingly to the Druids as the master architects of the reproduction of the Plough.

Despite this initial conclusion, when I looked at the early Christian Church, I found some evidence to indicate that certain factions within the Church would have been prone towards reverence of the stars and of Ursa Major in particular.

In the whole of Christian antiquity, at least in the Eastern Church, there is no writer who is so attractive, whose glory so disputed, or the study of whom is so difficult as Origen (185 – 254 AD). He was praised during his lifetime by saints like Alexander of Jerusalem and Gregory Thaumaturgus, but was condemned by his own bishop (Demetrius) and expelled from the Church. After his death, he had enthusiastic defenders among the greatest saints and most illustrious doctors, and yet his teaching was condemned by the Council of Constantinople in 553 AD in a decision which was confirmed by Pope Vigilius.

Upon the death of Clement of Alexandria in 215 AD, Origen became master of the Catechetical School where he had already gained a formidable reputation. He went to Rome during the pontificate of Zephyrinus and in his presence Hippolytus gave a discourse in the honour of the Saviour. It is quite likely that friendly relations resulted from this first contact and some writers have claimed that subsequently, Origen adhered to the schism of Hippolytus. Porphyry wrote of him: "In his conduct he lived as a Christian and in opposition to the laws. But in his beliefs concerning the divinity he was Greek, applying the art of the Greeks to foreign fables. For he was always studying Plato; the works of Numenius, Cronius, Apolophanes, Longinus, Moderatus, Nicomachus and of those learned in the Pythagorean doctrines constituted his reading, and he made use also of the books of the Cheremon the Stoic and Cornutus. It was from these that he learned the allegorical method of the Greek mysteries, which he then adapted to the scriptures of the Jews."

In '*The History of the Primitive Church*' by Lebreton, Zeiller, Fliche & Martin translated by E C Messenger we are told, "It is also from Hellenism that he derives his belief in the pre-existence of souls, the conception of heavenly beings as spherical bodies, and of the souls of the dead as luminous bodies."

Allen Scott's book, *Origen and the Life of the Stars* summarises Origen's views in relation to the stars in his final paragraphs: "The stars and the planets are living and rational creatures, whose bodies are ethereal and made of light. They are self moving beings, spherical, of vast size, and located far from the earth and yet still within our own cosmos. Origen agrees with earlier philosophical traditions that their precise movement is a tribute both to their intelligence and to divine providence. Scriptural references to heavenly bodies worshipping God and praying are not just metaphors, since like all rational creatures, they are part of God's creation and subordinate to his will.» And yet they too are sinners and stand in need of divine redemption. Their presence in bodies is linked to pre-existing sins, and this also effects both the brightness with which they now shine and their particular place in the sky. Satan and his evil angels are stars which had sinned especially badly and fallen into even lower types of bodies, but the planets and stars visible in the evening sky did not sin as much. In contrast to the demons, now they are doing penance for their sins by providing the times and seasons of the earth, and they will do so until the end of time. They certainly do not cause events on earth, but they can serve as signs of the future, and this and the cunning of demons has lent credence to astrology.»

When human beings rise from the dead, they ascend through the heavens. The resurrection body is ethereal and luminous, like the bodies of the stars, and resurrected humanity visits heavenly bodies, to which they (it would seem) have a physical kinship. The heavenly spheres are places of instruction for human souls, and are also tentatively likened to cities. Resurrected souls, however, have a higher density and eventually go beyond the fixed sphere ('the firmament') and ascend to a higher earth, the 'earth of heaven', or even above that to the true heaven."

This should be read in conjunction with the first two chapters of Revelations quoted in a previous chapter and the writings of Hippolytus – *The Refutation of all Heresies,* where, discussing the Hellenistic tradition, he says: "These (constellations), 'The Bears', however, he says, are two hebdomads, composed of seven stars, images of two creations. For the first creation, he affirms, is that according to Adam in labours, this is he who is seen 'on his knees' (Engonasis). The second creation however is that according to Christ, by which we are regenerated; and this is Anguitenens, who struggles against the Beast, and hinders him from reaching Corona, which is reserved for man. But 'The Great Bear' is, he says, Helice, symbol of the mighty world towards which the Greeks steer their course, that is, for which they are being disciplined. And, wafted by the waves of life, they follow onwards, (having in prospect) some such revolving world or discipline or wisdom which conducts those back that follow in pursuit of such a world. For the term Helice seems to signify a great circling and revolution towards the same points." This in turn should be studied in conjunction with an extract from Hermes Trismegitus, an anthology of philosophical *hermetica,* "Now, the divine intellect, being androgynous since it existed as life and light, engendered rationally a second intellect as craftsman; and the latter, being god of fire and spirit, crafted seven controllers, which encompass the perceptible world in orbits. And their control is called destiny."

The beliefs of Origen were a reinforcement of his predecessor Clement who in his work, *The Stromata,* proposed the immutability of angels and set forth immutability as the highest point possible in the ascent of the human soul: "Observe the sun, the moon, the firmament, and the other creatures which are in some respects greater than we are: they have not received liberty, but are fixed in such a way that they fulfil only the commandments, and can never depart from them." *The Stromata* discusses what it sees as two great problems, the relations between Hellenism and Christianity and those between gnosis and faith.

In summary therefore, the master of one the foremost Christian schools and one who most probably influenced many of the early Bishops sent to Gaul, believed that the stars were alive and were angels and human souls. Additionally, since he was known to follow the Hellenic tradition, it is probable that he believed 'The Great Bear' to have special significance.

He establishes a relationship between the sensible and the intelligible worlds, the former being the symbol and the latter the reality, signified by the symbol, with the exegesis:

> If there are secret relations between the visible and the invisible, earth and heaven the flesh and the soul, the body and the spirit, and if the world arises from the union of these, there exists also in scripture a visible element and an invisible one. It has a body – the letter which is seen by everyone; a soul – the hidden meaning which it encloses; and a spirit – the heavenly things it figures and represents.

Origen therefore, had a Gnostic orientation and applied the Hellenic practice of numerical analysis to the Scriptures. This being so, he set himself against men such as Irenæus, the second Bishop of Lyons following the martyrdom of St Pothinus in 177 AD and who was a major influence on the early Church in Gaul. Irenæus wrote much and two of his works have come down to us: The *Exposition and Refutation of False Gnosis* (which soon became a textbook for the members of the orthodox Church) and the *Demonstration of the Apostolic Teaching*. His primary aim was to unmask Gnosticism and to bring its systems into the full light of day. At the same time he indignantly condemned the use of numerical analysis (gematria): "When you read this, my friend, I am certain you will laugh at their folly which thinks itself to be wisdom. But indeed it is lamentable to see sanctity, the greatness of truth, and the ineffable power and the dispensations of God thus twisted by these people and treated with *alpha* and *beta* and numbers."

We know considerably more about the Gnosticism of the early Christians since parts of the Nag Hammadi scrolls, which were discovered in 1945, have started to be published. They believed in "the primacy of immediate experience . . . Whoever comes to experience his own nature – human nature-as itself, the 'source of all things,' the primary reality, will receive enlightenment. Realising the essential Self, the divine within, the Gnostic laughed in joy at being released from external constraints to celebrate his identification with the divine being".[1] The Orthodox Church on the other hand saw the route to God through the Church and the Sacraments and developed social rituals which welded the Church members into a web of community responsibilities.

The conflict between these two contradictory philosophies became so strong that Gnostics within the Church would need to have hidden their Gnostic beliefs from the Bishops and officials within the orthodox Church. In Gaul, this would have been particularly true following the anti-Gnostic tradition started by Irenæus.

Any involvement of the early Christians in the establishment of the earthly Plough must have been by Gnostics and therefore unknown to the official Church hierarchy. There would need to have been an underground movement within the Church sympathetic to the Druidic tradition which, in some ways, was so similar to the Hellenic tradition. They would need to have believed that the stars had special significance and that 'the seven stars' were somehow worthy of such a massive earthly construction. Maybe the words of John in the Apocalypse were sufficient.

---

[1] *The Gnostic Gospels* by Elaine Pagels

Gregory of Tours (539 594 AD) in *The History of the Francs,* includes several passages which indicate that the early Christians were very particular about the buildings and locations, which were selected to be used for the first churches: "One of the disciples went to the city of Bourges and preached to the people that Christ our Lord had come to save mankind. Only a few believed him. These were ordained as priests. They were taught how to chant psalms and they were given instruction in building churches and in celebrating the rites due to Almighty God. As yet they had little chance of building a church, so they asked for the use of a house of one of the townsfolk, so that they could make a church of it. The Senators and the other leading men of the place were still committed to their own heathen religion, and those who had come to believe in God were from the poorer classes, in accordance with what the Lord said when he rebuked the Jews: 'The publicans and the harlots go into the kingdom of Heaven before you.' They did not obtain the use of the house for which they asked; and they therefore went to see a man called Leocadius, the leading Senator of Gaul, who was of that same family as that Vettius Epagatus who, as I have already told you, suffered martyrdom in Lyons in the name of Christ. They told him of their Christian faith and explained what they wanted. 'If my own house' he replied, 'which I posses in Bourges, were worthy of being put to such use, I would be willing to offer it to you.' When they heard him, they fell at his feet. They said that his house was indeed suitable to be used for religious ceremonies and offered him three hundred golden pieces for it, together with a silver salver. Leocadius accepted three of the golden coins for luck and refused the rest. Up to this moment, he had believed in heathen gods, but now he became a Christian and turned his house into a Church. This is now the most important church in Bourges, constructed with great skill and famous for the relics of Stephen the martyr."

"In the city of Tours Bishop Eustochius died in the seventeenth year of his episcopate. Perpetuus was consecrated in his place, being the fifth Bishop after St Martin. When Perpetuus saw how frequently miracles were being performed at St Martin's tomb and when he observed how small was the chapel erected over the Saint's body, he decided that it was unworthy of these wonders. He had the chapel removed and he built in its place the great church which is still there some five hundred and fifty yards outside the city. It is one hundred and sixty feet long by sixty feet broad; and its height up to the beginning of the vaulting is forty five feet. It has thirty two windows in the sanctuary and twenty in the nave, with forty one columns. In the whole building there are fifty two windows, one hundred and twenty columns and eight doorways, three in the sanctuary and five in the nave. The vault of the tiny chapel which stood there before was most elegantly designed and so Bishop Perpetuus thought it wrong to destroy it. He built another church in honour of the Apostles Peter and Paul, and he fitted this vault over it. He built many other churches which still stand firm today in the name of Christ." "At this time the church of the blessed martyr Symphorium of Autun was built by the priest Eufronius." "After the death of the Bishop Rusticus, St Namatius became the eighth Bishop of Clermont-Ferrand. It was he who built by his effort the church which still stands and which is considered to be the oldest within the city walls. It is one hundred and fifty feet long, sixty feet wide inside the nave and fifty feet high as far as the vaulting. It has a round apse at the end, and two wings of elegant design on the other side. The whole building is constructed in the shape of a cross. It has forty two windows, seventy columns and eight doorways." « "The wife of Namatius built the church of St Stephen in the suburb outside the walls of Clermont-Ferrand."

Fig 102 The Cathedral of St Jean at Fouvière in Lyons

These passages clearly indicate that the construction of churches was an important priority for the early Christians and that the type of building and/or the location of it was of such importance that instead of simply finding a property or constructing one, they approached the 'leading Senator of Gaul' to find a property that was 'suitable'.

The Roman Emperor Claudius (268-270AD) decreed the abolition of Druidism and this was the death knell to the powers of Druids as both judges and priests. This left the way clear for the Christians and it would seem eminently logical that the bishops of the new religion should eliminate any remaining competition from the Druids by building their churches on sites, which the superstitious Celts already believed to be sacred.

This short insight into some aspects of the early Church provides the opportunity to see that there may have been an underground movement, linked somehow to a Hellenic tradition which could have been instrumental in the establishment of an earthly Plough as a symbol of the 'mighty world towards which they steer their course'. Additionally, (or maybe alternatively) the idea that 'one like the son of man', held 'in his right hand', 'seven stars', might have been sufficient to provoke a motivated group of believers to create 'the seven stars' in the heart of Gaul. The one major piece of evidence which does point to early Christian involvement is the fact that the line from St Quentin through Verdun, goes directly to Ephesus (the home of St John) and then on to Jerusalem. If not, this line (together with the line to the Temple of Isis at Philae) implies a link between the Druids, Hellenistic tradition, the Egyptians and Temple of Solomon (being the oldest monument in Jerusalem) which may be a focal point for 'the ancient knowledge' which is so written about (but not disclosed) by those who touch against these subjects.

The Druids, together with the nobility, had constituted the ruling class among the Celts. They controlled the judiciary and the care of occult sciences and powerful superstitions whereby they enveloped the entire life of the people. The temples possessed broad domains and had treasures of precious metals, so abundant they became proverbial. The power of the Druids declined after the enormous extortions of Julius Caesar had affected the temple treasures. Druid convocations between Dreux and Chartres gradually diminished and the migration of Druid disciples to Britain, ceased. Tremors of discontent became evident under Augustus and Tiberius: the latter, at least, is said to have found himself constrained, "to abolish the Gallic Druids and similar soothsayers and physicians." But they persisted even after Claudius (268-270 AD) who, according to Suetonius, "completely abolished their fearfully cruel religion."[1]

Janet and Colin Bord in *The Secret Country* tell us "By the time the decree of Nantes was issued some bishops had realized that it would be necessary to use new tactics in order to subdue the heathen practices of the people. This new attitude was shown in a letter of A.D. 601, from Pope Gregory to Abbot Mellitus, who was about to visit England.

> "When (by God's help) you come to our most reverend brother, Bishop Augustine, I want you to tell him how earnestly I have been pondering over the affairs of the English: I have come to the conclusion that the temples of the idols in England should not on any account be destroyed. Augustine must smash the idols, but the temples themselves should be sprinkled with holy water and altars set up in them in which relics are to be enclosed. For we ought to take advantage of well-built temples by purifying them from devil-worship and dedicating them to the service of the true God. In this way, I hope the people (seeing their temples are not destroyed) will leave their idolatry and yet continue to frequent the places as formerly, so coming to know and revere the true God."

The Christians not only absorbed traditional sacred sites into their own, they also christianized the ancient gods, so that, for instance, Brid became St Bridget, St Brigit, or St Bride; Santan (the holy fire) became St Anne; Sinclair (the holy light) became St Clare. They also positioned their feasts to coincide with pre-existing festivals, and in this way they succeeded in obliterating all but the minutest traces of the once so powerful religion of Nature.

But this process took many centuries. As late as 1649 the General Assembly of the Church of Scotland appointed a commission to examine and eliminate the 'Druidical Customs' which were still followed as the 'old places of worship'. In the early years, the missionaries faced great difficulties, not least of them being the problems they experienced when they came to site their churches, as is amply demonstrated by the hundreds of traditions which are still current today.

The majority of the stories concerning churches relate to the siting of the buildings, and most tell of how, at dead of night, the building work completed during the day was undone by unknown hands, and the building materials moved to another site, often on a hilltop (though not invariably; sometimes they were moved downhill to marshy ground, and we will discuss this later). Finally the builders would have to agree to the local wishes and build the church on the site which was thus indicated. Such

---

[2] *The Age of Constantine the Great* by Jacob Burckhardt

Fig 103 Stonehenge viewed from the north

stories almost certainly demonstrate an incompatibility between the desires of the incoming Christians and those of the still-powerful 'pagans', who in some respects were still the more influential. They tolerated the building of the Christians' churches, but it had to be done on their terms. They were fully aware of the importance of the position of a sacred building, and apparently they believed that for it to be completely effective it should stand upon one of the lines of the earth current, or leys. Most pre-Reformation churches are found to lie upon leys, and most are on sites which have geomantic significance."

The fact that the cathedrals were constructed at the centre of the major cities may be explained therefore if we assume that the Romans merged their Gods with the Celtic Gods (as we know they did) and then built their temples on Druid religious sites. "The Gods assumed not only Roman names but also the art forms of classical anthropomorphism. Taran had to be called Jupiter and was depicted as such, Teutates as Mercury or Calumus as Mars. Other deities retained their names with a Roman name. Thus we have Belanus or Apollo Belanus, Appolo Grannus, Mars Camulus, Minerva Belisana and the like. Then the Roman Gods received special cognomens in addition; some we can derive from localities. Thus we have Diana Ardoinna (Ardennes) Mars Vincius (Vince in southern France), Mars Lacavus (at Nimes). Otherwise, the Romanised gods were associated with a non-Romanised, perhaps kindred deity; so Veriogodumnus was associated with Apollo in Amiens; and Sirona who is conceived somewhat as Diana or Minerva in Bordeaux. A host of deities retained their Celtic Names, mostly with the prefix Deus, Sanctus or Augustus eg., Nemausus in Nimes, Vesontius in Besançon, Acionna in Orléans and Bemilucius in Paris. Until late in the fourth century the mightiest God continued to be Teutates-Mercury, who still offered vigorous resis-

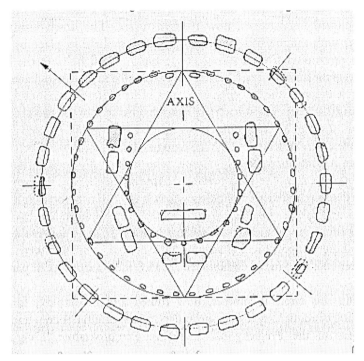

Fig 104 The groundplan of Stonehenge overlaid by the 'Jerusalem Diagram' as depicted in John Michell's Dimensions of Paradise

tance to St Martin of Tours."[1] It was the Romans who built their towns and cities around their temples and, in the early part of the 4th century, "After ten years of favour towards the Christians and of continued efforts to overthrow the ancient religion of the Empire the demand for Christian churches increased and many of the heathen temples ceased to be used. Some of these temples Constantine turned into churches, and some that they might not be used again for the old religion, he was content to unroof and leave as a sign of a faith that had passed away."[2] This is illustrated well in Lyons, the principal Roman city in Gaul and the first Christian stronghold. There, the Roman city of Lyons was constructed on the site of the old Celtic stronghold on the side of the hill known afterwards as Fouvière, and the site of the current cathedral (Fig 102). The most ancient Druid construction known to us is at Stonehenge (Fig 103).

Built between 1600 and 1900 BC, it has been shown (with the aid of a computer) to be an astronomical clock which predicted the principal movements and alignments of the Sun and the Moon (*Stonehenge Decoded* by Gerald S Hawkins). The dimensions of Stonehenge and the circles (and other shapes) it contains, have been shown to correspond exactly to the dimensions inherent to classical images of sacred geometry. (*The Dimensions of Paradise* by John Michell) (Fig 104) The knowledge of mathematics and astronomy and engineering ability, which was needed to construct Stonehenge indicate quite conclusively that the Druids did possess the necessary expertise to locate the seven points of the earthly Plough accurately.

---

[1] Stuart Piggott – *Ancient Peoples and Places – the Druids*
[2] T Scott Holmes, DD – *The Origin & Development of the Christian Church in Gaul*

The wonder of The Plough is that it was constructed so precisely over such large distances. As a matter of curiosity, I entered the co-ordinates of Stonehenge into my computer and attempted to find links with the seven stars or with the pentagram it contained. I could find no noteworthy direct connections through any of the seven points. The only line of significance was the Stonehenge – Donnersberg line, which at a bearing of 104° 30', is exactly parallel to the east – west arms of the pentagram (Fig 105). Since I knew that Stonehenge was designed as an astronomical clock, I set out to discover the day of the year when the sunrise azimuth[1] would co-incide with the angle of 104° 30' and discovered that in 1994 it occured on 23rd February. And in 1000BC it occurred on 3rd March. Intrigued, I checked the bearing of the Donnersberg – Chartres line and confirmed it to be 253°, the angle of the sunset azimuth, four days prior to the Spring Equinox. This suggested that the complex plan could well be linked, not only to the constellation of Ursa Major but also to the movements of the Sun. When I checked the angle of the sunrise azimoth at Chartres on Midsummer Day, it was 51° 58' in 1994 and 51° 18' in 1000 BC. At Stonehenge, it was 49° 15', which was, within the limits of my measuring ability, the same as the angle between the Rennes-le-Château – Chartres – Bonne Mare line (which represents the line through the north pole of the Heavens) and the line of orientation of Notre Dame de Chartres. (Fig 106). On realising this, I felt compelled to consider the possibility that the Chartres orientation was in some way connected to the angle of midsummer sunrise, at some date in the past when the angle was smaller than it is now.

I cannot with any certainty tell you when 'the seven stars' was duplicated in Gaul. If it was the work of the Druids, it is not difficult to see how the cathedrals of Chartres, Reims, St Quentin and Verdun came to occupy sacred territory which had been used for religious ceremonies by the Celtic priests. The fact that there is nothing tangible in the forests of Bonne Mare and Landonvillers would signify that the construction of The Plough took place before the Roman practice of marking every religious site with a temple and before the Christian tradition of constructing churches, where the tendency was "to make the entire structure and every stone a symbol of its power and glory" *(The Age of Constantine the Great)*. The fact that the St Quentin-Verdun line goes to Jerusalem however, would then need to be explained by an ancient link between the Druids and the Jews of the Old Testament. This may be accounted for by the belief (in some places) that the Celts were one of the twelve tribes of Israel.

For The Plough to have been the work of the early Christians, there would need to have been a secret underground movement inside the orthodox church which affected the choice of location for many of the early cathedrals. There is little conflict amongst historians about the identity of the first Christians in Gaul and the timing of their mission. *The History of the Primitive Church* tells us that, "The oldest apostolic claim in Gaul is that of the church in Arles, which already at the beginning of the fifth century regarded Trophimus, its founder as a disciple of St Peter. But this is unfortunately closely linked with the ambition of Arles at the time to be recognised as the first of the Episcopal sees in Gaul merely because, having become the administrative capital, Pope Zosimus momentarily invested its bishop with the title of Papal Vicar. The beginnings of Christianity at Lyons were not later than the reign of Hadrian, in the first half of the second century. An inscription, preserved at Marseilles and coming doubtless from that neighbourhood, which seems to refer to 'two martyrs Volusianus and

---

[1] Azimuth: The angular distance, usually measured clockwise, from the south point in the horizon to the intersection with the horizon of a vertical circle passing through a celestial body.

Fortunatus, burnt to death', may well be at least as ancient." This confirms what we are told in *The Origin & Development of the Christian Church in Gaul*, which says, "It was Pope Zosimus in 417 AD who ventured to declare that Trophimus of Arles was the first who sent forth Christian missions to Gaul. The martyrdom of St Photinus and many of his flock occurred in the summer of 177 AD during the reign of Marcus Aurelius (161-180 AD). The events of the year 177 AD were not evidence of the begin-

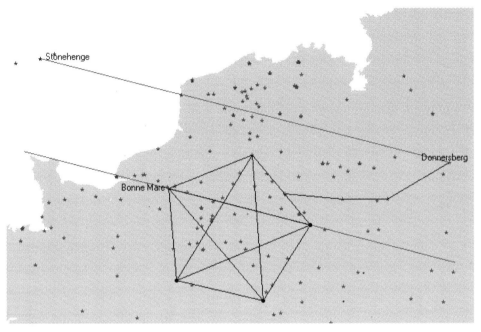

Fig 105 The Donnersberg-Stonehenge line, parallel to one of the arms of the pentagram

ning of a movement; they formed a crisis in that movement. Photinus, the Bishop of Lyons was ninety years of age when he suffered and we cannot imagine that he was sent there except as a man in full possession of his physical powers. We cannot be very wrong in allowing him a ministry of thirty years. The missionary work was not confined to Lyons; Lyons was only the centre. Vienne was expressly mentioned as one of the cities of the newly organised Church. It is certainly clear in any case that the work of the Church in Gaul must have been going on for some considerable time before the year 177 AD.

Photinus, Irenaeus, Attalus, Alexander and many others bore Greek names. The last three were certainly from Asia Minor . . . Was then the mission to Lyons a special effort on the part of the church in Asia Minor? Not a word is said by Irenaeus as to the mission at Lyons being due to the initiation of Polycarp, nor is there any reliable evidence that the churches of Asia Minor ever attempted missions in Gaul. Like Rome itself, Lyons was full of foreigners, and the appeal of the Christians in Lyons, to Eleutherus, and the fact that Irenaeus, when Bishop of Lyons, regarded the permanence of the orthodox tradition of the Church as depending on the continuity of the Roman episcopate, seem to prove that the mission to Lyons came at least through Rome, if indeed it did not emanate from Rome. In the year 189 AD or perhaps a few years earlier, Irenaeus, in behalf of the Church in general as well as of the Church at

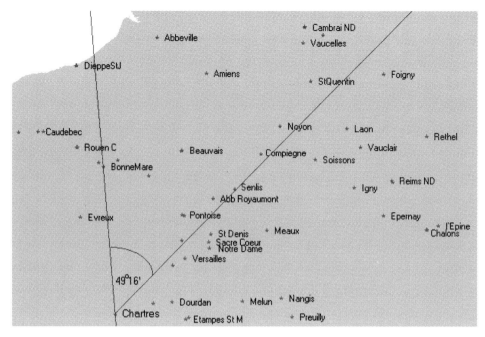

Fig 106 The angle between the line of orientation of Nôtre Dame de Chartres and the line of the pointers is the same angle as the sunrise azimuth at Stonehenge on midsummers day

Lyons, wrote strongly to Victor condemning his severity and urging him not 'to cut off whole churches of God, who observed the tradition of the ancient custom'."

This appeal seems a strange contrast to the zeal with which he condemned and persecuted the Gnostics but does imply diocese other than Lyons and a movement which was unorthodox, relative to the rule, as stipulated by Rome.

Gregory of Tours tells us that at the time of Decius, (249 – 251 AD) "seven men who had been consecrated as bishops were sent to preach among the Gauls." He specifies their destinations as Toulouse, Tours, Arles, Narbonne, Paris, Limoges and Clermont Ferrand and implies that they were sent by Sixtus, Bishop of Rome. The arrival dates of these first missionaries imply that any unofficial movement with Hellenic or Gnostic orientations, could only have arrived in Gaul from the end of the 3rd century onwards (at the earliest). This second round of bishops would probably have originated from Asia Minor and they may well have been seen as 'them' rather than 'us' by the existing bishops and their disciples. In *The Age of Constantine the Great,* we are told; "A host of unworthy persons had invaded the Church and even forced their way to the episcopal thrones. Among these evils, Eusebius mentions in particular the bitter feud between bishops and between individual congregations." This supports the idea of a dichotomy within the Church. However, if the 'unworthy persons' mentioned by Eusebius, were Celts with Druidic affiliations, it could also support the idea that the first churches were built on Druid sites and that, therefore, the earthly representation of 'the seven stars', was conceived and designed by the Druids and unknowingly enhanced by the Christians.

Since there is no tangible evidence which tells us who the architects of The Plough were, and given the paucity of information available, the probabilities must be compared and the more likely alternative chosen.

Assuming that the Druids were the architects, it is possible to substantiate all seven points and their extended connections. If we assume that the Christians were the architects, we are left with question marks over three of the sites. This hypothesis seems to be confirmed by the alignments with the other cathedrals in Gaul: the locations of some 46 cathedrals which link with five or more of the seven sites would need to have been precisely chosen and it is unlikely that any secret movement within the Church could have had so much success without being discovered. It is a much simpler scenario to assume that these sites were already in existence as Druidic religious sites and that they were supplanted by the Christians.

Additionally, from what we know of the Druids, it is probably also true that they were more likely to have been able to navigate themselves to the seven sites (and the other connecting sites) than the early Christian Bishops. In view of this, I conclude in favour of the Druids as the planners, architects and builders of the earthly Plough. The fact that its existence has remained secret until now can only mean that the construction had great significance amongst the highest orders of Druid priests and was not commonly known by the privileged Bards and Ovates. Their motivations, (other than honouring the most visible star constellation in the Northern hemisphere) are not obvious and the implications of this 'heaven on earth' are discussed in the next chapter.

During the process of my research, I discovered that the position of Polaris relative to the pole of the ecliptic, changes slowly year by year and at the same time, the position of Ursa Major (and therefore the pointers) also changes. In view of this, it occurred to me that it would be worth analysing the changing positions of these stars over time to determine when the dimensions in the sky most closely approximated those on the ground. To do this work, I purchased 'Sky watch 2.0', a computer programme which facilitates the examination of star positions (relative to the pole of the ecliptic and relative to one another) at dates going back to 5000 BC and going forward to 4000 AD. I produced star charts for the constellation of Ursa Major and Polaris for the years 2500 BC, 1500 BC, 500 BC, 100 AD, 1100 AD, 2000 AD and 2500 AD. (Appendices 9-15).

During the 5000 year period, Polaris moves from a position remote from the pole of the ecliptic towards the Pole and seems to reach its zenith (before moving away again) in the current period. The distance between the pointers compared with the distance between Marak and Polaris varied between 15.5% and 16.1% but never approached the 13.85% ground measurement, mentioned in Chapter 2. (Bonne Mare to Chartres compared with Bonne Mare to Rennes-le-Château). The angle between the pointer line and the line between the furthest pointer Marak and Polaris varied for each of the 7 epochs examined and (as far as I was able to measure with my limited resources) was at its smallest in the 1100 AD chart when it was 1.2° and at its greatest on the 500 BC chart when it was 3.8°.

CHAPTER 8

Who knew the significance of the pattern?

Despite my conviction that the pattern was laid down by the Druids, I was intrigued by the precise alignments which were made when Clairvaux Abbey was moved in 1135 (see Fig 107) :-

* The line from the abbey at Clairvaux II to the centre of Nôtre Dame Cathedral in Reims misses the centre of Abbey St Remi in Reims by 28 metres
* The line from the centre of Abbey Mont St Michel to the abbey at Clairvaux II misses the centre of Nôtre Dame in Chartres by 19 metres
* The line from the basilica at Caudebec to the abbey at Clairvaux II misses Bonne Mare by 123 metres
* The line from the cathedral at St Flour to the centre of Nôtre Dame Verdun misses the centre of the abbey position at Clairvaux II by 195 metres

Additionally, the line from Cîteaux (the first Cistercian abbey founded by Robert of Molesmes and Etienne Harding) through Clairvaux II, passes 128 metres from the centre of the cathedral in Dijon and 460 metres from the centre of the basilica in Stenay but <u>passes precisely through the tip of the regular pentagon held within the body of 'The Plough' and therefore the left hand tip of the pentagram.</u> (Fig 109)

Such accurate alignments through the abbey at Clairvaux, rendered even more accurate by the movement of the abbey from its original position, could (just possibly) be a coincidence. More likely however, it indicates that someone involved in the establishment of Cîteaux and the displacement of Clairvaux Abbey, was aware of the existence of 'The Plough' and the pentagram it contained.

The Cistercians were established coincidentally with the formation of the Knights Templar whose early seat of power was in Troyes. The similarity of name between the French town of Troyes and the ancient Greek city of Troy itself creates an interesting link with the 'The Bear' since it is known from the works of Homer that Arcadians (bear people) were present at the seige of Troy and early Greek histories tell us that Troy was founded by settlers from Arcadia.

To establish the possibilities more clearly, and in an attempt to identify the person who knew of the existence of the earthly 'Plough', I examined the events surrounding the establishment of the Cistercians and the Templars and the early expansion of the two organisations. To make my analysis easier to follow, a list of possibly significant dates is included at the end of the chapter.

Many books have been written which make much of the to-ing and fro-ing of the Count of Champagne to Jerusalem and the subsequent activities of the Templars. *The Sign and the Seal* proposes that the Templars were searching for the Ark of the Covenant and the *Holy Blood and the Holy Grail* traces a close link between the Templars and the Prieuré de Sion. All the literature agrees that it is highly likely that Hugues de Champagne's first visit to Jerusalem was in response to information which he was given by one of the knights returning from the first crusade. It is widely acknowledged that his first visit there in 1104, confirmed him in the view that something of importance was to be found beneath the Temple Mount.

It is generally accepted that the Templars did discover a cache of information, which they brought back to France (probably in 1127). This information was subsequently used in the design and construction of the many Gothic cathedrals and abbeys that were built during the 12th, 13th and 14th centuries. A study of the foundation dates and locations of the first Cistercian abbeys provides the opportunity to hypothesise about the decisions and discoveries that were made.

If the positioning of the second abbey at Clairvaux in relation to Chartres, Mont St Michel, Nôtre Dame Reims and Abbey Saint Remi was deliberate, then the significance must have been known to someone before the beginning of the 11th century:

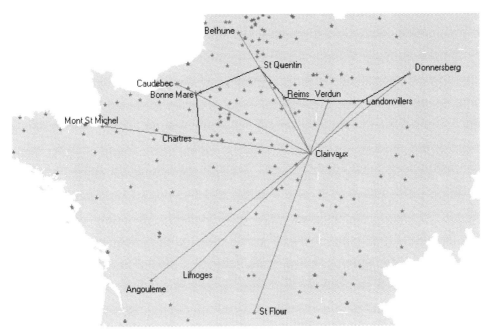

Fig 107 The connections between Clairvaux II and The Plough

the position of Chartres was established in ancient times (as we have already discussed) and the abbey at Mont St Michel was built on the site of an ancient Celtic funeral mount. An oratory was constructed there in 708 AD by St Aubert, Bishop of Avranches and this was replaced by a Benedictine monastery, which started construction in 966 AD and which was completed in 1023 AD. The cathedral in Reims was positioned in the early 5th century and Abbey St Remi, could well have been constructed on the site of the first Christian church in Reims, which was established in the 3rd century. If the abbey was not built on the exact location of this original church but was constructed on a different site, it would be important to note that it was built in the early 11th century.

The most likely answer to this problem of timing, is that all four basilicas were constructed on ancient Celtic/Druid sites and that (therefore) the connections had been established long before any Christian construction took place. If this is so, and the connections with Clairvaux were meant to go through Chartres and Reims, then Clairvaux must also have been an ancient Druid site of some significance. Additionally, if the line from Cîteaux to Clairvaux was meant to intersect one of the five points of the pentagram (which it does) then either the position of Cîteaux was chosen to make this happen, or it too was located on a Druid site.

I decided that the answer to this puzzle could lie in the orientation of the abbey at Cîteaux, since this orientation would only have been chosen by the those who constructed the abbey. Any such connection, would imply that Robert of Molesmes, Alberic, Etienne Harding or someone who advised them was aware of The Plough and the pentagram it contained. Robert, Alberic and Etienne Harding started their life as Benedictine monks. They had been cloistered at Molesmes (30 kilometres south of Troyes) and had decided in 1075 to return to the 'asceticism of the early mystics'. This decision led to the foundation of Cîteaux in 1098. If the location of their first monastery in relation to the position of Cîteaux (which was only going to be constructed 17 years later) and to the orientation of the abbey itself, showed a precise connection to The Plough or the pentagon, it would be reasonable to assume the following: that they were also aware of the future location of Clairvaux and consequently chose the location and/or bearing of Cîteaux to fit their future plans.

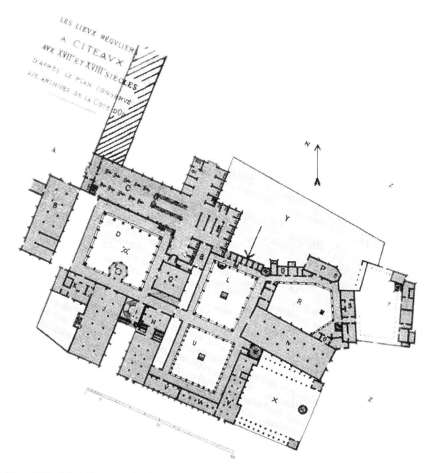

Fig 107a The diagram indicating the orientation of the ancient abbey at Cîteaux

When I visited Cîteaux, I was disappointed to find that the old abbey was destroyed during the French revolution and that it was impossible to plot the orientation of the abbey church from the sparse ruins that remain. In the bookshop of the existing abbey, I did manage to find a '*Chronologie de l'histoire de Cîteaux*' by Frère Marcel Lebeau, which contained two items of considerable interest. The first was a note in the chronology that in 1101, Cîteaux Abbey was moved 'half a league' (2 kilometres) further south and the second was a plan of the abbey that included a north pointing compass arrow.

The official guide book to Cîteaux states that the abbey was moved half a league in 1101 because the monks needed a better source of water. This does not correspond with the information contained in '*A Concise History of the Cistercian Order*' by a Cistercian monk, which says; "Through wild and rugged paths they journeyed on, chanting the divine praises until they arrived at the forest of Cîteaux, in the diocese of Chalon, in the province of Burgundy. Here they beheld a vast solitude, chiefly inhab-

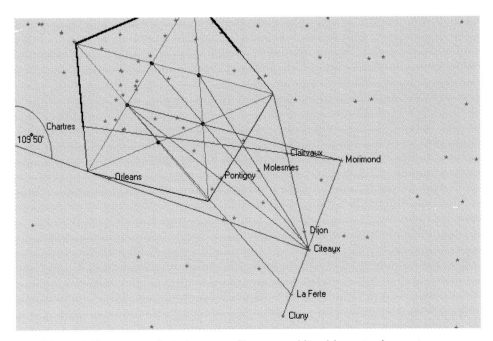

Fig 108 The connections between Cîteaux and its abbeys to the pentagram

ited by wild beasts, that found shelter in the thickets of undergrowth and brambles which luxuriated in the parts left vacant by forest trees. Through it ran a small stream, which took its rise from a fountain, about five leagues from Dijon called *sans fonds*, because it was so deep that no one had ever found the bottom. The stream from this fountain sometimes overflowed its banks and left in the hollows of the adjacent banks, stagnant pools which fostered the growth of bullrushes and various aquatic plants. From these features of its locality, it derived its name 'Cîteaux' which created the foundation for the subsequent name of the order; Cîtorns, *Cisterciens* or (in English) Cistercians. In this forbidding situation, St Robert and his companions beheld, either by some special indication from Heaven or by previous choice and arrangement, the spot most eligible for their new foundation, and the austere life which their hearts were growing to practice." Additionally, it is perhaps important to note that Robert, the first abbot of Cîteaux, had at that time been involved with five different abbeys and, despite his yen for the austere life, would have been aware of the necessity for an adequate supply of water. Given these facts, it is unlikely that the reason the abbey was moved, three years later, was because of an inadequate supply of water.

Using the second piece of information I had located, I plotted the orientation of the abbey as indicated on the plan and found it to be 111° E. However, since I was not certain of the accuracy of the map, I decided to assume that the orientation lay between 109° E and 113° E. Having obtained this orientation, I studied the lines from Cîteaux to the pentagram, to see if any of them had a bearing that lay between these angles. I was excited to discover that the line from Cîteaux to the left corner tip of the pentagram, has a bearing of 109° 50′, which (given the error latitude I had allowed in the plan) is on the same line as the orientation of the abbey. I also discovered that the line which represents a girdle or sash, from the right shoulder to the thigh of the five pointed figure, goes directly to the abbey at Cîteaux.

These alignments led me to look more carefully at the foundation of the first abbeys under Cîteaux and Clairvaux:

Cluny
    1075 Molesmes
    1098 Cîteaux I
    1101 Cîteaux II

                    1112 St Bernard joins Cîteaux
                    1113 La Ferté
                    1114 Pontigny
                    1115 Morimond
                        Clairvaux I

                                            1118 Trois Fontaines
                                            1119 Fontenay
                                            1121 Foigny
                                            1128 Igny
                                                Reigny
                    1135 Clairvaux II

The connections between Cîteaux and its abbeys were astounding:

* Cluny, La Ferté, Cîteaux and Morimond lie in an exact straight line
* La Ferté, whose precise location I had not been able to plot, would lie on one of the extended arms of the pentagram and would join one of the points of the interior regular pentagon, through Pontigny, if the position of the abbey was in the woodland known as 'réserve de la Ferté'
* Cîteaux, Pontigny and one of the points of the interior regular pentagon lie in a straight line
* Cîteaux, Molesmes and one of the points of the interior regular pentagon lie in a straight line
* Morimond lies on a straight line formed by two of the points of the interior regular pentagon
* Morimond, Clairvaux and Chartres lie in a straight line
* Cîteaux, Clairvaux and one of the points of the pentagram lie in a straight line
* Cîteaux lies on a line formed by two of the points of the interior regular pentagon

* The line formed by the orientation of Cîteaux passes through one of the points of the pentagram

This incredible series of coincidences convinced me that the first Cistercians (or someone in a position to influence them) must have been aware of The Plough and the pentagram it contained. If this conviction is valid, then these first Cistercians would definitely have known where they wanted Clairvaux to be situated and it would have been they who made contact with Hugues de Champagne. The alternative is that the connections were all just a giant co-incidence and that one day, for no good reason, the count of Champagne decided to donate the plot of land of Clairvaux, owned by one of his vassals, to the fledgling order of Cistercians that had established itself at Cîteaux.

The one certainty is that in 1115, there was contact between Hugues de Champagne and Etienne Harding, the then Abbot of Cîteaux and that following the meeting, the parcel of land at Clairvaux was passed on to the Cistercians. Simultaneously, Bernard was made abbot of the new monastery at the age of twenty-five. I do not know who instigated this contact, nor do I know, other than by deduction, who chose the piece of land that was to house Clairvaux Abbey. As we will see from the history below, a good case can be made in favour of either person.

As a way of checking the relationship between the position of Clairvaux II and the pentagram, I plotted the connections between the pentagon, the pentagram it contains and the first five abbeys founded under Clairvaux. (Fig 109) The alignments were far more numerous than I would have expected by chance:

* Trois Fontaines lies on a line which extends one of the arms of the pentagram
* The line from Foigny to Chartres passes close to one of the points of the interior pentagon
* Foigny, Igny and one of the points of the interior pentagram are in a straight line
* Abbey St Remi, Igny and one of the points of the interior pentagon are in a straight line
* The line from Igny to Chartres goes close to one of the points of the interior pentagon
* Fontenay, Pontigny and one of the points of the interior pentagon lie in a straight line
* Fontenay, Reigny and one of the points of the pentagram lie in a straight line
* Reigny, Pontigny and Igny lie in a straight line.

To complete the analysis, I studied the orientation of Clairvaux II as presented in the copy of the 1708 engraving in the official monastery guide. There, the abbey is depicted as lying just over 94°E (within the limits of my ability to measure accurately from the picture). Assuming, as I did with the diagram of Cîteaux, that there can be a 2° error either way, I had computed the orientation of the abbey to be between 92 and 96 degrees East. When I then examined the location of Clairvaux in relation to the ground plan, I was amazed to discover that the line from Clairvaux to one of the points of the interior pentagon, lies on a line 96° East. In other words, within the error limits I had specified, the abbey at Clairvaux was pointing to one of the interior points of the pentagon, which was so strongly signed by the positions of the other abbeys.

The first abbey at Clairvaux was established in 1115 and twenty years later in 1135, it too was moved. The abbey church was moved in an easterly direction and by approximately 500 metres. The effect of the two movements (Cîteaux and Clairvaux) was that very accurate and precise alignments were made between these abbeys, the key locations of The Plough and the end points of the interior and exterior pentagon it con-

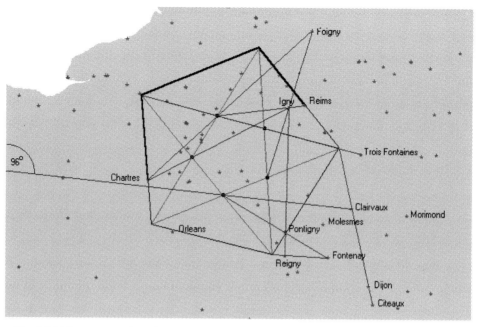

Fig 109 The connections between Clairvaux II, its first abbeys and the pentagram

tains. In addition, these connections were multiplied by the alignments created through the first abbeys founded under both Cîteaux and Clairvaux. Such a large number of connections can not be a coincidence and since the orientation of the abbeys could only have been decided at the time, the connections are clear and unequivocal evidence that someone involved in the establishment of these first Cistercian abbeys, knew of The Plough and the pentagram it contains.

In Troyes, the seat of the court of Champagne, there had been a leading school of cabalistic studies since 1070 AD. The Qabbalah was known as the soul of the soul of the Jewish Law and means *secret or hidden tradition.* According to Eliphas Levi, the three greatest books of Qabbalism are the *Sepher Yetzirah,* the Book of Formation; the *Sepher Zohar,* the Book of Splendour; and the *Apocalypse,* the Book of Revelation. All the books are steeped in the mystery of sacred numbers and I will quote here, two extracts from the Book of Formation which relate to the number seven:

> *With the seven double letters He also designed seven earths, seven heavens, seven continents, seven seas, seven rivers, seven deserts, seven days, seven weeks (from Passover to Pentecost) and in the midst of them his Holy Palace. There is a cycle of seven years and the seventh is the release year, and after seven release years is the Jubilee. For this reason, God loves the number seven more than any other number under the heavens.*
> *(Chapter 4, verse 9)*

> *To prove this there are three faithful witnesses: the universe, the year and the man. There are the twelve, the balance and the seven. Above is the dragon, below is the world and lastly the heart of man: and in the midst is God who regulates them all. (Chapter 6, verse 2)*

Could the twelve, the balance and the seven relate to star constellations; and if so which

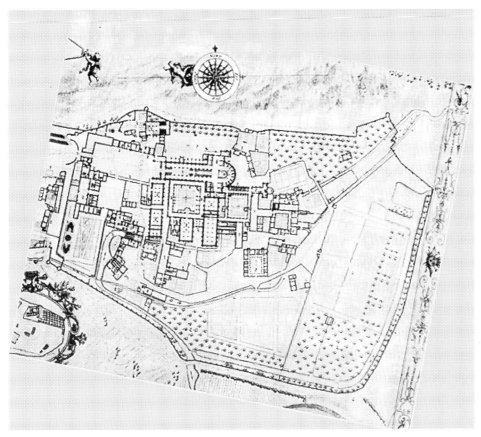

Fig 109a Orientation of the Abbey at Clairvaux in the 'Plan de l'Abbaye de Clairvaux' by Dom Milley in 1708 (Bibliothèque de Troyes, Carteron 1)

ones? We have already shown the link between the Apocalypse and the shape on the ground. Could the Qabbalistic school in Troyes have known of the ground pattern and have been the source of mystery and intrigue which we know surrounded the activities of the Count of Champagne and his family's involvement with the Templars and the Cistercians?

Hugues de Champagne was born in 1077 AD. He was the third son of Thibaud I who at the time of Hugues's birth was Count of Blois, Chartres, Sancerre and Champagne. As was usual with the third son, he would not have expected to take the principal titles from his father and may well have been pointed towards the church. During his formative years it is likely that he was educated by monks and being high born, he would have attended one of the leading scholastic institutions of the time.

When he was nineteen, the first crusade left for the Holy Land and it is not difficult to imagine that such an important event had a singular effect on him. His eldest (half) brother, Stephen Henry, who was married to Adèle, daughter of William the Conqueror took a sizeable contingent and joined his brother-in-law Robert, Count of the Normans on this first crusade. We can only conjecture as to why Hugues, who was known to have had a great affection for his brother and was old enough to have been married for a year, was not included in the party. We must conclude that it was a decision of his own making, particularly as he had been involved in an assembly of bishops and nobles in Reims which had discussed the crusade and had included the famous crusader, Robert, Count of Flanders. The evidence can only mean that he felt he had good reason to stay at home.

A leading figure who drummed up support for the first Crusade was Peter the Hermit, one of the Calabrian monks of Orval, who was known to have stayed in Jerusalem in the years that followed the campaign. As one of the recruiters-in-chief, this monk would certainly have visited all the principal and titled families of the Empire and in so doing, he would probably have met Hugues de Champagne. If Hugues' intellect had already been exposed to Plato, Hellenic numerical analysis (gematria) and the mysteries of the Qabbalah, he could well have spoken to Peter the Hermit about these matters, and in particular about the then current whereabouts of the tablets of the law, the Mosaic code and therefore the Ark of the Covenant. If this subject interested him, it is not difficult to imagine that Hugues asked Peter the Hermit, Stephen Henry and other nobles who were setting off for the Holy Land to discover what they could about these lost and priceless treasures. Did this initial interest spark an incredible quest for the Ark of the Covenant? Did this relate in some way to theGrail of the *Grail Romances* of Chrétien de Troyes, a member of the court of a later Count of Champagne? (See *The Sign and the Seal* by Graham Hancock)

One year after the first crusaders had departed, (1097) Hugues is known to have spent Easter at the monastery of Molesmes, which was 30 kilometres south of Troyes and some 6 kilometres south of Les Riceys, and surrounded by the families of the house of Tonnerre; Bar-sur-Seine, Châtillon-sur Seine, Montbard and Tonnerre. (Fig 110) Here he would have met all three monks who were to be responsible for the founding of Cîteaux and the new Cistercian order; Robert (who came from one of the noblest families of Champagne and the same family as St Bernard), Alberic and Stephen Harding (an Englishman). The monks also included nobles of high birth who had been living as hermits in the forest of Collan before they invited Robert to lead them and before he 'saw fit to remove their habitation to Molesmes'. Given the reported austerity of the monks at Molesmes and their desire to live strictly in accordance with the rule of St Benedict, the arrival of the court of the Count of Champagne with its attendant wealth seems incongruous. One can only assume that he was influenced by his brother, the then Bishop of Châlons-sur-Marne, who accompanied him. Interestingly, this first visit by Hugues and his party may have been the first step in the split between Robert and other like-minded monks who wished to stick to the simple and impoverished life to which they aspired and those other monks who 'refused to obey their Abbot and insisted on keeping possession of parochial tithes and who assumed habits of a richer and warmer sort than the rule allowed.'

There would (at first glance) appear not to have been a close relationship between Hugues and Robert. This can be concluded from the fact that, at the beginning of 1098, when Robert and his group obtained permission from the Papal Legate to leave Molesmes and found a new monastery, they left Champagne and made for the heartland of Burgundy, south of Dijon. The books describing the life of St Robert all tell of a horrific journey until they came upon a 'suitable place' to resume their life of poverty. One historian[1] tells us: "*Robert took with him the ecclesiastical vestments and vessels necessary for celebrating the holy mysteries, and also a large breviary for the ordering of the divine office. Except for this, they had nothing. Two accounts are left of their march; one that they left the convent gates, not knowing whither they were going, and that sought the*

---

[1] J D Dalgains; Stephen Harding (Saint) Abbot of Clairvaux

wildest and most rugged paths, and at last arrived at Cîteaux, where a voice from heaven bade them rest. Another account says that they had already pitched upon Cîteaux, before they left Molesmes, as being the most lonely and uncultivated spot they could find." Given the alignments from Cîteaux and the fact that the abbey was located on land donated by Robert's cousin, it seems most likely however that the group knew exactly where they were going and only missed their desired location by 'half a league'. The trip from Molesmes to visit Hugues de Diem (the Papal Legate) in Lyon had probably taken Robert through Dijon (the location of the Court of Burgundy) and it is likely that he would have mentioned his intentions to his cousin and confirmed any agreement about the land at that time. A footnote from *A Concise History of the Cistercian Order* by a Cistercian monk might be relevant: *'In the Menologium etc by Henriquez, two letters are given in notes to St Bernard's life; the first from St Robert to Eudes, Duke of Burgundy, imploring the assistance of this prince; the second, from Eudes, promising with much respect every favour within his power. Eudes, therefore, could not have been ignorant of St Robert's departure from Molesmes, with the intention of founding a new monastery.'*

On June 2nd of the same year (1098) something extraordinary happened in the house of Champagne: Stephen Henry left the head of the crusade the day before the surrender of the city of Antioch. The city had been under siege from the Christians since October 1097.

The great army that surrounded the city soon ran out of food and Fulchres of Chartres reports: *In the year of the Lord 1098, after the region all around Antioch had been wholly devastated by the multitude of our people, the strong as well as the weak were more and more harassed by famine.* At the end of March, Stephen had written to his wife Adèle and said; 'You may know for certain, my beloved, that of gold, silver, and many other kinds of riches I now have twice as much as your love had assigned to me when I left you. For all our princes, with the common consent of the whole army, against my own wishes, have made me up to the present time the leader, chief and director of their whole expedition.' The letter goes on to talk about the successes and difficulties of the various campaigns but nowhere does it give any indication that he was losing stomach for the fight or for the continued advance towards Jerusalem. On June 2, nine weeks later, Fulchres tells us; *'Stephen, Count de Blois, withdrew from the siege and returned home to France by sea. Therefore all of us grieved , since he was a very noble man and valiant in arms. On the day following his departure, the city of Antioch was surrendered to the Franks. If he had persevered he would have rejoiced much in the victory with the rest. This act disgraced him.'* Fulchres was a cleric and left Europe with the army of Robert of Normandy, Stephen of Blois and Robert of Flanders, so that his chronicle was a first hand account of events as he saw them. He later became chaplain to Baldwin, King of Jerusalem.

James Brundage reports that when Stephen left the Crusade, he first travelled with a large group of men to Alexandretta, about 40 miles north of Antioch. Within five days he heard that Antioch had been surrounded by a huge Saracen army and he returned to reconnoitre the situation from a nearby mountain. When he could see that there was nothing his tiny force could do against the might of the Turkish army, he and his men immediately boarded ships bound for Constantinople. They met the Byzantine forces of the Emperor at Akshehir and accompanied the Emperor back to Constantinople. From there, they set out for home by way of Italy.

What was it that made Stephen Henry, take the fastest route he could back to Epernay and his wife Adèle? Was he simply dispirited and homesick? Had he had a major disagreement with 'the princes'? Was he aware of the contrivance between

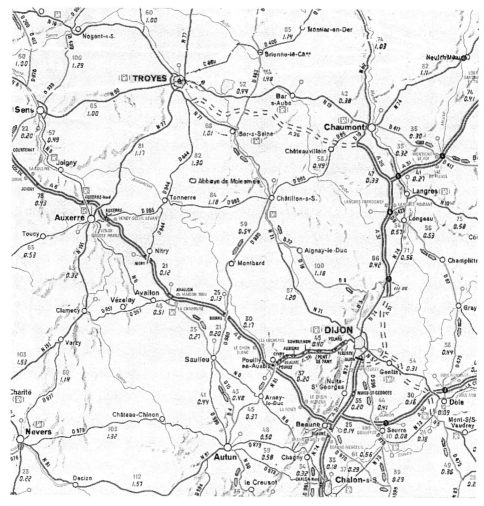

Fig 110 A modern map showing the relative locations of Dijon, Auxerre, Tonnerre, the Abbey Molesmes and Troyes

Bohemond and Firouz the Armenian, when Bohemond asked the Christian leaders to let the lord who took the city of Antioch first be the one to control it? Did Stephen Henry receive a message from his wife that made him want to rush back to her?

At least one report claims that she "angrily denounced him."[1] Did he discover something, of such great importance, some incredible piece of information, that he had to take it back personally, to France? Given that he was a 'noble man', his reasons must have had massive significance for him, to persuade him to leave his post and journey back to Champagne in disgrace. It is interesting to compare the words of Fulchres of Chartres when Hugues, brother of Philippe the King of France, left the campaign one month later; "*Then Hugues the Great, with the goodwill of the princes, went away to Constantinople; thence to France.*"

---

[1] Ordericus Vitalis 10.11 (ed. Le Provost IV 118-119)

Robert, Alberic and Stephen Harding had left Molesmes in Champagne and founded Cîteaux, in Burgundy south of Dijon, in 1098. The following year, 1099, the sequence of extraordinary events continued. Three weeks after Easter, the monks at Molesmes, who had so turned against the rule established under Robert, when he had been there as Abbot, that they had '*seized on Alberic (the Prior) who still endeavoured to carry out Robert's principles, beat him severely and thrust him into a dungeon*', presented themselves to the Pope in Rome. They 'represented to Urban II, the widowed state of the church at Molesmes, deprived of its first Abbot and Pastor'. What was behind this apparent contradiction? Had they had some insight which made them yearn for a strict regime of poverty and penance or was there something more insidious happening behind the scenes?

Could it be that Hugues de Champagne did not want Robert housed in Burgundy where he would have little chance to meet and talk with him? If this was the case, did he arrange with Geoffrey, the Prior of Molesmes that he send a delegation to Urban II (who came from the house of Châtillon) to request his assistance in returning Robert to Molesmes, in exchange for some favour? If he did, Hugues either wanted information from Robert that only Robert possessed or he wished to prevent Robert from passing information he had learned in Champagne to the house of Burgundy. Whatever the motivations of the people involved, the result was the same: The Pope wrote to the Papal Legate in Lyons who convened a synod which decided that Robert should return to Molesmes. From that time onwards, Robert seems to have come to terms with a different style of leadership when (as we shall see) he accommodated the court of Champagne at Molesmes and founded several new monasteries.

Stephen Henry, the elder brother of Hugues de Champagne arrived back from the Holy Land in 1098. In 1099, (the year Robert returned to Molesmes) and 1100 when Philippe, the Bishop of Châlons-sur-Marne and brother to Hugues and Stephen Henry, died, Hugues would have had many opportunities to talk with his brother Stephen Henry. He would thus have been able to obtain any information which he had brought back with him, about Jerusalem and about the Ark of the Covenant. In the following year, the princes returned from the Holy Land with their retinues. One can be sure that stories and rumours of the wonders of the Holy Sepulchre and the ancient secrets of the Bible were rife as the repatriated soldiers sought to impress an eager audience with tales of their exploits.

In 1101, Hugues again spent Easter at Molesmes. Robert had been re-instated as abbot for some time and was therefore able to participate in any discussions which took place with the group of assembled nobles. In addition to the count of Champagne, they included; Hugues, count of Reynel, Hugues, count of Ramerupt (a vassal of the count of Champagne) and Hugues the seneschal of the count of Burgundy. If continuing conversations did take place about the secrets held in Jerusalem, the inclusion of the seneschal of the count of Burgundy, could only mean that the count of Champagne's motivation for having Robert return to Molesmes did not involve keeping information from the house of Burgundy. It must therefore have related to information which Hugues could get from Robert. This may be the first real clue which suggests that Robert of Molesmes had access to information which had been handed down since the time of the Druids and that he was the person behind the positioning of the abbeys. It is perhaps important that at that time, Hugues de Champagne and Constance his wife donated to Molesmes, '*la seigneurie*' (the lordship) over Rumilly-les-Vaudes (a village between Molesmes and Troyes) plus four steers with the land they rested on and sufficient corn to feed them.

After this meeting in Molesmes, two significant events took place. After three years in its first emplacement, the monastery at Cîteaux was moved half a league further south and Stephen Henry, count of Blois and brother of the count of Champagne returned to the Holy Land. We can only speculate about the motives behind both these seemingly unusual events. The only thing we <u>do</u> know is that the events must fit with the preceding and subsequent history.

We certainly know that the abbey at Cîteaux was <u>not</u> moved because of a shortage of water as given out in the official records: *The Life of Stephen Harding* by Dalgairns gives a clear and concise description; *'This stream had also a strange peculiarity connected with it, that in the time of rain it was languid and shallow, but when the heat dried up all the rivers, it ran merrily along in a copious stream, as if it defied the power of the sun.'* If as I suspect, the abbey was moved to more accurately delineate the pentagon contained within The Plough, there were two possible instigators: either they were influenced by the Duke of Burgundy following information which he (perhaps) received via his seneschal, or, Albéric and Stephen realised themselves that the first emplacement was incorrect. *The Life of Stephen Harding* tells us; *'At length, Eudes (the Duke of Burgundy) heard of the exaction, and determined to free them from it forever, by assigning a portion of his ground to the lord of Beaune, out of the produce of which he was to help himself to twenty shillings; and the Viscount in return, freed the monks for ever from all claims which he himself, or his heirs, might have upon them. This was indeed the last service which the good duke rendered them, for he set out for the Holy Land that very year in which he conferred this benefit on the monastery.'* (1101). This tells us that coincidentally, at the very time the monastery was moved, the Duke of Burgundy granted a parcel of land via the Viscount of Beaune and it is possible therefore, that directly or indirectly, he influenced the relocation. Could it be that the Duke of Burgundy had obtained information via his seneschal and if so, did this information originate with Hugues de Champagne or with Robert of Molesmes?

The involvement of Eudes, Duke of Burgundy in these puzzling events did not end there: In that same year (1101), he left for the Holy Land. Was it simply a coincidence that he left at the same time as Stephen Henry and that like Stephen, he was killed at Ramelah in 1102? What had Eudes been told by Hugues the Great, who had left the crusade one month later than Stephen Henry and who had represented the house of Burgundy? What were Eudes and Stephen Henry looking for?

The orthodox reports tell us that once Jerusalem was in the hands of the Christians, it had to be continually defended against the infidel. It could be of course, that these two lords embarked for the Holy Land to defend the Holy Sepulchre: Stephen Henry to expunge the disgrace of his previous departure and Eudes (who had been Duke of Burgundy since 1078) to add his forces to beleaguered army of protectors, that had stayed to guard the Christian possessions in the Holy Land. Alternatively, they returned, possibly at the instigation of Hugues de Champagne, to get additional information about the whereabouts of the mystical prize, the Ark of the Covenant. There is one truly puzzling aspect of their journey: if Stephen Henry did leave the siege of Antioch in 1098 in disgrace, how did he imagine he would be received favourably by crusading lords still in the Holy Land and by Baudouin, King of Jerusalem on his return? We are told by James Brundage that in early 1102 he and others landed at St Simeon, the port city of Antioch, and were welcomed by Tancred.[1] Steven Runciman

---

[1] Albert of Aachen 8.41 (RHC *Occ* 4.582)

tclls us: *'The Duke of Aquitaine, The Count of Bavaria and the Count of Nevers (later to be William II of Tonnerre) arrived with their few surviving comrades at Antioch by the Autumn of 1101; but the leaders of the Franco-Lombard Crusade were still in Constantinople. Alexius found it hard to forgive them their follies. Even Raymond, on whom he had built great hopes, had disappointed him. At the end of the year, the western princes decided to continue their pilgrimage, and Raymond asked leave to rejoin his wife and his army at Lattakieh. The Emperor willingly let them go and provided ships to convey them to Syria. About the new year, Stephen of Blois, Stephen of Burgundy, the Constable Conrad and Albert of Biandrate disembarked at St Simeon and hastened up to Antich, where Tancred gave them a warm welcome.'* Brundage tells us that; *'Near Beirut, the crusaders met King Baldwin 1 of Jerusalem, who escorted them to Jaffa, where they arrived on 22 March and where they remained for eight days. On Palm Sunday, 30 March, they journeyed to Jerusalem where they fulfilled their vows by worshipping at the sacred shrines and where they celebrated the feast of Easter.'*[1]

All the historians agree that immediately after Easter, Stephen Henry and 'Stephen' (Eudes?) of Burgundy embarked for home, but that their ship was grounded by a storm off Jaffa. It was only when they were waiting for a replacement ship that they heard of the Moslem force that was marching up from Egypt and decided to help in the coming battle. This indicates quite clearly that Stephen Henry and the Burgundian lord(s) that accompanied him did not journey to the Holy Land intent on joining the armies of Christians there. The history of their movements tells us that their purpose was to visit Jerusalem and that once their purpose there had been achieved, they immediately embarked for home. It was an accident that they became embroiled in the action which led to their deaths.

Stephen Henry's journey, and his very return suggests that he knew he would be favourably received and that his original departure had not occurred as a result of homesickness or a lack of stomach for the fight. His actions tell us that there was something known only to a privileged few which motivated his previous flight and which now obliged him to return to Jerusalem.

A short extract from the *Histoire des Ducs et des Comtes de Champagne*, relating to the period (1102) gives us a further clue that Robert of Molesmes was not the simple recluse that Church historians would have us believe and that there could well have been some secret conspiracy between Robert and the count of Champagne: "At about that time, Hugues made his way, with Constance his wife, to Epernay to make a visit to the Countess Adèle his sister in law; Geoffrey his seneschal accompanied him. He found Adèle in the company of her three sons, William (some literature name the third son Henry, later to become Bishop of Glastonbury and then Winchester), Thibaud and Stephen. Count Stephen Henry was missing from that family reunion; he had gone back to Palestine, he was not to return to them; perhaps he had already fallen under the arrows of the infidels. (Following the capture of the Christian forces at Ramelah he is reported to have been executed at Ascalon in 19 May 1102).[2] One of the subjects of conversation was the generosity of Hugues towards the abbey at Molesmes; Adèle congratulated her brother-in-law. Precisely the same day, a visitor arrived at the Château at Epernay; it was the illustrious Abbot of Molesmes, Robert, one of the most revered and celebrated monastic reformers of his time; the Church, who conferred sainthood on him did nothing but confirm the testimony of his con-

[1] Albert of Aachen 8.42-45, 9.1 RHC Occ IV 582-584, 591); Fulcher 2.17.1-5 (Ed Hagenmayer 433-435)
[2] Comte de Riant; 'La légende du martyre en Orient de Thiemon, archevêche de Salzbourg (28 Septembre 102).'

temporaries. Robert, accompanied by three monks from his abbey, presented himself to the countess Adèle, he had business to discuss with her. Hugues made use of the situation to renew the gift already made of 'the lordship' of Rumilly-les-Vaudes . . ."

This single narrative is sufficient to throw doubt on everything we previously had been led to understand about Robert of Molesmes. This man, who had created consternation when he had organised his departure from the post of Abbot of two abbeys to join or to set up groups who would live apart from the world and work in simplicity and poverty was visiting the home of the countess of Blois in her husband's absence, to discuss certain things. Was it just a coincidence that he happened to call at the very time Hugues de Champagne was visiting her and that her three sons were present? As Hugues of Champagne had no sons it may have looked at that time as though one of Adèle's sons, might succeed to the title (as in fact one of them did). If so, this meeting may have been organised to discuss the future guardianship of the information then shared by Robert and Hugues. Alternatively, Robert may have called, hoping that Adèle would have heard from her husband Stephen Henry. If so, we can only surmise what piece of news he hoped to obtain. Whatever the reasons for his visit, there was obviously more to this elderly Abbot (now 73 years old) than hagiography tells us.

During the 12th century, twelve peers of France constituted the high court of justice of the kingdom: six ecclesiastics (The Archbishop of Rheims and the Bishops of Beauvais, Laon, Châlons, Langres and Noyon) and six lords (the dukes of Normandy, Burgundy and Guyenne and the Counts of Flanders, Champagne and Toulouse). Because of this it was to be anticipated that Hugues found himself called to various conclaves and synods to discuss and decide on issues of the day.

In 1104, he attended a synod in Troyes (the seat of his own court). This synod included amongst the 27 named by Arbois de Subainville; Richard, the Papal Legate; Robert of Molesmes; Robert, Bishop of Langres (brother of the Grandfather of Hugues then Duke of Burgundy); André, Count of Ramerupt; Rainier of Châtillon; André, Lord of Baudement and Geoffrey, seneschal to Hugues. Whilst the synod had met in Troyes where, in theory, the count would have had every opportunity to discuss any topics he wished with the other attendees, his actions following the synod showed that this was not the case. Instead of staying at home, when the conference was complete, Hugues accompanied Robert, the Bishop on his journey back to Langres. There are many reasons why Hugues might have wanted to make this journey but the most obvious reason was that there was something private he wanted to discuss; something he did not wish to talk about in front of the others. The most obvious subjects (given the benefit of hindsight) were the joint mission of Eudes (Robert's grandson) and Etienne Henry (Hugues's brother) to the Holy Land and the activities of the monks at Cîteaux, which was in the Bishop's diocese and therefore part of his jurisdiction.

Whatever it was they discussed, it seems to have spurred Hugues into action: First he called a group of high ranking nobles to a meeting in Molesmes. Attendees included Hugues II, Duke of Burgundy; William II, count of Auxerre, Nevers and Tonnerre; Hugues, count of Reynel; Erard, count of Brienne; André, count of Ramerupt; Milon, count of Bar-sur-Seine; Jeffroi, lord of Chaumont and Bassigny; Roger de Joinville; Ponce of Trâinelle and Thibaud, Hugues's nephew. This group was significant in the following respects:

1) William II had been active in the Holy Land, had accompanied Stephen Henry to Jerusalem and had only recently returned.

2) William, Jeffroi, André de Montbard and Roger de Joinville were all related to Bernard de Fontaine (Saint Bernard) on his mother's side and were therefore part of the house of Tonnerre. Although he was not mentioned, it is perhaps worth reminding ourselves that Bernard's father was a knight in the service of Hugues, Duke of Burgundy.

3) André de Ramerupt and Milon, count of Bar-sur-Seine were both at the Troyes synod, a few months earlier.

4) Hugues started to involve Thibaud his nephew, implying that he was already grooming him for his future role as successor to the titles of Champagne and Blois.

5) The location of the meeting was the abbey at Molesmes which made it easier to be held in conclave and the contents kept secret. It also meant that Robert, the Abbot of the Monastery could more easily be involved. The meeting could just as easily have been held at Tonnerre which is only 35 kilometres west of the abbey of Molesmes.

Did William bring information from Jerusalem which he shared with Hugues de Champagne, with Robert of Molesmes and with the other nobles in the houses of Tonnerre and Champagne? Whatever it was he told them provoked a further meeting in Dijon attended by Hugues, Duke of Burgundy; Robert, Bishop of Langres; the Bishop of Chalon-sur-Saone; the Abbot of St Germain in Auxerre; the seneschal and high constable of Hugues the Duke of Burgundy; Gui of Vignory; Rainord of Grancy (another relation of St Bernard) and William of Fouvent. This seems to have been a follow up briefing for other selected Bishops and nobles. When the meeting was finished, Hugues accompanied the Abbot of St Germain back to Auxerre, from where he could easily call on William of Tonnerre and then Robert of Molesmes on his way back to Troyes.

At this time, (1104) Bernard de Fontaine was 14 years old. He would have already started to make an impression on those around him. His father's service and fealty to the Count of Champagne would mean that he was already known to Hugues. It may be that the future of Bernard was also discussed at the meetings, which included so many members of his extended family.

It was during this same year that the marriage of Hugues de Champagne to Constance, daughter of Philippe I of France was annulled. The two of them were married in October 1095 and only two months prior to the Council of Clermont which excommunicated Philippe I (Constance's father) because of his 'relations' with Bertrande de Montfort, wife of Foulques Réchin, Count of Anjou. It seems surprising therefore that the Church should wait almost ten years before pronouncing that the marriage of Hugues and Constance was invalid because of consanguinity. Perhaps the extract (below) from the letter of Yves, Bishop of Chartres to the Papal Legate, Bishop of Lyons gives us some clues: 'With the permission of God we are obliged to make known under the evil eye of the King of France and his son the King designate, the incestuous union which exists between Constance, daughter of the King, and the count of Troyes. We have been sustained by the authority of the law and by the support of men of good will. Now, these two princes wish to hurry the dissolution of this marriage: they wish to make the most of the eagerness with which they made this decision.' This would suggest that the action to have the marriage annulled came from Constance. Arbois de Subainville tells us that Constance wanted the annulment and was 'ashamed of the obscurity which seemed to please her incapable spouse.' This is perhaps confirmed by the fact that less than two years later (Easter 1106) she was married in Chartres to Bohemond, prince of Antioch and son of Robert Guiscard. The same noble who knowing he had connived with the Armenian, Firouz, to gain entry to Antioch for the Christian armies, extracted promises from the Christian princes regarding the city: *". . . let one of us put himself ahead of the rest, and if he can acquire or contrive (the capture of) the city by any plan or scheme, by himself, or through the help of others, let us with one voice grant him the city as a gift."* According to Runciman, Bohemond's marriage to Constance was 'arranged' by Adèle, the Countess of Blois who also introduced him to her brother, Henry 1 of England.

With his marriage annulled and the enthralling stories of the mysteries of Jerusalem to inspire him, Hugues de Champagne left for Jerusalem, accompanied by Hugues de Payens. This is the first we have heard of this man who was later to become famous as the official first Grand Master of the Knights Templar. Much has been written about his unknown origins but the most feasible and most likely solution to this apparent mystery is the one dismissed by R P Dom Marie; that he was not one of the lords of the region but was simply one of the vassals of the count of Champagne.

The signature of Hugues de Champagne was missing from all documents which might have told us of his presence in France until the entry in the grand charter which Hugues prepared in favour of the abbey at Molesmes and which was dated 1108. For this reason, it is commonly accepted that the count of Champagne and Hugues de Payens were in the Holy Land for at least three years; 1105, 1106 and 1107. I have no information about their activities during this period and find it strange that their business in the Holy Land was never mentioned by any of the many chroniclers of the time. Hugues himself, did not avoid a fight, since we know that he was wounded in 1102 during the battle between the emperor Henry IV and Robert II, Count of Flanders. However, it is most likely that if he had joined any of the campaigns organised by King Baudouin of Jerusalem, his arrival there and his exploits would have been mentioned by those who were keeping the records. We are only left with the possibility that his activities were clandestine and that he spent his time searching for the sacred things he craved. Charles Addison tells us (in relation to the Templars) that; *"The two most distinguished members of the fraternity[1], were Hugues de Payens and Geoffrey de St Omer, two valiant soldiers of the cross, who had fought with great credit and renown at the siege of Jerusalem."* This means that Hugues de Payens was involved in the first crusade and that he reached Jerusalem. We must therefore deduce that along with William, Count of Tonnerre, **he** was the one who brought back the information concerning the treasures in Jerusalem. This would certainly explain how this unknown knight aquired the status which later resulted in him becoming the first grand master of Knights Templar.

The Count of Champagne and his faithful knight were away from France for four years but were not successful in their primary quest. Based on the evidence of subsequent events, it is reasonable to assume however, that they unearthed sufficient material to convince them that the ultimate prize did exist but that they needed more information about its precise location before they could continue. In the year of their return to France, the monks had disappeared from their abbey at Orval. Could it be that these colleagues of Peter the Hermit were the ones who continued the search in Hugues' absence? If so, it is not difficult to imagine that it galled the Count of Champagne to have left the quest in the hands of people he did not control. One report

---

[1] The Knighthood of the Temple of Solomon – *pentalcon*, lib. iii p82.

suggests that Hugues returned without Hugues de Payens which would perhaps make more sense.

Back in France, the first information we have of Hugues de Champagne after his return, is his meeting at Châtillon-sur-Seine with the group of nobles he had met with at Molesmes, four years earlier: William II, count of Nevers and Tonnerre; Milon, count of Bar-sur-Seine; Roger of Joinville; Geoffrey of Chaumont and Ponce of Traînelle. The reports do not say so, but the meeting would probably have included Gobert de Châtillon (in whose home this meeting took place), André de Montbard and André de Ramerupt, who were both subjects of the count and who had been present at the previous meeting. It is logical to presume that the purpose of the meeting would have been to debrief the nobles on the outcome of his trip.

If Hugues did believe that he would eventually find the Ark, it is not difficult to imagine that he and his close colleagues spent time after Hugues' return devising a grand master plan. He would have known that to hide, interpret and use the Ark, they would need secrecy, privacy, schooling and freedom of movement. Hugues's involvement with monks during his own schooling and subsequently, especially his involvement with Robert of Molesmes, had taught him that these religious foundations had unique rights and privileges. It is not difficult to see therefore, how he came to the conclusion that he needed to form a religious order. Additionally, if he believed that the possession of the Ark of the Covenant would give him extraordinary powers, as it was reputed, then he probably also believed that he would need a large army of dedicated knights to uphold and protect the new order he envisaged. This hypothesis fits well with the events between Hugues' return to France in 1108 and his second trip to Jerusalem in 1115.

In particular, it fits with Hugues' founding of an independent monastery at Cheminon in 1110, (located only three kilometres north-west of the future location of Trois Fontaines and directly on the arm of the pentagon through 'Bonne Mare') and with the establishment of 'The Militia of Christ', the forerunners of the Templars in 1111 .Some writers claim that the existence of this organisation may be confused with the order of St John of Jerusalem, described by Yves of Chartres as 'la milice du Christ' in a letter dated 1114. However, Charles Addison tells us; "... *in the year 1118 (nineteen years after the conquest of Jerusalem by the Crusaders,) they had rendered such good and acceptable service to the Christians, that Baldwin II, King of Jerusalem, granted them a place of habitation within the sacred inclosure of the Temple on Mount Moriah, amid those holy and magnificent structures, partly erected by the Christian Emperor Justinian, and partly built by the Caliph Omar, which were then exhibited by the monks and priests of Jerusalem, whose restless zeal led them to practice on the credulity of the pilgrims, and to multiply relics and all objects likely to be sacred in their eyes, as the Temple of Solomon, whence the poor fellow soldiers of Jesus Christ came thenceforth to be known by the name of 'the Knighthood of the Temple of Solomon.'"* This clearly indicates that the nucleus of knights who were later to become 'the Templars' had been operating for some considerable time, prior to 1118.

Hugues's realisation that the monks of Cheminon were not going to be the start of the expanded religious order that he wanted, coincided with a series of other inter-related happenings:

1) In 1109, Alberic, the Abbot of Cîteaux, died and Etienne Harding, then 43 years old, became the new Abbot. Both men had served under Robert of Molesmes and Robert could well have advised Hugues on Etienne Harding's qualities.

2) In 1110, Hugues married Elizabeth, sister of the count of Burgundy. This action would have meant him spending time in Burgundy and he could well have started an acquaintance with Etienne Harding at Cîteaux.

3) Etienne Harding banned Eudes the Duke of Burgundy from holding his court at Cîteaux, an action which might have prompted Hugues to believe that he could form a relationship with Etienne Harding.

4) In 1112, Bernard de Fontaine arrived at Cîteaux with a contingent of 30 nobles from the houses of Tonnerre, Montbard, and Burgundy. Their purpose was to become postulents in the new Cistercian order.

It is difficult to imagine how a young man of 22 years of age, was able to persuade his elder brothers, uncles and other nobles who were all older than he, to give up everything (in some cases, wives and children) and accompany him to a life of austere simplicity at Cîteaux. *"There were amongst them, men of middle age, who had shone in the council of princes, and who hitherto had worn nothing less than the furred mantle or the steel hauberk, which they now came to exchange for the poor cowl of St Benedict."* The many biographers of St Bernard would have us believe that it was the force of Bernard's piety that made them join him and of course this may have been true. Another possibility however, is that these nobles followed Bernard, believing that their action marked the birth of a new and expanded religious order. Bernard's qualities had been the subject of considerable discussion amongst the hierarchy of the house of Champagne, as had the ambitions of the count himself: if Hugues suspected that Bernard was the key, he would have known that Bernard needed to be located under someone who would train him and work with him to hone his potential and to create the network of monasteries that might be needed. His actions indicate that he had given up on the abbey at Cheminon and had decided (perhaps on the advice of Robert of Molesmes) to work with Etienne Harding. This would seem to be confirmed by the fact that Cîteaux changed from being a poor and struggling community of 12 monks prior to Bernard's arrival, to a thriving and expansionist monastery that founded four new affiliates in three years; La Ferté in 1113, Pontigny in 1114 and Morimond and Clairvaux in 1115. Interestingly, all these abbeys are part of the pattern which connects to the pentagon held by the plough. (Fig 108) This implies that the same person(s) who chose the revised position of Cîteaux in 1101, influenced the selection of the locations of La Ferté, Pontigny, Morimond and Clairvaux.

Previously, I speculated that the source of information regarding the pentagram and The Plough was Robert of Molesmes and it would be reasonable to ask, if this were the case, why these new abbeys were not established under Molesmes?

Molesmes was a Benedictine monastery. The Benedictine rule was centralised at Cluny and none of their many abbeys had the autonomy to expand and create new affiliates at will. The Cistercians, under Etienne Harding, took a completely different approach: each Cistercian community conserved its autonomy and could expand if it wished. Control and perpetuation of the rule was only maintained by the attendance of each abbot at the annual general chapter and by annual visits to each direct affiliate. It was almost as though Etienne Harding eliminated the Clunic structure in order to ensure that the order would expand. What was it that changed his vision from a life of contemplation in relative poverty to one of organisation, expansion and growth? Had Bernard or some of the nobles that went with him to Cîteaux, been briefed to influence Etienne Harding regarding the benefits of expansion and the ways it might be achieved? The annual general chapter was a completely new idea and it had the effect of uniting all the abbeys in the order. In fact, it was so successful, that it was later copied by the Benedictine, Dominican and Franciscan orders.

Hugues had married Elizabeth in 1110 when she was 20 years old and he was 33. Four years later, he announced that he wanted to join the order of St John (the Hospitallers) in Jerusalem and that he wished to spend the rest of his life in the Holy Land. He even noted his intentions in three separate documents; charters in favour of the abbeys at Montiérmary, Montier-la-Celle and Saint Remi in Reims. Since the order of St John had become a religious order in 1113 and its members took the vows of poverty, chastity and obedience, Hugues was stating his wish to leave his wife forever. Elizabeth was having none of it and she sought the assistance of Yves, Bishop of Chartres. Yves wrote to Hugues and reminded him of the words of the scriptures concerning marriage; '*that a man shall leave his mother and father and cleave to his wife and that they shall be two in one flesh*', and that if he was to start a life of continence without the consent of his wife that he would not be fulfilling his conjugal obligations. It would seem that this influenced Hugues, who left for the Holy Land in August 1114 and who is known to have been back in France one year later.

Given that the journey to Jerusalem took four months, we can calculate that he only stayed in the Holy Land for a short period (four months) before starting back for France. What was the purpose of this short visit? If he had decided that he was going to take notice of the letter from the Bishop of Chartres and that he was not going to join the order of St John, what had he expected to achieve in four months? There are two possible reasons why his visit to Jerusalem was such a short one; either he had gone there to confirm information he had previously been given and once it was confirmed he left, or he discovered something during his visit which made him believe that he should return immediately to France.

We are told that Hugues's travelling companion was Richard, Bishop elect of Verdun. The fact that Hugues de Payens did not travel with him either means that Hugues de Payens was still in Jerusalem and had remained there when Hugues de Champagne returned in 1108, or that (apart from the coincidence of meeting pilgrims who were journeying to the Holy Land at the same time) Hugues de Champagne was travelling alone. Either way, it points to Hugues being the instigator of the entire affair. On balance, we can speculate that the brevity of his stay indicates that when he arrived, he was able to confirm the information he had previously received; that the Ark was buried beneath the Temple Mount. At the same time, a minimum of investigation would have shown him that considerable excavation would be required to retrieve it. Whilst he was there, there is little doubt that he would have spent some time in the company of the French King of Jerusalem, Baudouin I. This king, according to *The Holy Blood and the Holy Grail*, was obliged to the *Ordre de Sion*, an organisation whose founder members were also the founder members of the Knights Templar and which therefore included Hugues de Champagne. For this reason, he would have been accommodating to any special requests the count of Champagne might have made.

On the assumption that Hugues wished the excavation to be carried out by a small group of loyal and trusted men, it is possible that he negotiated with the King and promised to send a group of knights, to guard the King and Jerusalem in exchange for permission to excavate beneath the Temple Mount. It may even be that Hugues did not mention his plans to excavate but only promised a group of the best and most trustworthy knights to guard the King, who had housed himself in the Al Aqsa Mosque, believing that the knights would get the opportunity to excavate, once they were in situ. It is unlikely that Hugues would have taken Baudouin completely into his confidence since he would not have wanted the King to find, and take dominion over the Ark, in his absence.

Having completed his negotiations, Hugues returned to France in 1115 and immediately set about the implementation of his plans. He met with Etienne Harding and agreed to the establishment of Clairvaux, with Bernard (who was 25 years old) as abbot. Presumably, he met with Bernard and talked to him (if his uncle, André Montbard had not already done so) regarding his hopes and expectations for the future. It is interesting that Hugues had to promise the title of Viscount de La Ferté to Josbert de Grancey, the landowner, in order to get the exact piece of land he was looking for.

In the same year, Robert of Molesmes died at the age of 86. He was canonised one hundred and six years later in 1221. Since the emplacements of monasteries established after Robert's death were linked closely to the pattern of the pentagon held by The Plough, we must assume that if Robert was the source of knowledge regarding the ground pattern, he had passed much of what he knew to someone else before he died – the two most likely candidates for this information were Hugues de Champagne and Etienne Harding, Abbot of Cîteaux. A third but less likely possibility is Bernard of Clairvaux who is known to have had sympathy for the Celtic lure. As Victor Murray tells us: *"He used to say jokingly to his friends that whatever was of value in the Scriptures he had gained chiefly by prayer and meditation in the woods and in the fields, and in this he often had no other teachers than the oaks and the beeches. And again; Believe me, for I know, you will find something far greater in the woods, than in books. Stones and trees will teach you that which you cannot learn from masters."*

In 1116, Hugues de Champagne donated a piece of land to Bernard, three kilometres from the abbey he had founded at Cheminon and in which he had subsequently lost interest. This was to be the location of the first filial of Clairvaux at Trois Fontaines, officially founded and occupied in 1118. In that same year (1116), Etienne Harding called the Abbots of La Ferté, Pontigny, Clairvaux and Morimond to first General Chapter in Cîteaux. The only Abbot who did not attend was Bernard who was laid low by a serious illness. J D Dalgairns tells us: *'In the midst of the holy conference, an unexpected visitor comes into the chapter house in the dress of a bishop. The abbots ought to have risen to beg the blessing of this prince of the Church, thus suddenly appearing amongst them. Instead of this, he prostrated himself on the ground in the presence of Stephen and his brethren. This was no other than the celebrated William of Champeaux, once the great doctor of the schools, now Bishop of Châlons; in that lowly presence he informed the Abbot of Cîteaux that Bernard was hard at death's door and would certainly die if he were allowed to continue administering the affairs of his abbey. On his knees therefore, the venerable bishop begged of Stephen to transfer his authority over St Bernard to himself for the space of a year. The Abbot of course willingly acceded to this request, backed as it was by the humble guise of William, and St Bernard was accordingly, by virtue of his vow of obedience, compelled to give himself up entirely into his hands. For the space of a year therefore, he was removed to a habitation built for him outside the walls of Clairvaux, and was put under the hands of a physician, whom he was ordered implicitly to obey.'* This illness of Bernard probably explains the delay between the initial gift of Hugues de Champagne and the actual formation of the abbey at Trois Fontaines.

Whilst Bernard was struggling with his health, Hugues was working hard to enlist the services of knights he could trust. In 1118, when a small group of nine knights had been assembled and were preparing to embark on their trip to Jerusalem, the 'Order of the poor knights of Christ and the Temple of Solomon' (the Knights Templar) was officially founded. One can only presume that it was necessary to establish an 'order', to commit these first knights to absolute secrecy and to focus their resolve. Normally, the knights would have taken a vow of loyalty and pledged obedience to the 'rule'. In this particular instance however, it is reported that the rules of the new order involved vows of chastity and poverty. If this is true, then one must deduce that there were religious connotations to the order's existence. The one thing we can be sure of, is that these nine knights did not get together to form a new order and journey to the Holy Land for no reason. They were embarking on a quest, but a quest that did not require their founder and sponsor to be with them. The count of Champagne had decided not to join the group on the initial 'dig', and therefore, to ensure that they retained absolute fidelity to him, he selected the knight who had helped him with all the initial ground work, Hugues de Payens, to be the first leader of the order.

The official founders of the order of the poor knights of Christ and the Temple of Solomon, were: Hugues, count of Champagne; André de Montbard (Bernard's uncle); Bisol (some say Godefroy or even Geoffrey) de Saint-Omer; Archambaud de Saint-Aignan (St Amand) and Novard de Montdidier, Godbemar (Gundemar) and Rossal.

In 1119 Hugues de Payens, presented himself to King Baudouin I of Jerusalem together with the first Templar knights and it is reported that they were well received. Charles Addison tells us: *"They renounced the world and its pleasures and in the Holy Church of the resurrection, in the presence of the Patriarch of Jerusalem, they embraced vows of perpetual chastity, obedience and poverty[1], after the manner of monks."* They were accommodated in a wing of the Royal Palace on the Temple Mount, reportedly on the foundations of the ancient Temple of Solomon. The public reason for their existence was that they were 'to keep the roads from the coast to Jerusalem free from bandits'. In fact, the task of protecting pilgrims was that of The Knights Hospitaller of St John, and for the first seven years of their nine year sojourn, it is known that the Templars stayed within the confines of the Temple Mount and concentrated on excavation. *The Holy Blood and the Holy Grail* states that in 1120, the Count of Anjou joined the Knights Templar.[2] The Count of Anjou was in fact Fulques who was later to become Fulque V of Jerusalem after he married Melissande daughter of Baudouin II.

In the years between the beginning of 1119 and the end of 1124, not much of note seems to have happened: the count of Champagne was occupied with affairs of state and after establishing abbeys at Fontenay and Foigny, little is heard of Bernard de Clairvaux. The only incident of significance, was the rejection by Bernard of King Baudouin II's offer to establish a monastery in the Holy Land. The offer from Baudouin indicates that Bernard was being talked about in Jerusalem but the action by Bernard would tend to confirm that he was not a co-conspirator with the count of Champagne and that Bernard's involvement (whether in innocence or by design) was to come later.

Sometime in 1124, Elizabeth, the wife of Hugues of Champagne announced that she was pregnant. Hugues immediately took steps to prove that he was impotent. He claimed that her child must be the result of an adulterous affair, and ceded his title, by

---

[1] There were three kinds of poverty. The first and strictest (altissima) permitted the possession of no property whatsoever. The second (media) forbade the possession of individual property, but sanctioned any amount of wealth when shared with the fraternity in common. The lowest allowed separate property in some things such as clothing and food, whilst everything else was shared in commom. The second kind of poverty was adopted by the Templars.

[2] They give no documentary back up for this claim but state that 'it is clearly on record'. It is confirmed in The History of the Knights Templar by Charles Addison who uses the contemporaneous writer, William of Tyre as his primary source. Fulque's entry also shows that the status of 'married knight' was usable within the order at that time.

charter, to his nephew Thibaud, Count of Blois. In the early part of 1125, he officially
joined the order of the poor knights of Christ and the Temple of Solomon' and set off
to join the other Templar knights in Jerusalem. Since all the other knights were supposed to be in Jerusalem, one can only surmise in whose presence Hugues pronounced
his vows of obedience to the order's rule. Could it be that one of the group had returned
to France with information which triggered Hugues into action and that this knight
of the order was present to witness Hugues's commitment? If so, to have precipitated
such a dramatic reaction, the news must have been compelling,. Without doubt, the
message implied that the group had been successful and that they had found the Ark.
Why else would someone, who was reputed to be more powerful than the King of
France, have renounced his wealth and title and set out yet again for the Holy Land?
There is of course the possibility that the count knew that the child could not be his
and was so devastated by his wife's adultery, that he renounced all and joined the
Templars. Another explanation of his actions suggests that he believed he <u>had to</u> join
the order; that he knew that the other knights had taken a vow to ensure that no one
other than a member of the order would be permitted to have access to the Ark. For
this reason, and to overcome the problem put in his way by Yves of Chartres 11 years
earlier, Hugues got doctors to attest to the fact that he was impotent and claim that
Elizabeth's baby was the result of an adulterous affair on her part, leaving him free to
take a vow of obedience to the rule of the Templars. Either way, we know that in late
1124/early 1125, Hugues left Troyes to join the rest of the group in Jerusalem.

Hugues stayed in Jerusalem for almost two years and returned to France with the
entourage of Knights which constituted the entire 'order' at the end of 1126. It is this
return of the group, which more than anything else, points to the fact that their intentions had nothing whatsoever to do with protecting pilgrims. It is widely conjectured
that the Templars discovered some cache of scrolls or manuscripts, containing ancient
knowledge including the architectural secrets of sacred geometry, proportion, balance
and harmony which were incorporated into the Temple of Solomon. Any such documents would have been written in Hebrew and since the Templars had no way of
knowing the form of the hoped for 'tablets', or any container which housed them, it is
entirely possible then the Templars thought that they had found the Ark and that when
Hugues de Champagne arrived, he too thought mistakenly that the Templars had
found the Ark. During the time gap between Hugues' arrival in Jerusalem and the
group's departure, one can only assume that he inspected the find very carefully and
painstakingly retrieved the scrolls from their hiding place. Once free, he would have
ensured that they were scrupulously wrapped and shielded for their long journey. The
Templars arrived back in France early in 1127, and presumably took their find to
someone who could arrange the interpretation of the ancient tablets/scrolls. Since we
know that a revolution in church architecture started at this point and was sponsored
by the Cistercians, we must assume that they took the sacred parchments to either
Stephen Harding or to Bernard of Clairvaux.

If the first Templars took some vow which designated who could and who could not
see and touch the Ark, and they first took their find to Bernard or Stephen Harding,
it would indicate one of two possibilities: either the Templars knew by now that their
find was not the Ark, or that their vow limited access to those who had taken vows of
poverty, chastity and obedience. This latter alternative would have allowed the knights
to take their find to Bernard or Stephen Harding, believing it to be the Ark of the
Covenant. The strongest evidence for the proposition that the knights did believe that
they had discovered the Ark and/or its contents, was the fact that excavations had

ceased and the entire group had left Jerusalem to guard the precious cargo on its way back to France. If they had believed that their find was important, but was not the Ark, they would have recommenced their excavation work with renewed enthusiasm.

The various biographies of Saint Bernard say little about his life and activities between the foundation of Clairvaux in 1115 and the return of the Templars in 1127. He is reputed to have suffered severe bouts of illness (as we have seen) and was no doubt involved in the establishment of the new monasteries at Trois Fontaines, Fontenay and Foigny. The most significant action (in relation to this unfolding story), which gives us a good idea of Bernard's views at the time, was his Apology to the Clunisians, which was written in 1124 or 1125. In this lengthy Epistle, we find the following extract:

> *"I come now, to larger violations which do not seem small to us because they are in wider use. I will bear in silence the excessive elevation of your churches their huge length, their unjustifiable size, their sumptuous decoration, their paintings full of studied elegance the effect of which is to distract those who pray, and thus to dissipate their fervour and which reminds me, somehow, of the ancient Jewish ritual."*

This tells us that Bernard was (amongst other things) interested in architecture and that his views about size at least, must have changed between writing this and the construction of abbeys and cathedrals which he controlled and influenced in subsequent years.

There is a conflict in the records covering the periods relating to the death of Hugues de Champagne. Hugues's death is officially recorded in the register of deaths at Chartres as 1126, which would mean that he died in the Holy Land and did not return to France in 1127 with the rest of the Templars. On the other hand, Hugues is reported to have attended the Council of Troyes in 1128. If this is true, he would most likely have returned to Jerusalem afterwards with Hugues de Payens in 1130.[1]

Bernard is known to have prepared the 'rule' for the warrior monks based on the rule of the Cistercians, which committed the knights to poverty, chastity and obedience. This rule was officially drawn up at the Council of Troyes in 1128. However, there must have been an initial 'rule' to coincide with the formation of the order in 1118. On that basis, there must have been contact and discussion between Bernard, Hugues de Champagne and (probably) André de Montbard (Bernard's uncle and one of the first nine Templar knights) prior to the establishment of the order and their departure for Jerusalem. It is difficult to imagine that they asked Bernard to write the rule without first explaining the objectives of the order that they wanted to create: It is possible therefore that Bernard would have suggested that the establishment of the official 'rule' should await the results of their forthcoming expedition.

In January 1128, Bernard convened the council of Troyes. Attendees included Matthieu d'Albabo, the Papal Legate, thirteen Archbishops and Bishops including the Bishops of Orléans, Troyes, Sens, Reims, Chartres, Soissons and Laon. Other religious persons attending were Reynaud de Semur, Abbot of Vezeley; Etienne Harding, Abbot of Cîteaux; Hugues de Macon, Abbot of Pontigny; Gui, Abbot of Trois Fontaines; Ursion, Abbot of Saint-Denis de Reims; Herbert, Abbot of St Etienne de Dijon and Gui, Abbot of Molesmes. The lay attendees included the Count of Champagne (Thibaud), the Count of Nevers and 'several other princes'[2]. All of these attendees were persons who are known to have been well-disposed towards either Hugues de

---

[1] Guillaume de Tyr, Hist., 1. XII, c VII dans Histoire des Croisades Occidentales.,
[2] Monsieur de Villfore; La Vie de St Bernard

Champagne, or Bernard of Clairvaux or both of them. Some of the literature reporting the Council of Troyes, claims that whilst he convened the council, for some unknown reason Bernard de Clairvaux did not attend. This is contradicted by Richard in *Analysis des Conciles,* by Hefele in *Histoires des Conciles* and by Vacandard in *Vie de Saint Bernard.*

Hugues de Payens, presented himself to the council and stated his desire to create an order of Warrior Monks from the nucleus already in existence. The council agreed and (as had been anticipated) charged Bernard with prescribing the rule.

The important question raised by the Council of Troyes is: why was it necessary for Bernard to convene such a powerful religious assembly and to make a formal request that the Templars be given full religious status as monks? There are three possible reasons: the first is that the work had not yet started on the documents brought back from Jerusalem and one of the unofficial tasks of Etienne Harding or Bernard himself if he did attend, was to inform the assembly of the find and to enlist their support in the translation and interpretation of the documents. In this scenario, the manuscripts/tablets would have been taken into the interiors of the delegated monasteries where no lay person would have had access to them. By being declared monks, the Templars would have been allowed into the inner sanctums of the monasteries working on the precious documents and they would have been able to ensure that the find and the information it contained, was not lost to them. Alternatively, some work had started in a limited way at Cîteaux and/or Clairvaux and the Templars had discovered that the cloistered monks were not giving him access to the libraries and *scriptoria* where they were working and where the documents were being housed. Hugues de Champagne, or in his absence Hugues de Payens who had devoted his life to this endeavour, would have been concerned by this loss of control. In such circumstances, it is not difficult to imagine the conversation that would have taken place between Hugues and Bernard and why the solution proposed by Bernard, involved official monk status for the Templars. It was a clever solution, since Bernard would have wanted to assist Hugues but would also have wanted to protect the integrity, seclusion and privacy of his abbey's inner sanctums. A variation on this hypothesis, is that Bernard knew that they were going to have to enlist the services of learned monks in monasteries outside the Cistercian order. In such an event, having the Knights Templar recognised as a religious order gave the Templars access to and control over the work undertaken by these other monasteries.

A second, but less likely reason for the new religious status, was that work had started on the manuscripts and that they already knew that they had not located the Ark. Perhaps the documents told of the location of the Ark in Ethiopia but stated that the only person allowed access to it was a guardian monk! On this basis, they might have believed that their retrieval of the Ark would be facilitated by having the official status of monks.

We can certainly conjecture, that following the council of Troyes, the work of translation and interpretation would have commenced in earnest. The Knights Templar in their new official status as warrior monks, transported portions of the precious documents/tablets to designated abbeys where learned individuals were waiting to start work on them. The knight assigned to protect each fragment may well have stayed close to his sacred charge to ensure its secrecy and its safety. Once completed, he would then have been able to transport the original document, together with any copies and translations back to the Templar headquarters in Troyes.

The third possibility is that someone (Hugues de Payens or André de Montbard) judged from the reaction to their return, that the warrior monk would have significant appeal and that an official order thus constituted would gain many recruits and therefore, much wealth and influence. *The Holy Blood and the Holy Grail* tells us: *"During the two decades following the council of Troyes, the order expanded with extraordinary rapidity and on an extraordinary scale. When Hugues de Payens visited England in late 1128, he was received with 'great worship' by King Henry I. Throughout Europe, younger sons of noble families flocked to enrol in the order's ranks, and vast dominions – in money, goods and land were made available from every quarter of Christendom. Hugues de Payens donated his properties and all other recruits were obliged to do likewise. On admission to the order, a man was compelled to sign over all his possessions. Given such policies, it is not surprising that Templar holdings proliferated. Within a mere twelve months of the council of Troyes, the order had substantial estates in France, England, Scotland, Flanders, Spain and Portugal."*

In 1130, Hugues de Payens returned to Jerusalem with a 'veritable army', which had been recruited in the west. In view of this we can be certain that by the time of his return, he knew that they did not have the Ark. If we knew the exact purpose of his mission to England in 1128 we would also know his awareness of the status of the sacred tablets/scrolls. Did he go to England to recruit young men to the Templar ranks in anticipation of his forthcoming return to Jerusalem or did he take to England some part of the sacred manuscript, which itself received 'great worship', in order to enlist the help of learned religious scholars in its translation and/or interpretation? Either way, it is clear that between 1127 and 1130 the inner circle were made aware of enough of the sacred information that they had retrieved from the Temple Mount to convince them that they should return and continue their search. They probably felt encouraged when they discovered that they had unearthed ancient and sacred texts, which translated the mystery of number and geometry into the harmony of design that had been incorporated into Solomon's Temple. Hugues de Payens' return to Jerusalem with such a large following is a clear indication that the initial find had only served to fuel the zeal of the Templars for their ultimate prize, the Ark of the Covenant.

From 1130 both Hugues de Champagne and Hugues de Payens seem to have disappeared from history. If Hugues de Champagne did not in fact die in 1126, is it possible that they both returned to the Holy Land in 1130 and if so, then they might well have led the first expedition into Ethiopia in search of the Ark, leaving others to control the order in their absence?

Back in France, the work on the documents brought back from Jerusalem had started to have an impact and in 1130, the first signs of a new departure in religious architecture were being manifested. The current guidebook at Clairvaux tells us; *"It is Louis VI who, as early as 1130, in the fullness of the reign of St Bernard, and paradoxically with his agreement, allowed Sugar to start work on the basilica of St Denis. The big vessel of light developed the first Gothic experiences refining Clunic magnificence. But he also experimented with 'proportion' that new concept which Abelard, enemy of St Bernard, encouraged at the Sorbonne."*

Abbot Sugar was a Benedictine and, like Etienne Harding, was an Englishman. He befriended the King of France and was even made Regent when Louis left for the second crusade in 1147. His approach was visionary and the progressive construction of the St Denis Basilica proclaimed the new Gothic style and used 'light' to illuminate the spirit. On the bronze doors of the western portal, Sugar had written; "The dejected spirit rises to the Truth, by way of material things, and seeing this light it is resuscitated from its previous submersion."

Sugar is known to have had friendly relations with Bernard de Clairvaux since his acceptance of Bernard's Apology to the Clunisians. It is entirely possible therefore, that he (Sugar) and the abbey of St Denis were given access to parts of the sacred writings which had been brought back from Jerusalem. However his impetuous use of the new information produced a reaction from Bernard: he made pronouncements against the excessive use of ornaments and is reputed to have said, "There is no decoration, only proportion."

Bernard's enthusiasm for the architectural information deduced from the Jerusalem material can in turn be deduced from his answer to his own rhetorical question; "What is God?" He said; "He is length, width, height and depth."

Significantly, in 1130, work also started on the cathedral in Sens; a town in the heart of Champagne and only 28 miles from Pontigny.

Following the council of Troyes in 1128, a virtual explosion started in Cistercian houses throughout Europe. In the 15 years between 1113, when the first filial of Cîteaux was established at La Ferté and 1127, the year the Templars returned from Jerusalem, 29 monasteries had been established including Cîteaux. Four of these 29 houses were Clairvaux and its subsidiaries.

In the seven years from the beginning of 1128 to the end of 1134, 49 new Cistercian monasteries were established, 14 of which were filials of Clairvaux. Additionally, the abbey at Fontenay was moved from La Rocherie and the magnificent new abbey we now know was constructed. In the four years from the beginning of 1135, to the end of 1138, a further 54 Cistercian monasteries were established of which 25 were founded by Clairvaux or its direct filials. (It may be significant, that Bernard's cousin, Godfrey de La Roche-Vaneau, was Prior of Clairvaux from 1128 to 1138 when he became Bishop of Langres) Also, at the beginning of the latter period, (1135) Clairvaux itself was moved and a magnificent new abbey church was constructed.

In other words, between 1118 and 1128 Clairvaux created 3 new abbeys and between 1128 and 1138 Clairvaux created 39 new abbeys and reconstructed two of the most important. By 1145, (30 years after the establishment of Clairvaux and only 18 years after the council of Troyes) there were 350 Cistercian houses throughout the various parts of Western Europe. These new monasteries were all constructed in the new architectural style which incorporated the harmonious relationships of so-called sacred geometry. The secret information which was incorporated into these new abbeys was closely controlled.

Expansion of the philosophy amongst the Bishops was limited to the work at Sens (which the Templars presumably thought they could control), St Denis and the construction of the north-west tower and the Royal Portal at Chartres where Bernard had struck up a close relationship with Geoffrey, the new Bishop who had developed considerable enthusiasm for the new formula. Even the cathedral at Verdun, which underwent massive reconstruction between 1136 and 1160, was rebuilt in the 'Norman-Bourguignon' style with numerous ornamented columns and portals and could not therefore have been given access to the new design information.

The close relationship between the early Templar Grand Masters and Bernard and the access which the religious status of the Templars gave them to the libraries and scriptoria of the monasteries was sufficient to ensure that secrecy and control was maintained. Once Bernard died however, (1153) the formula was sufficiently dissipated by the construction of new abbeys that it could develop and progress under its own momentum leading to the Gothic cathedral style that we now know. The revolution started with the construction of Nôtre Dame in Paris (1163) and then progressed to the other cathedrals which were built or reconstructed after the middle of the 12th century. In amongst all this activity, the events we need to examine more closely are the movements of the abbeys at Fontenay and Clairvaux. There is little information, in fact, about the movement at Fontenay. The only thing we know is that the new abbey was located on land donated by Rainard de Montbard (Bernard's uncle) and Stephen de Bag of Auton. This latter purchased the château at Touillon from Laudry, brother of Rainard (and therefore another uncle of Bernard) and one of the group of thirty relatives and friends who had gone with Bernard to Cîteaux. The only discrepancy in this information, is that Fontenay was moved in 1131 and Rainard (according to Ivan Gobry) died in 1123.

Fig 111 The nave at Fontenay Abbey

We can only assume that Rainard's donation of land covered the first emplacement as well as the eventual final location. Certainly, it is likely that Laudry disposed of his land prior to taking his vows in 1113.

We have considerably more information about the movement and reconstruction of the abbey at Clairvaux. In 1132/33 Bernard had been called to Rome by Pope Innocent II, to help him in his negotiations with the Emperor.

He stayed in Italy until after the council of Pisa in the middle of 1134 and was not at Cîteaux for the General Chapter of 1133 nor for the death of Etienne Harding on 23 March 1134. The *'Oeuvres de Saint Bernard'* tells us that; *Saint Bernard, after having spent a year almost entirely in Lombardy, obtained at last permission to return*

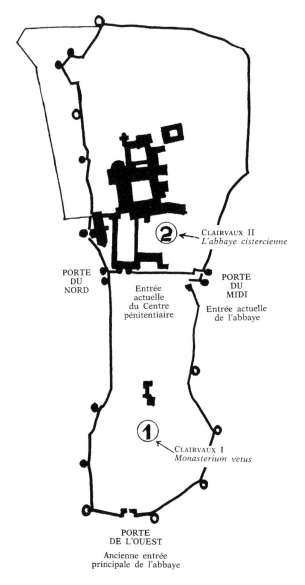

PORTE
DU
NORD

Entrée
actuelle
du Centre
pénitentiaire

CLAIRVAUX II
L'abbaye cistercienne

PORTE
DU
MIDI

Entrée actuelle
de l'abbaye

CLAIRVAUX I
Monasterium vetus

PORTE
DE L'OUEST

Ancienne entrée
principale de l'abbaye

Fig 111a The relative locations of Clairvaux I and Clairvaux II
scale: 1 centimetre = 100 metres

home to Clairvaux. He obtained leave from the Sovereign Pontiff in the beginning of Spring, 1135.

The biography of Saint Bernard tells us: '*So this monk (Godfrey[1], the Prior of Clairvaux) and several others who took care of everyone and their services (Bernard's brother Guy), obliged the Saint (Bernard) whose mind was in Heaven, to humble himself and come down to details which were necessary for the running of the house. With his permission, they made him realise that the monastery was situated in a remote and secluded place and that it could not house enough people because the number who wished to live there was increasing and they could not be accommodated in the existing buildings; the church was not even sufficient for the monks themselves.*

They also added that they had noticed land lower down from the Monastery, clear land with a river, and there was enough space there to supply all the needs of the Monastery: thanks to the meadows, the worked fields, the planted fields and even vineyards and because the nearby forest did not make a limit or boundary it would be easy to replace it with stone walls that the area could provide easily and in sufficient quantity.

At first the servant of God did not agree with his monks. He told them «You see, this house was built with great effort and it cost a great deal to construct the aqueduct to bring water to the kitchen and other work places. If we abandon all the buildings that we have constructed everyone will have a bad opinion of us and believe that we are thoughtless, fickle or that the excess of wealth (that we do not have) makes us extravagant. And as you certainly know that we have no money, remember the words of the Gospel: «that the one who wants to build a tower must calculate its cost, otherwise, if after the beginning he gives up his works, one will say: this mad man has begun something that he cannot finish»

To this the monks answered in these words: «If once the buildings were completed, God had stopped sending people here, your answer would be understandable and there would be no need to build anything. But as God multiplies his flock each day, either we have to reject those he sends or we must build new buildings to welcome them; there is no doubt that the one who prepares new monks for this house also must erect new buildings for them. And we would be rather mercenary if by fearing the expense we missed that which was necessary to accomplish his work and that we would render ourselves responsible for the inconvenience and disorder.»

Hearing their arguments, the Abbot was touched by their deep faith and their ardent love. He came to agree with them after much prayer to God on the subject and after having understood His will through several revelations.

The monks were very pleased when he told them that he agreed with the building. The very famous Thibaud, Count of Champagne of holy memory, already knowing the new project, gave a lot of money for the expenses and promised to give even more in the future.'

It is clear from this account, that the monks had planned the expansion and movement of the monastery, with the assistance of Thibaud the new Count of Champagne, during Bernard's absence and that Bernard was initially opposed to their suggestions. This presents us with various possibilities:

1) Bernard was aware of the importance of the precise location of each abbey and believed that Clairvaux should not be moved, despite its pitifully small facilities, until someone proved to him that the original emplacement was in error by a factor of 500 metres.

---

[1] The Prior of Clairvaux in 1135 was Godfrey de La Roche Vanneau, cousin of Bernard.

2) Bernard was never aware of the relevance of the position of the abbey before or after its movement and that the explanation for his initial reticence is as outlined in the biography.

Whatever the real explanation, it means that someone else (other than Bernard) was the guardian of the information which connected the positions of the Cistercian abbeys to the pentagram and The Plough. The most likely candidates were Thibaud, who had presumably been passed the information by Hugues his uncle, or Godfrey, the Prior of Clairvaux who had been passed the information by Etienne Harding prior to his death and who in turn, had received it from Robert of Molesmes. A third possibility is that the secret information regarding the pentagram and The Plough was held within the house of Tonnerre. That deduction is possible from the bulk of circumstantial evidence which points in that direction:

* Robert of Molesmes came from the house of Tonnerre
* Between 1068 and 1071 Robert de Molesmes had been Abbot of St Michel de Tonnerre
* The abbey of Molesmes was sited only 35 kilometres from Tonnerre
* Cîteaux was established on land owned by the viscount de Beaune, who was related by marriage to the mother of St Bernard who in turn came from the house of Montbard and thus Tonnerre
* Many of Bernard's family entered Cîteaux with him and therefore there were Montbards (and therefore people from the house of Tonnerre) at the heart of the Cistercian expansion from the beginning
* Pontigny was established on land donated by the Canon of Auxerre at a time when the William was Count of Tonnerre, Nevers and Auxerre
* Clairvaux was established on the dominions of Hugues de Champagne and on the land of Josbert de Grancey, cousin of Bernard and a member of the house of Tonnerre.
* Fontenay was established on land owned by Rainard de Montbard, a member of the House of Tonnerre
* William, Count of Tonnerre was the person who met with Hugues de Champagne after his return from the Holy Land and who could well have provoked Hugues's first visit there.
* Geoffrey de La Roche-Vanneau, the Prior of Clairvaux at the time of the construction of Clairvaux II was Bernard's cousin and had been the first Abbot of Fontenay until 1128
* One of the two lay attendees at the Council of Troyes was the Count of Nevers (and Tonnerre?)
* One of the founders of The Knights Templar was André de Montbard, uncle of Bernard de Clairvaux and a member of the House of Tonnerre.

When I read the history of Tonnerre, I was struck by a series of interesting facts that might well indicate a link between this house, The Plough and the pentagram it contains. The first was the fact that the Bishop of Langres had temporal sovereignty over the counties of Bar-sur-Seine, Langres and Tonnerre and that this Bishopric was normally occupied by lords of the first families of the country; amongst others, the families of the dukes of Burgundy, the counts of Tonnerre and Bar-sur-Seine. Could this sovereignty have accounted for Hugues de Champagne's trip to Langres, with Robert the Bishop, in 1104 and immediately prior to his meeting with William, Count of Tonnerre and others?

Another interesting piece of information was that the Monastery of Saint Michel, situated in Tonnerre was established in 6th century and was one of the oldest monasteries in France. Robert of Molesmes was Abbot of this monastery from 1068 to 1071 when he was 40 years old and only left to return to Moutier-la-Celle at the command of his superiors. Could this monastery have held the ancient information about the incredible pattern on the ground which had been set down by the Celts?

Challe, the author of the *Histoire du Comté de Tonnerre* mentions that the sole document from the 10th century, which mentions Tonnerre, was written by a monk of St-Germaine d'Auxerre, Radulphus. He quotes a small passage, which includes the phrase; *". . . il vit, du côté du **septentrion**, sortir et marcher vers l'occident, . . ."* which translated means; ". . . he saw, from the north, coming out and marching towards the west, . . ." This was the first time I had seen the word **septentrion**, which as translated by the Harraps French-English dictionary as '*Litt:* North'. This ancient French word meaning 'north' could well come from the three words; *sept en trillion* – seven in a trillion. If this is so, it could refer to the seven stars of Ursa Major (seven stars in a trillion) and could well be a word derived from the ancient Celtic habit of refering to the north in terms of the 'the seven stars'.

One of the most interesting facts that emerged, was that on the death of Milon III, the county of Tonnerre fell into the hands of Rainard Hugues, his son and Bishop of Langres. He is described as 'one of the grand figures of the century, a man of letters, able to read and write in both Latin and Greek. This was the same Bishop of Langres who; *". . . whilst he was in charge of Tonnerre, he founded in its territory the abbey of Molesmes, and his generosity started the fortune of the monastery that was later to be so rich and so strong."* This link between the house of Tonnerre and the first abbey of Robert of Molesmes only strengthens the likelihood that somewhere in the relationship between this house and crusading saint, lay the link, which resulted in the first Cistercian houses forming a complementary pattern to the ancient ground plan that already existed.

In the last analysis, it is impossible for us to know precisely who was behind the positioning of the first Cistercian abbeys and the motivations of those who were responsible for the extraordinarily rapid growth of the Cistercians. In addition, we can only wonder at the power and influence of the Knights Templar and the Gothic revolution in Church architecture. What we do know, is that the beliefs and energy of a small number of people resulted in a building programme, which bears witness to the secret knowledge of a pattern so intricate, accurate and magnificent, that it defies explanation.

Perhaps it just another coincidence, but the circle through the point where the Langres – Clairvaux line crosses the Igny – Troyes line, passes close to Igny, Abbey Saint Remi in Rheims, Trois Fontains, Clairvaux, Molesmes and Pontigny. (Fig 112) A wider circle through the same point passes through Verdun, Senlis, Nôtre Dame in Paris and Vezeley and even wider circles through Cîteaux and Chartres and through Bonne Mare, Arras, Douai, Mons, Marchiennes and Charleroi.

Because of these circles and the coincidence that the first Cistercian Abbeys were founded in the same period as the Grail legends were first committed to verse, it might be appropriate to end with some reference to the works of 'The Grail', that first introduced the 'round table' to us. To do this, I quote from Flavia Anderson; "Wolfram von Eschenbach, a native of north Bavaria, wrote his poem Parzival in German verse. As he died in 1220 he must have brought out his work within about thirty years of Chrétien de Troyes' death. He frequently refers to Chrétien's version with great contempt.

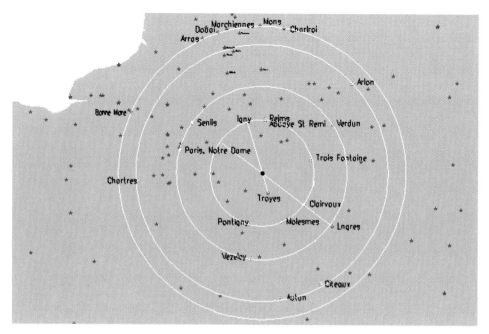

Fig 112 The circles connecting many of the key locations

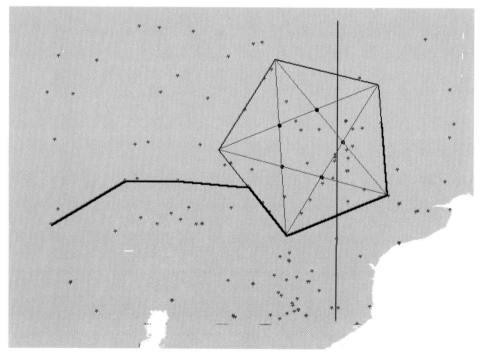

Fig 113 The Plough, Meridian and Pentagram; do they represent the Grail and its mysteries?

They both admit to drawing from earlier sources, so that it is beside the point as to whose poem predated the other. Wolfram claims to hold the true version from Kyot, the singer; a Provençal who found the tale of Parzival written in Arabic by a Jew in Toledo: "It is interesting to remember that Toledo in Spain was at first a Punic settlement and that it was in Toledo that Wolfram von Eschenbach claimed that the true story of Parzival and the Grail had been found from a writing discovered by a Provençal troubadour; a certain Kyot. I give the words of Parzival as translated by Jessie Weston:

Since I did but as Kyot bade me, for he would I should hide the tale'
And tell none the secret, till the venture so far were sped
That the hidden should be made open, and the marvel of men be read.
For Kyot of old, the master whom men spake of in days of yore,
Far off in Toledo's city, found in Arabic writ the lore
By men cast aside and forgotten, the tale of the wonderous Grail;
But first must he learn the letters, nor black art might there avail.
By the grace of baptismal waters, by the light of our Holy Faith,
He read the tale, else 'twere hidden: for never, the story saith,
**Might heathen skill have shown us the virtue that hidden lies
In this mighty grail,** or its marvels have opened to Christian eyes.
'Twas a heathen, Flegetanis, who had won for his wisdom fame.
And saw a wondrous vision (**from Israel's race he came,
And the blood of the kings of old time, of Solomon did he share**).
He wrote of the days long vanished, ere we was as a shield might bear
The cross of our Holy Baptism 'gainst the craft and the wiles of Hell.
And he was the first of the earth's children the lore of the Grail to tell.
By his father's side a heathen, a calf he for God did hold,
How wrought the devil such folly, on a folk so wise of old?
And the heathen, Flegetanis, **could read in the heavens high
How the stars roll on their courses, how they circle the silent sky,
And the time when their wandering endeth – and the life and the lot of men
He read in the stars, and strange secrets he saw, and he spake again
Low with bated breath and fearful, of the thing that is called the Grail.
In a cluster of stars was it written, the name, nor their lore shall fail.**"

Many more links can be found between the many stories of the Grail and the picture of the cup of The Plough holding the Pentagram. The most symbolic, is the tale of the Fisher King who was long ago wounded by a spear thrust through both thighs, and that the wound would have been healed had Parzival asked concerning the mysteries which he saw. This corresponds well with the passage of the meridian through the pentagram, where in one direction the line crosses an arm and a leg and in another (108° further round) it passes through two thighs.(the first two figures of Fig 123)

One of the more tenuous links between the picture of The Plough holding the pentagram (Fig 113) and the early Cistercians is the illustration at the begining of the book of the Apocalypse, in St Etienne Harding's Bible. This precious manu-script is still intact and is kept in the archives of the library in Dijon. The engrav-

Fig 114 The illustration which starts the Apocalypse in St Etienne Harding's Bible

ing shows us St Michael's sword (intersecting the head of the dragon) in the place of the meridian, St Michael in place of the pentagram, the centre of the shield for the internal pentagram and the dragon itself replacing the seven stars. This picture perhaps becomes more apt when we realise that the Druids called the constellation of Ursa Major, 'King Arthur's Chariot' and that Arthur was known as 'The Dragon King'.

CHAPTER 9–
Conclusion

I had hoped that an analysis of the activities of the people surrounding the first Cistercians would give me a tangible clue to the meaning and origin of the design. In particular, I had hoped that Hugues de Champagne's activities in Jerusalem might have been based on an attempt to discover an answer to some mystery to which he had become a part. I had even hoped that there might have been some clue to the secrets of the Templars and their interest in things esoteric, in order to discover any possible link with the shapes I had uncovered. Unfortunately, whilst I can speculate about Hugues' intentions and about the identity of those who chose and/or influenced the positions of the first monasteries, I have nothing tangible to offer and the link between Hugues de Champagne's initial involvement and the subsequent Templar secrets remains a mystery.

The following is a summary of the facts revealed by my research:

A ground pattern, which is a duplication of the seven stars of Ursa Major, exists in Northern France

The seven points, which make up the pattern, include 4 major cathedrals and an acknowledged Celtic site

The pattern has been designed and constructed to contain two equal angles of 108° which is the internal angle of a regular pentagon

The regular pentagon within the design contains a pentagram which in turn contains a further pentagon, and this pattern was known to someone involved in the construction of the first Cistercian abbeys, which are positioned to align with key points in the plough and the five shaped figures that it contains

The construction must have been undertaken by the Celts or Druids and may even go back to 2500-3000BC

There appears to be a coincidental link with the legend of the Holy Grail whose stories were first committed to writing at the time the first Cistercian Abbeys were founded

The line of the pointers aims precisely towards the small town of Rennes-le-Château in the foothills of the Pyrenees.

The ground pattern has been constructed so that the ancient meridian exactly bisects the base of the plough, grail or chariot.

Two of the cathedrals are precisely aligned with Ephesus and Jerusalem

One of the seven points is connected with the Temple of Isis in Philae through the centre of Nôtre Dame in Paris

Two lines drawn through five of the seven points of The Plough are exactly parallel to one another

The phrase 'The mystery of the seven stars' contained in the book of Revelations, is linked via gematria to the pattern on the ground.

The seven points are intersected by circles with the same centre and this centre is midway between Chartres and Donnersberg

The dimensions of the outer circle and the diameter of the circle are exact multiples of ancient units of measurement used by the Egyptians and the Greeks, and the building blocks appear to correspond with numbers which have been identified as ancient sacred units of measure.

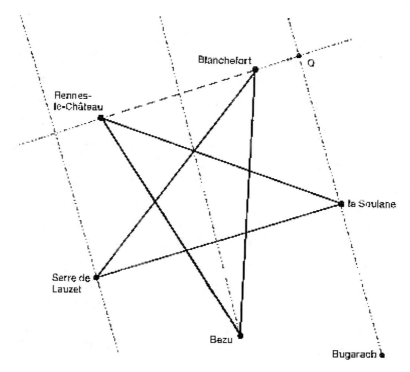

Fig 115 The pentagram first illustrated by Henry Lincoln

A set of coincidences that is worthy of mention is the pentagrams that have been uncovered in and around the Polaris position, Rennes-le-Château. In the 1970's, Henry Lincoln awoke a large UK television audience to the mysteries of Rennes-le-Château and its surroundings through a series of three fascinating programmes. In them, he explained how Rennes is one of the five points in a natural pentagram, which seems to be imprinted on the landscape. (Fig 115) He explained about the parchments that had been uncovered by Abbé Saunière, the parish priest of Rennes-le-Château and thatthese parchments contained codes to some mysterious hidden treasure.[1] In the same programmes, he illustrated the pentagram contained in Nicolas Poussin's painting *Les Bergers d'Arcadie – Et in Arcadia Ego* (Fig 116) and suggested that Nicolas Poussin was aware of the mystery. Apparently he (Poussin) discussed it with the brother of Nicolas Fouquet, the powerful minister of finance who then wrote a letter to his brother, which said; "He (Nicolas Poussin) and I have planned certain things of which

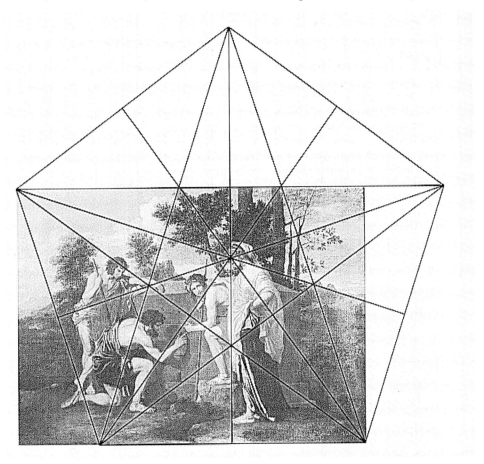

Fig 116 Les Bergers d'Arcadie and the pentagram, discovery of which Henry Lincoln attributes to Professor Christopher Cornford of the Royal College of Art.

in a little while I shall be able to inform you fully; things which will give you, through M. Poussin, advantages which kings would have great difficulty in obtaining from him and which, according to what he says, no one in the world will ever retrieve in centuries to come; and furthermore, it would be achieved without much expense and could even turn to profit, and they are matters so difficult to inquire into that nothing on the earth at the present time could bring a greater fortune nor perhaps ever its equal." More recently, David Wood has published two books which illustrate an extended pentagram,which again has Rennes-le-Château in the key right hand posi-

---

[1] *The Holy Blood and the Holy Grail* by Michael Bagient, Richard Leigh & Henry Lincoln and *The Holy Place* by Henry Lincoln

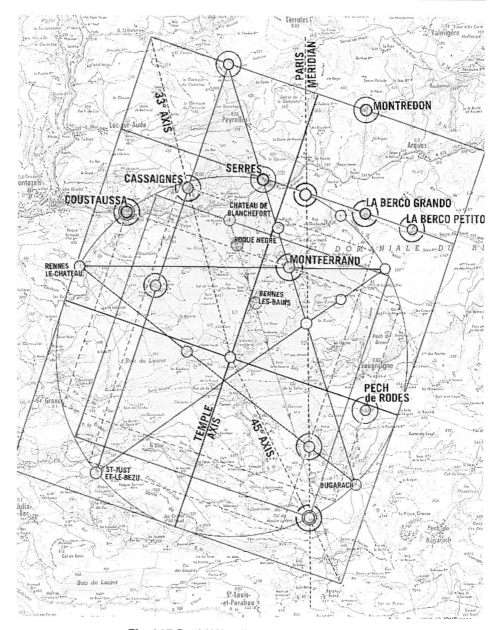

Fig 117 David Wood's extended Pentagram

tion.[1] (Fig 117) Interestingly, simple observation uncovers a regular pentagon in the centre of the the Poussin painting which I am amazed that everyone has overlooked. (Fig 118)

In addition to the encrypted messages in the parchments uncovered by Saunière, the stones on the grave of Marie de Nègre (Figs 75 & 77) have been decoded by various authors and it is commonly accepted that one of them says that '. . . Poussin and Teniers

---

[1] *GenIsis* and *Geneset.*

hold the key . . .' Both these painters created paintings which incorporated the phrase 'Et in Arcadia Ego'; one of which is a painting of Mary Magdalen with a skull at her knees and is duplicated on the front of the altar in the church at Rennes-le-Château. The phrase was reputed to be the motto of the house of Blanchefort and is incorporated into one of the inscriptions on the grave of Marie de Nègre.

The phrase 'Et in Arcadia Ego' means 'And I am in Arcadia' or 'I am also in Arcadia'. Which led me wonder where 'Arcadia' might be. '*The Holy Blood and the Holy Grail*' says; "the very name Arcadia derives from Arcades, which means 'people of the Bear'. The ancient Arcadians claimed descent from Arkos the patron deity of the land, whose name also means 'bear'. According to Greek myth, Arkos was the son of Kallisto, a nymph connected with Artemis, the huntress. To the modern mind, Kallisto is most familiar as the constellation Ursa Major – the Great Bear."

This connection between 'Arcadia' and 'Ursa Major' made me wonder if the phrase 'Et in Arcadia Ego' could mean 'I am also in the Great Bear'. Could the pentagrams which abound at Rennes-le-Château and which can be uncovered in Poussin's painting be the link? Could the 'I' in 'I am also in the Great Bear' refer to the pentagram which can be found in both places? If so, the pentagram itself must have some special significance.

Manly P Hall states that; "The pentagram is the formula of the microcosm – the magical formula of man. It is the one, rising out of the four – the human soul rising out of the bondage of animal nature. It is the true light – the 'Star of the Morning.' It marks the centre of five mysterious centres of force, the awakening of which is the supreme secret of white magic." (Fig 119)

There is no literature which links the Druids to the shape of the pentagram. However, the pentagram shape does fit into a stylised plan of the original Stonehenge which I obtained from *The Secret Teachings of all Ages* by Manly P Hall. (Fig 120) If this imposition of the pentagram is correct, it would appear that the strange horseshoe shape of the ten large inner stones may well have combined with the position of the altar stone to create the pentagram shape.

The number 'Five' (the number of sides and angles of the pentagram) had a special significance in ancient times: *The Serpent in the Sky* by J. A. West tells us; "To the Pythagoreans, Five was the number of 'love' or 'life', because it represented the union of the first male number, Three, with the first female number, 'Two'. Four terms are necessary to account for the idea of matter, or substance. But these four terms are insufficient to account for its creation. It is Five, the union of male and female, that enables it to 'happen'.

It is for this reason that the pentagram and the pentagon have been revered as sacred symbols through the ages. In ancient Egypt, the symbol for a star was drawn with five points. The ideal of the realised man was to become a star, and to become 'one of the company of Ra'.

The pentagram, made up of the Golden Section segments, is the symbol of unremitting activity; 'Five' is the key to the vitality of the Universe, its creative nature. In mundane terms, 'Four' accounts for the fact of the sculptor's statue, but does not account for the 'doing' of it. Five terms are required to account for the principal of 'creation'; 'Five' is accordingly the number of 'potentiality'. Potentiality exists outside time. 'Five' is therefore the number of eternity and the principal of eternal creation, union of male and female – and it is for this reason, and along these lines of thought, that the ancients came to hold 'Five' in what looks to us like a peculiar reverence." His description would seem to fit well with the later representation of Christ by a pentagram.

Fig 118 Nicolas Poussin's painting – Et in Arcadia Ego with my own pentagon and pentagram superimposed. – The figure is created by linking key points in the picture; the shepherdess's nipple to the crouching shepherd's forehead to the triangle in the bright spot on the upright shepherd's arm (this line is parallel to the top of the tomb); the shepherdess's nipple via the kneeling shepherd's arm to the point of the angle in the same shepherd's calf; the shepherdess' nipple to the white spot on the crouching shepherd's sandal.

One of the most interesting features of the pentagram thus devised, is that the staff of the crouching shepherd seems to be in a similar position to the meridian in the mirror image of the pentagram prescribed by The Plough. Additionally, the tip of the staff bisects one of the five sides of the exterior pentagon. (See fig 122 for comparison). At the same time, the vertical line down the centre of the tomb, being pointed at by the crouching shepherd, bisects the bottom side of the pentagon – It is interesting that the shepherd's staff cuts the pentagons and the pentagram just as the ancient meridian cuts the ground pattern.This inevitably provokes the question whether Poussin (who is reputed to have known some significant secret) was aware of the pattern and its connection to the area close to Rennes-le-Château.

Fig 119 The pentagram which is claimed to be the figure of the microcosm – the magical formula of man.

Arcadia was a province of Greece and there is evidence in the Bible[1] which suggests that the Spartans, who were the strongest and most well known of the Arcadians, were 'of the stock of Abraham'. *The Holy Blood and the Holy Grail* quotes a text from the secret dossiers of the Prieuré de Sion[2] which claims that they were in

---

[1] 1 Maccabees 12,21

[2] UN JOUR LES DESCENDANTS DE BENJAMIN QUITTÈRENT LEUR PAYS CERTAINS RESTÈRENT DEUX MILLE ANS APRÉS GODEFROI VI DEVIENT ROI DE JERUSALEM ET FONDAIT L'ORDRE DE SION – De cette légende merveilleuse qui orne l'histoire, ainsi que l'architecture d'un temple dont le sommet se perd dans l'immensité de l'espace et des temps, dont POUSSIN a voulu exprimer le mystère dans les deux tableaux, les Bergers d'Arcadie, se trouve sans doute le sécret du trésor devant lequel, les descendants paysans et bergers du fier sicambre, méditent sur 'et in arcadia egeo', et le Roi 'Midas'. Avant 1200 à notre ère – Un fait important est l'arrivée des Hébreux dans la terre promise et leur lente installation en Caanan. Dans la Bible, au Deuterone 33; il est dit sur BENJAMIN: C'est le bien aimé de l'Éternel le couvrira toujours, et résidera entre ses épaules.

Translated, this reads: 'ONE DAY THE DESCENDANTS OF BENJAMIN LEFT THEIR COUNTRY SOME OF THEM REMAINED TWO THOUSAND YEARS AFTERWARDS GODEFROI VI BECAME THE KING OF JERUSALEM AND ESTABLISHED THE ORDER OF SION – POUSSIN wanted to express the mystery of this wonderful legend which adorns history, as well as that of the architecture of a temple whose summit is lost in the immensity of space and time, in the two paintings. Les Bergers d'Arcadie doubtlessly contains the secret of the treasure before which peasants and shepherds, descendants of the proud race, meditate on 'et in arcadia egeo', and King *Midas*. Prior to 1200 up until our era – a significant event is the arrival of the Hebrews in the promised land and that they gradually settled in Canaan. In the Bible, in Deuteronomy 33, it is written of BENJAMIN: He is the beloved of the Eternal One who will always cover him, and who will live between his shoulders.'

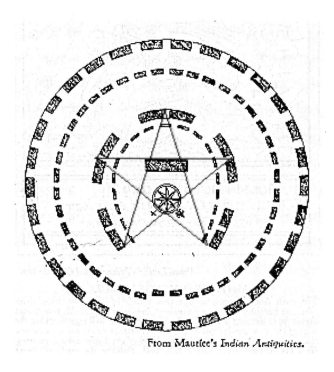

From Maurice's Indian Antiquities.

Fig 120 The pentagram which fits neatly into the above plan of Stonehenge

fact the descendants of the tribe of Benjamin. They also state that; "There is the legend of King Belus' son, of one Danaus, who arrives in Greece with his daughters, by ship. His daughters are said to have introduced the cult of the Mother Goddess which became the established cult of the Arcadians. According to Robert Graves, the Danaus myth records the arrival of the Peloponnesus of 'colonists from Palestine'.[1] Graves states that King Belus , is in fact Baal or Bel – or perhaps Belial from the Old Testament. It is also worthy of note that one of the clans of the Tribe of Benjamin was the clan of Bela. « In Arcadia, the cult of the Mother Goddess not only prospered but survived longer than in any other part of Greece. It became associated with the worship of Demeter then of Diana or Artemis. Known regionally as Arduina, Artemis became tutelary deity of the Ardennes; and it was from the Ardennes that the Sicambrian Franks first issued into what is now France. The totem of Artemis was the she-bear – Kallisto, whose son was Arkas , the bear-child and patron of Arcadia. And Kallisto, transported to the heavens by Artemis, became the constellation of Ursa Major, the Great Bear."

---

[1] Robert Graves, *Greek Myths*

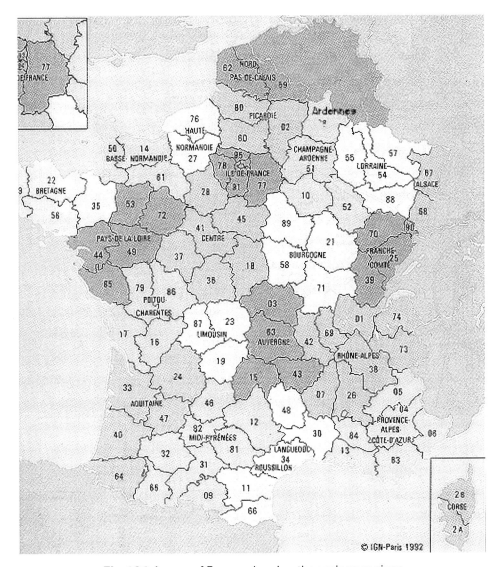

Fig 121 A map of France showing the various regions

It is well-known that the Arcadians came to Gaul from Greece and it is suggested that they migrated up the Danube, then up the Rhine and established themselves in Western Germany and the North West corner of France.(The Ardennes) Certainly, the establishment of towns with Trojan names such as Troyes and Paris (both associated with The Plough/Chariot and its five pointed passengers) might well have a direct relationship with ancient Troy. I include a map (Fig 121) to show the relationship between the Ardennes, Champagne and the Ile de France. The literature relating to the mysteries of the Grail and other ancient lore may give us further clues to the Plough-Pentagram relationship, although the information that does exist is rather tenuous.

A Guide to Glastonbury's Temple of the Stars by K E Maltwood quotes W T Olcott in *Star Lore of all Ages* and tells us; "The great Plough appears to revolve around the heavens once in twenty four hours, though it is the Earth that is really turning . . . In

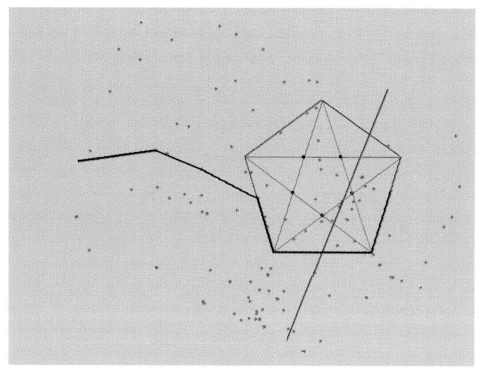

Fig 122 The Plough holding the pentagram which is being intersected by the meridian

Ireland it was 'King Arthur's Chariot', and the Druids so name it. The French call it 'The Great Chariot', and 'David's Chariot', which is interesting, for the effigy bird appeared to hold the Old Vicarage at Barton St David, with the church and the cross of St David in its beak. In the Middle Ages, in different countries, Ursa Major was known as the 'Chariot of Elias', 'Thor's Wagon', 'Wagon of Odin', 'Car of Osiris', 'the abode of the seven sages who entered the Ark with Minos', 'the Wagon of Our Saviour', and 'The Brood Hen'. To sum up, the constellation of the Great Bear or Plough was held to be the fiery Brood Hen, and appears to have carried Osiris, Minos, David, Elias, King Arthur, Thor, Odin and Our Saviour endlessly round the starry heavens every twenty four hours. The Welsh Bard sings: 'I have presided in a toilsome chair, over the circle of Sidin – the circle of the Zodiac – whilst that is continually revolving between three elements: is it not a wonder to the world that men are not enlightened?'"

Brinsley le Poer Trench who claims in *The Temple of the Stars* that there is a line of 'Arthurs', tells us; "There is for us, an interesting connection here between two of the names bestowed upon this constellation and King Arthur, or The Arthur as we would prefer to call the Office. These two names are 'The Great Bear' and 'The Great Plough'. Arthur, by derivation, means 'Chief of the Bear People', and there is a legend applied to at least one of the Arthurs that when the Druids came to fetch him to become King, he was ploughing in a field with oxen. « John Whitehead, discussing the word *Arwiragus* wrote: 'The Gaelic-Pict name it represents appears to be *Arc-wyr-auc*, Ar'wirane, 'The Bear-Folk Chief'. The Gaelic 'c' could become 't' in Pictish, both aspirated giving *Arth-wyr*, 'The Arthur'.

(a)

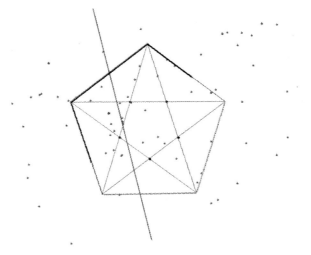

(b)

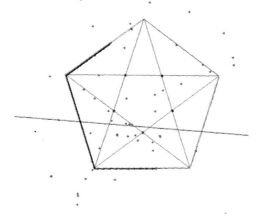

(c)

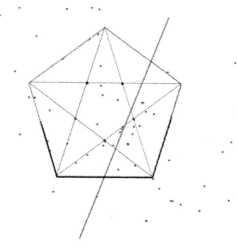

Fig 123 a, b, c

(d)

(e)

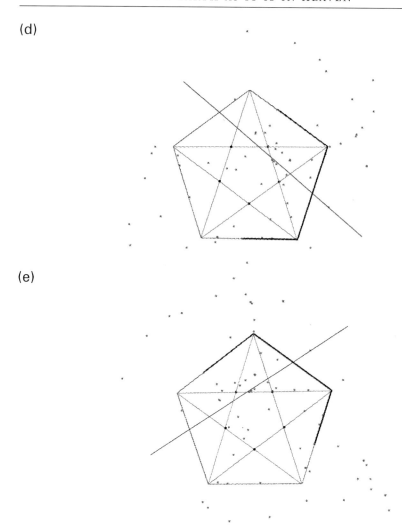

Fig 123 (a–e) The 5 positions of the shield, knights and lance

Gareth Knight, in *The Secret Tradition of the Arthurian Legend*, says; "It is the same ancient sources, in their Greek-Irish recension, that give the stories of the ancient Tuatha de Danaan – the children of the Goddess Dana – who had four treasures that have come down in Arthurian and Grail myth and legend, and later in the suits of Tarot, and the four traditional magical instruments related to the Elemental Quarters – the Lance, the Sword, the Cup and the Stone (or Shield). «The Tuatha de Danaan on a May day or Beltane, in a mist, came 'through the air and the high air' to Ireland, from a place with four cities, each with four wise men to teach the young men 'Skill and knowledge and perfect wisdom'.

In the words of Lady Gregory: 'And they brought from these four cities their four treasure: a Stone of Virtue from Falies, that was called the Lia Fail, the Stone of Destiny; and from Gorias they brought a sword; and from Finias a spear of victory;

and from Murias the fourth treasure, the Cauldron that no company ever went away from unsatisfied.[1]

In Arthurian legend we have the same treasures appearing: Arthur's sword Excalibur, that came from the Faery workshops of The Lady of the Lake and which was returned to her at the end of Arthur's mission; The Lance that gave the Dolorous Stroke that brought the evil enchantment upon the Land of Logres in the Grail Legend; The Cup that is representative of the Holy Grail itself, although the actual form of the Grail is never seen by mortal eyes; The Stone which appeared floating in the river, with a king's sword in it, to be drawn only by he who had the destiny of terrestrial kingship in the case of Arthur, or of spiritual kingship in the case of Galahad."

Jessie Weston, the most celebrated writer and researcher of the Grail mysteries, attempts to pinpoin the origins of the Grail stories in *The Quest for the Holy Grail*. She comments on three theories, one based on Christian origin, another on folk-lore and a third based on ritual. In her chapter on folklore, she says; "The weak point, and it is a fatally weak point, of the method employed by the defenders of both Christian and folklore theory, is that both alike content themselves with a discussion of the nature and the origin of the Grail, and its attendant talisman, the Lance, each, as it were, *per se,* and independent of the other, and disregard, more or less, the setting in which they are placed.

Yet surely no theory of the origin of the story can be considered really and permanently satisfactory, unless it can offer an explanation of the story as a whole; of the relations between the two chief talismans, and of the varying forms assumed by the Grail: why it should be at one time a food-providing object of unexplained form, at another a dish; at one moment the receptacle of streams of blood from a lance, at another, the cup of the Last Supper: here 'Something' wrought of no material substance, there, a Stone; and yet everywhere and always posses the same essential significance; in each and every form be rightly described as *The Grail."*

In *From Ritual to Romance*, she attempts to create a link between the Grail stories and Ancient Mysteries embedded in the hellenized cults of Asia Minor. In this respect she writes; "Here the evidence, not merely of the evidence of the mysteries, but of their widespread popularity, is overwhelming; the difficulty is not so much to prove the case, as to select and co-ordinate the evidence germane to our enquiry." In the following chapter where she illustrates the links back to Mithra and Attis she tells us that . . . "the conception of Seven Heavens, ruled by the seven Planets, which we find in Mithraism, is due to the influence of Babylonian siderial cults." Without intending to, Jessie Weston, one of the foremost authorities on the stories of the Grail, finds an abundance of evidence to link the Grail mysteries to the ancient beliefs and rituals of Asia Minor and thus to Apollo, Pythagoras, geometry, Plato, Gematria, the Qabala, the Israelites and the seven Planets. What she did not do, because she was never privileged to see the plan that had been laid out in northern Europe, was make the connection to the shapes contained within the Great Bear on the ground and therefore the mythical connection with the star constellation which dominates the northern hemisphere and which circulates around the pole of the heavens. The closest connection she finds to the pentagram is covered in passing in *The Quest of the Holy Grail* where she writes:

'The final stage is the initiation into the higher Secret of the Mysteries, that of regeneration and spiritual life. It is quite obvious that here the experience must, of necessity, pass on a higher, a non-material plane, and the source of spiritual life must

---

[1] *Guardian of the Grail* by John Whitehead

be other than a material, food-supplying Vessel. And so we have the Holy Grail, which, we are told, was not of wood, nor of any manner of metal, nor was it in any wise of stone, nor of horn, nor of bone, and therefore was he (Sir Gawain) sore abashed. The Grail, at this stage, is wrought of no material substance. The test here demanded of the Quester is that he shall ask concerning the nature and use of this mysterious Vessel; but, as we have seen, he does not ask, after he falls asleep, and though instruction may be given, his ears are closed. Frequently, as in the Bleheris-*Gawain* form, he is required to re-weld a broken sword; his failure to do this bars him from achievement.

Is it a far-fetched hypothesis to assume that here the Sword represents the will-power, which, welded to its hilt, the 'pentangle', the mystic symbol which is supposed to give power to the Other-world, will enable the initiand to forego the final test, that of retaining his consciousness during the vision of the 'Holy' Grail, so that, the vision passed, he can, in full and clear remembrance of what he has seen, demand without fear or denial what this mysterious Vessel is, and whom, or what purpose, it serves? As students are well aware, the Sword of the Grail romances is a very elusive and perplexing feature. It takes upon itself various forms; it may be a broken sword, the re-welding of which is an essential condition of achieving the quest; it may be a 'presentation' sword, given to the hero on his arrival at the Grail Castle, but a gift of dubious value as it will break, either after the first blow, or in an unspecified peril, foreseen, however, by its original maker. Or it may be the sword with which John the Baptist was beheaded; or the sword of Judas Maccabæus, gifted with self acting powers; or a mysterious sword *as estranges ranges*, which may be identified with the preceding weapon. In this latter form we find that the scabbard may bear the mysterious inscription, *'mémoire de sens'* (the sense memory), and one of the finest of our Gawain romances, *Sir Gawain and the Green Knight*, assigns to that hero, as his distinguishing badge, the 'pentangle' (the pentagram)."

One can only surmise what Jessie Weston would have made of the parallel lines disappearing into the the pentagon and the pentagram (pentangle) it contains and the fact that these shapes are all hidden within the cup made by the body of the Plough: it is easy to see how Gawain's sword disappearing into the scabbard bearing the 'pentangle' (pentagram) inscription is a powerful metaphor for the parallel lines disappearing into the regular pentagon and the pentagram in contains. If the plough pattern was established in ancient Celtic times and the story of the pattern was handed down verbally and woven into stories and tales over the centuries, it is entirely likely that the Grail romances were a commentary on the complex geometric pattern that was laid down by Celtic religious leaders many centuries earlier. The fact that the Grail romances were written at a time when we know that someone involved in the establishment of the first Cistercian abbeys was intimately aware of the pattern on the ground would seem to suggest another coincidental link between the stories and the intricate shape that was embedded into the landscape of northern France. The hypothesis that the stories of the Grail emanated from legends, which in turn were based on stories that Celtic religious intelligentsia had designed to explain their intricate creation and that the creation itself was made to honour and depict complex juxtaplay between the Gods that existed amongst the constellations, is a far more easy theory to swallow than the tales of talismen and magic that so often accompany mention of The Grail.

In summary, the legends and paucity of facts point to a remote past when the Arcadians, the bear people, direct descendants of tribe of Benjamin first settled in the Ardennes. From there, they spread throughout Gaul and their religious leaders, well-versed in astronomy and mathematics laid down a master design of the story they saw in the heavens. The plan,

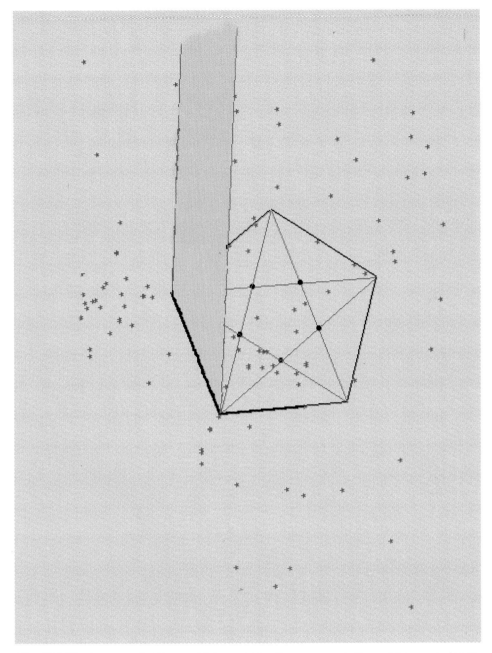

Fig 124 The two parallel lines which could be the representation which gave rise to the legend of the sword in the stone.

or the perceived heavenly plan on which it was based, was known to the Hellenists and early Christians Gnostics who were steeped in the science of gematria.

St John (if he was the writer of Revelations) incorporated his perception of the Divine Christ, his 'Arthur' into the plan so that Christ became the stone inside the Grail. This then was the story that was gradually turned into myth until it became entwined with magical yarns of Gods, semi-Gods and heroes until it finally evolved into the legends of the Elixir of Life, the Philosopher's Stone and the Holy Grail as we know them in part, today. The great chariot carrying Gods (or in more modern times knights) around the pinacle of the heavens, holding their shield and spear and with their sword hidden, has been the inspiration of religious leaders since time began. Only since the origin and constitution of the stars has been known and our modern day scientists have given us electric light and television have we ceased to look up and wonder at the pictures that are woven above our heads. In ancient times, these same starry patterns were at the centre of people's mystical belief and their propositions regarding the origins of the stars and their courses were central to their religious beliefs.

The ground plan somehow became known in its precise detail to the early Cistercians. Based on the information outlines in chapter 8, the knowledge had most likely been guarded and protected in the Monastery of St Michel de Tonnerre (St Michael of Thunder) since its establishment in the 5th century. Later, when St Robert de Molesmes became abbot, he must have become aware of the information, which he then passed to those close to him such as Hugues de Champagne and St Etienne Harding. The only alternative is that the alignments with the first Cistercian abbeys were a giant coincidence, which resulted when these abbeys were located (unwittingly) in clearings which had once been ancient Druid sites. It would be possible to continue with an abundance of quotations from the many writers who have studied the mysteries of the so-called 'ancient knowledge' or who in more recent times have speculated about the various Grail texts and (still more recently) about the re-establishment of the Merovingian dynasty in France[1] and its links with the Arcadians. Ultimately however, much of it would be guesswork and speculation, reinforcing the fact that we can never know for certain who laid down the ground plan of the Great Bear and the other shapes that the plan contains. I consider that the plan is too accurate and on too vast a scale to be ignored. It seems to contain all the major elements inherent within the stories of the Grail;

> The Great Bear = Arthur, The Fisher King who has suffered serious disability (The positions of the seven stars in The Plough were changed in order to create the precise geometry that the architects required)
> The meridian = The Lance
> The Parallel lines = The Sword embedded in the stone
> The seven stars = The Chariot, Cup or Grail
> The cup made by the body of the Plough = The Grail
> The hidden pentagram(s) (depending on which of the five points we choose as the head) = The five knight(s)
> The pentagons and pentagram = The shield
> The inner pentagon = the floating stone or sacred wafer floating over the sacred vessel of the last supper
> The circles which go through the seven star points and which are centered at the same point = The round table.

I have chosen as the final picture, the body of the Plough together with the internal pentagon which sits over it. Together they resemble closely pictures of 'the Host' held by Christ over the cup of wine at the Last Supper – a traditional representation of the Grail. (Fig 125)

---

[1] *The Holy Blood and the Holy Grail* by Baigent Leigh & Lincoln

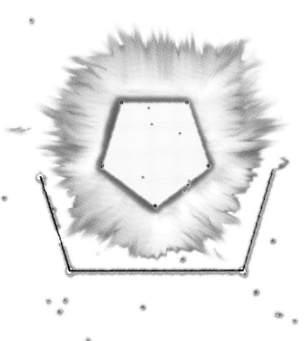

Fig 125 The cup of the plough and the interior pentagon which is so similar to the Host over The Grail

The only thing that I can say for certain is that **the pattern and its many connections exist.** From idle beginings, where curiosity led me to search for a pattern of the Great Bear amongst the cathedrals of northern France, I discovered what may be the oldest and most magnificent monument to man's achievement on earth.

In ancient times, man's courtship with the stars and the many Gods that the stars contained, was central his existence. The Hellenic tradition which was brought to northern Europe by the Arcadians and which is known to have had much in common with the traditions of the Druids, was based on the power of number and geometry. In these traditions may lie the link between the intricate and precise design that has been etched into the landscape of North Western Europe and the Grail stories. These stories were formulated in writing at the end of the 12th and begining of the 13th centuries but are acknowledged to have been based on some previous folklore or ritual, which had existed from much earlier times.

The principal dates and activities surrounding the establishment of the Cistercians and the Knights Templar

910	—	Benedictine abbey established at Cluny.
990–1028	—	Fulbert at Chartres cathedral school.
1020	—	Construction of Abbaye St Remi commenced.
1023	—	Construction of the new abbey at Mont St Michel commenced.
1029	—	Birth of St Robert, known as Robert of Molesmes, destined to be the first Abbot of Cîteaux. By his mother he was closely related to the Counts of Tonnerre and his father was a vassel of the Duke of Burgundy.
1043	—	Robert commenced his novitiate at the monastery of Moutier-la-Celle near Troyes.
1058	—	Robert became Prior of Moutier-la-Celle.
1065	—	Robert became Prior of St-Ayouls-de-Provins.
1066	—	Birth of St Etienne Harding.
After 1068	—	Robert became Abbot of St-Michel de Tonnerre.
1070	—	Rabbi Rashi founded the famous school of cabbalistic and esoteric studies in Troyes.
	—	Monks from Calabria (including Peter the Hermit) led by an individual called 'Ursus' (The Bear) became established at Orval.
	—	Birth of Hugues de Payens.
After 1071	—	Robert left St-Michel de Tonnerre and returned to Moutier-la-Celle.
1073	—	Robert was head of a group of Hermits in the forest of Collan. The seven original hermits were joined by six others who told of the writing of the life of the saints (hagiography) practised by the Bollandists.
1075	—	Foundation of the Abbey at Molesmes. Hugues de Maligny, related by marriage to the families of Châtillon, Noyers, Montbard, Riceys, etc., (and therefore a relative of St Bernard) agreed with his sisters, nephews and nieces to give to Robert and his companions some land that they owned between Laignes and Riceys in order that they could 'live more comfortably and to give to their newly born settlement, more scope for development.' Robert was part of the family of the Counts of Tonnerre, either of the Noyers or of the Maligny, Robert I then Duke of Burgundy.
1077	—	Birth of Hugues, Count of Champagne.
1086	—	Pope Victor III (Didier de Bonevent, Prior of Mont-Cassin).
	—	Etienne Harding joins Molesmes.

1088   Pope Urban II (Eudes de Châtillon, Prior of Cluny).

1090 — Birth of Bernard de Fontaine, son of Tascalin le Saur de Fontaine-les-Dijon and Aleth, Daughter of Bernard de Montbard who was grandson of one of the counts of Tonnerre and nephew of the Bishop of Langres. She was related by marriage to the Viscount of Beaune from the line of the Dukes of Burgundy and also to the family of Mont-Saint-Jean one of whom was Bishop of Autun, to the Couches one of whom was Bishop of Châlons and to the counts of Nevers, Brienne and Roucy.

1093 — Robert, Abbot of Molesmes formed a project with several of his companions to live strictly to the rule of St Benoit in a spirit of prayer and poverty.

— Hugues de Champagne, in concert with his mother and brother Philippe, gives a donation to Abbaye St Oyand in Le Jura.

1095 — Hugues de Champagne marries Constance, daughter of Philippe I of France

— Consecration of Philippe, brother of Hugues de Champagne, who had been elected to the post of Bishop of Châlons-sur-Marne in 1093.

— Bernard (at 5 years old) is sent to the school at Châtillon-sur-Seine, 65 kilometres north of Dijon and half way between Dijon and Troyes.

— The Council of Clermont is called by Pope Urban to excommunicate Philippe I. At this council, Urban preaches the first crusade.

1096 — Hugues de Champagne joins an assembly of Bishops and Barons in Reims. They include Manasses, Archbishop of Reims; the Bishops Philippe of Châlons-sur-Marne, Lambert of Arras, Hugues of Soissons and Elinand of Laon. The most important Barons included Robert I, Count of Flanders; Hugues, Count of Rethel; Dudon, Count of Mareuil and Erlaud, Vidame of Reims.

1097 — Hugues de Champagne spent Easter at Molesmes. Among those there at the time were his seneschel Gosbert-le-Roux; his brother Philippe, Gui de Vignory and Dudan, Vidame of Châlons-sur-Marne.

1098 — (January) Robert, accompanied by several companions, left Molesmes and visited Hugues de Diem, Archbishop of Lyons, to obtain permission to establish a new order.

— (March) The first Cistercian monastery was established in the forest of Cîteaux, on land donated by Robert's cousin Rainard, viscount of Beaune and a relation to the mother of Bernard de Fontaine.

— (March) Etienne Henri, elder brother of Hugues de Champagne, wrote a letter from the Holy Land to Adèle his wife, claiming that he had doubled his riches, had been made up to 'leader chief and director of the entire expedition' and was 'advancing steadily towards the home of Our Lord Jesus Christ'.

— Etienne Henri deserts the crusade and returned home to France.

— (July) Hugues, brother of Philippe of France, left the Holy Land for France via Constantinople.

1099 — Jerusalem was taken by the first crusade.

— A secret conclave was held in Jerusalem which included a certain 'Bishop from Calabria'. Its stated purpose was to elect the King of Jerusalem, Godfrey, Duke of Lorraine.

— Dedication of the first Abbey at Cîteaux.

— Geoffrey, Prior of Molesmes, sent a delegation to Urban II in Rome. Urban (Champenoise by birth) sent an official letter to the papal legate suggesting that he would be happy if Robert returned to Molesmes.

— (June) A synod was convened in Port d'Ancelle where it was decided that Robert should return to Molesmes. Robert left Cîteaux with two monks and Alberic (Aubry) became Abbot of Cîteaux.

— (August) Pope Pascal II (Rainier de Bieda, monk of Cluny).

— Robert, count of Flanders and Robert, count of Normandy return to France from the Holy Land.

1100 — Death of Philippe, Bishop of Châlons and brother of Hugues de Champagne.

1101 — Hugues de Champagne again spent Easter at Molesmes. With him was Constance his wife, Hugues count of Reynel, Hugues Count of Ramerupt and another Hugues, seneschel of the Count of Burgundy.

— The monastery at Cîteaux was moved 'half a league' (2 kilometres) further south. The official reason currently given for this re-location, is 'lack of water'.

— Etienne Henri, brother of Hugues de Champagne, returned to the Holy Land.

1101/1102 — Hugues de Champagne and his sister-in-law Adèle, wife of Etienne Henri, gave substantial donations to the Abbey at Molesmes.

1102 — Hugues de Champagne was wounded in the battle between Emperor Heny IV against Robert II, Count of Flanders.

— Death of Etienne Henri of Blois, brother of Hugues de Champagne, at Ramleh.

1103 — Death of the mother of Bernard de Fontaine.

1104 — (April) Hugues de Champagne made four large gifts of charter; one to the cathedral in Troyes, one to the cathedral in Châlons-sur-Marnes, one to the Abbey of St Loup and the last to the Abbey of Molesmes. These gifts and charters were made in Troyes during a synod which was presided over by the papal legate, Richard, Bishop of Albano. Also in attendance were Daimbert, Archbishop of Sens; Raoul, Archbishop of Tours and Manasses, Archbishop of Reims. The bishops attending were Yves of Chartres, Humbaud of Auxerre, Herve of Nevers, Marbode of Rennes, Robert of Langres, Notgaud of Auton, Hugues of Châlons-sur-Marne, Philippe of Troyes, Manasses of Soissons and Jean of Orléans. In addition there were a number of abbots and lords; Robert of Molesmes, Helgaud of Marmoutier, Lambert of Pothieres, Raoul of Moutier-la-Celle, Otton of

Montieranney, Milon, count of Bar-sur-Seine, Milon lord of Chaceney, Gui lord of Vignory, Rainier of Châtillon, André count of Ramerupt, André lord of Baudement and Geoffrey seneschel of Hugues de Champagne.

— (May) Hugues de Champagne travelled to Langres with Robert the Bishop (uncle of the duke of Burgundy).

— The Count of Champagne met in conclave at Molesmes with a group of high ranking nobles including; Hugues II Duke of Burgundy, William II Count of Auxerre, Nevers and Tonnerre (who had recently returned fromn the Holy Land), Hugues Count of Reynel, Erard Count of Brienne, André Count of Ramerupt, Milon Count of Bar-sur Seine, Geoffrey Lord of Chaumont and Bassingy and the leige lord of André de Montbard, Roger of Joinville and Thibaud Count of Blois and Ponce of Trainelle.

— Hugues de Champagne had another meeting this time at Jereton Abbey in Dijon. The attendees included Hugues Duke of Burgundy, Robert Bishop of Langres, the bishop of Chalon-sur-Saone, the Abbot of St Germaine in Auxerre, the seneschel and high constable of the Duke of Burgundy, Gui of Vignory, Rainord of Grancy and William of Fouvent.

— Hugues visited the monastery of St Germain in Auxerre accompanied by Brise-Loup Lord of Bercenay.

— Hugues' marriage to Constance was annulled.

— The Count of Champagne paid his last visit to Molesmes and set off for the Holy Land with Hugues de Payens.

1106 — Consecration by the Bishop of Châlons of the new church – Cîteaux II.

1108 — 'Ursus' and his monks are reported to be missing from Orval.

— Hugues de Champagne returned from Jerusalem and met in Châtillon-sur-Seine with William II Count of Nevers, Milon Count of Bar-sur-Seine, Roger of Joinville, Geoffrey of Chaumont and Ponce of Trainelle.

1109 — Death of Alberic and election of Etienne Harding as Abbot of Cîteaux.

1110 — Hugues de Champagne married Elizabeth, daughter of Etienne-le-Hardi Count of Varais and Macon and of Beatrix of Lorraine, sister of Rainaud, Count of Burgundy.

— Hugues de Champagne founded the Abbaye de Cheminon in the forest of Luiz.

1111/1112 — 'La Milice du Christ' was formed, being the forerunner of 'The order of the Temple'.

1112 — Bernard de Fontaine joined the Cistercians at 22 years of age and brought with him, his four brothers and 25 other relations and friends who were noblemen in the houses of Tonnerre, Montbard and Burgundy. Elizabeth, the wife of Guy, one of Bernard's brothers, withdrew to one of the filiates of Molesmes.

1113 — The first abbey was established under Cîteaux at La-Ferté-sur-Grosne, on land donated by Savaric-de-Dozny, Lord of Vergy and his nephew William, Count of Chalon. The offer was made via Goutier de Couches, Bishop of Chalon.

— William of Chapeaux became Bishop of Châlons-sur-Marne.

— The Pope granted the right to become a religious order to 'the Crusading order of St John of Jerusalem' (the Hospitallers). The head of the order was Peter Gerard.

1114 — Pontigny Abbey was founded under Cîteaux on land donated by Hildebert, Canon of Auxerre. The first abbot of Pontigny was Hugues, friend of Bernard and previously Lord of Macon.

— The Count of Champagne announced that he wanted to live the rest of his life abroad and that he intended to join the newly formed order of St John of Jerusalem.

— (August) Hugues de Champagne left for Jerusalem.

1115 — Morimond Abbey was established under Cîteaux. It was founded on land donated by a recluse John and the noble Odobric d'Aigremont and his spouse Adeline de Choiseul.

— Hugues de Champagne returned from Jerusalem.

— The Count of Champagne founded the first abbey at Clairvaux and Etienne Harding put Bernard de Fontaine in charge. The abbey was on the land of Josbert de Grancey, vassel of Hugues de Champagne and cousin of Bernard and who was promised the title of Viscount de la Ferté in exchange for the land. Bernard took with him his four brothers, his uncle Gaudry, his cousin Geoffrey de la Roche Vanneau, Geoffrey d'Aignay, Elbaud and Renier.

— Death of Robert of Molesmes.

1116 — Meeting of the first affiliates of Cîteaux (Bernard was too ill to attend).

1118 — The official founding of the Knights Templar under the leadership of Hugues de Payens, one of the vassels of the Count of Champagne.

— The foundation of the Abbey of Trois Fontaines under Clairvaux on land donated by Hugues de Champagne.

— Pope Gelase II (Jean Coniolo, monk of Mont-Cassin).

— St Bernard's father came to spend his final years at Clairvaux.

— Raymond le Puy succeeded Peter Gerard as the head of the Order of St Jean

1119 — Hugues de Payens presented himself and his eight knights to Baudouin, King of Jerusalem.

— Foundation of Fonteney abbey under Clairvaux.

— (October) Hugues de Champagne attended the Council of Reims and then accompanied the Pope and sheltered him from the forces of the Emperor in the château at Grandpré.

— Pope Calixte II (Guy of Burgundy, previously Archbishop of Vienne and papal legate).

— Chapter of the first nine affiliates of Cîteaux.

1120 — Hugues convened a meeting in Troyes which was attended by barons and ecclesiastics where, amongst other things, he gave the abbey of Montieramey the rights of justice in the village of St-Martin les Vignes.

1121 — Foigny Abbey was established under Clairvaux.

1122 — Baudouin II offered land in the Holy Land and 1000 ecus in gold for the construction of a monastery. St Bernard declined the offer and asked that it be transferred to the Order of Prémontre.

1124 — Hugues assembled an army for the King of France, which prevented the planned invasion by Henry V.

— Elizabeth, wife of Hugues de Champagne announced that she was pregnant. Hugues claimed that the child must have been the result of an adulterous relationship by his wife.

— Hugues de Champagne repudiated his wife and child, assigned his earldom and estates to Thibaud his nephew and officially joined the 'Order of the Temple' before travelling to join the other Knights Templar in Jerusalem.

— Pope Honorius II (Lambert de Pagnani).

1125 — Letter from Bernard to Hugues de Champagne.

1126 — Death of Huges de Champagne recorded at Chartres.

1127 — The Templars returned from Jerusalem.

— Bernard made excuses and claimed fatigue when the papal legate asked to see him regarding preparatory steps for the Council of Troyes.

1128 — (January) The Council of Troyes where the Templars are officially recognised as a religious-military order.

— Foundation of the Abbey at Igny under Clairvaux.

— Foundation of the Abbey at Reigny under Clairvaux.

— First Cistercian abbey established in England at Waverley (filiate of Cîteaux).

1128–1138 — Geoffrey, Bishop of Chartres and companion of Bernard on his trips to Italy and Aquitaine.

1129 — Ourscamp Abbey founded under Clairvaux.

— Council of Châlons.

1130 — Hugues de Payens returns to Jerusalem with a veritable army.

— Pope Innocent II (Gregoire Papareschi).

— Construction commenced at the cathedral in Sens (The archbishop of Sens was Henri de Sanglier 1122-1142, friend of Bernard).

1131 — Reconstruction of the cathedral at Noyons planned (work started 1145).

— Bernard travels to Flanders with Innocent II and recruits thirty postulants in St Quentin and Cambrai among whom were several future priors of Clairvaux, a future bishop of Auxerre and future abbots of Dunes and Clairvaux.

— Council of Reims.

— Fonteney Abbey moved from la Rocherie onto land donated by Rainard de Montbard (St Bernard's uncle) and Stephen de Bag, bishop of Auton who purchased the Château at Touillon from Gaudry, another uncle of Bernard and one of the thirty nobles who followed him to Cîteaux.

— Bernard wrote to Hugues de Payens the 'Book to the soldiers of the Temple: orientation to the new militia'.

	—	Assumed death of Hugues de Payens.
1132	—	Construction of the western facade and front nave of St Denis commenced.
	—	Foundation of the Abbaye de Fontaine Guérard.
	—	Bernard travelled to Rome and arrived in January 1133.
1134	—	Construction of the north tower started at Chartres.
	—	Council of Pisa.
	—	Death of Etienne Harding.
1136	—	Clairvaux II.
	—	Hugues de Macon became Bishop of Auxerre.
1137	—	Bernard's third trip to Rome.
	—	Death of Vilain d'Aigrement, relation of Bernard and Bishop of Langres.
	—	Bernard has a political battle with Cluny before he persuades the Pope to install Geoffrey de la Roche Vanneau, Prior of Clairvaux as the next Bishop.
1138	—	Accession of Conrad III (Hohenstaufen) brother of Othon as Abbot of Morimond.
1140	—	Council of Sens.
1143	—	Pope Celestine II Guy de Costello).
1144	—	Pope Lucius II (Gerard Caccianemici).
1145	—	Pope Eugene III Bernard Paganelli monk of Clairvaux, Abbot of St Anastase).
	—	The Royal Portal is started at Chartres.
1146	—	Bernard toured extensively and preached the 2nd crusade.
1147	—	The 2nd crusade.
1148	—	The Council of Reims.
1153	—	The death of Bernard of Clairvaux.
	—	The construction of the Gothic cathedral of Nôtre Dame is started in Paris.

Appendix 1

Alignments within 100 metres

Bonne Mare – <u>Chartres</u> – Albi – Alet les Bains – <u>RLC</u>
Dieppe – Bonne Mare – Montlucon – St Flour
Nôtre Dame, Rouen – Bonne Mare – Nangis
Alencon – Bonne Mare – Arras
<u>Notre Dame, Reims</u> – Bonne Mare – <u>Ruins, Landonvillers</u>
St Lo – Caen – Bonne Mare – Rethel – Virton – <u>Donnersberg</u>
Bonne Mare – Rethel – Virton – <u>Donnersberg</u>
Bonne Mare – Dourdan – Toulon
Bonne Mare -Lens – Gent W
Bonne Mare -Tournai – Anterp E
Bonne Mare – Gisors – Chalons-sur-Marne – Nôtre Dame en Vaux – Nancy
Bonne Mare – Ablis – Nimes
Bonne Mare – Mons SW – Mons NE
Bonne Mare – Wervick SW – Wevick N
Bonne Mare – Sedan W – Sedan E
St Pol de Leon – Bonne Mare – Orval
Savigny – Bonne Mare – Mortemer
Le Releque – Bonne Mare – Beauvais N
Bonne Mare – Port Royal – Grenoble
St Ouen, Rouen – Fontaine Guérard – Bonne Mare – Nôtre Dame, Paris

Alignments between 100 metres and 250 metres

Amiens – Bonne Mare – Sees – la Blanche
Notre Dame, Rouen – de Fontaine Guérard – Bonne Mare – Sacré Coeur, Paris
St Ouen, Rouen – ND Rouen – Fontaine Guérard – Bonne Mare – ND Paris – Sion
Bonne Mare – Nevers – Vaison la Romain
Bonne Mare – Mortemer – Liege – Cologne
Bruxelles E – Bruxelles S – Bonne Mare
Bonne Mare – Gent W – Gent C – Gent E
Lyons St Jean – Lyons Notre Dame – Bonne Mare
Caudebec – Bonne Mare – Clairvaux
Dijon – Bonne Mare – Fontaine Guérard
Fontenay – Bonne Mare – Fontaine Guérard.
Bonne Mare – St Germain en Laye – Pontigny

Alignments between 250 metres and 1000 metres

Evreux – Bonne Mare – Abbeville
Lisieux – Bonne Mare – Noyon
Lisieux – Bonne Mare – Beauvais
Bonne Mare – Gisors – Senlis – Epernay – l'Epine
Metz – <u>Verdun</u> – St Remi, Reims – Bonne Mare
Bonne Mare – Bourges – Puy de Dôme
Caen – Bonne Mare – Luxembourg
Bonne Mare – Tours – Angoulême
Nantes – Bonne Mare – Arras
Bonne Mare – Melun – Geneva
Bonne Mare – Dourdan – Trets
Bonne Mare – Mortemer – <u>St Quentin</u> – Bonn
Bonne Mare – Amiens – Antoing
Bonne Mare – Arras – Oudenaarde
Bonne Mare – Lille – Tourcoing
Bonne Mare – Meaux – Lillebonne
Bonne Mare – Le Puy – Uzes
Treguier – Bonne Mare – Arlon
Valance – Etampes St M – Bonne Mare
Bonne Mare – Lille – Waregem
Bonne Mare – Pontoise W – St Denis
Bonne Mare – Gisors – Toul
Lillebonne – Bonne Mare – Basel
Bonne Mare – Compiegne – Vauclair – Stenay
Bonne Mare – Le Puy – Arles
Vannes – Rennes – Bonne Mare – Mortemer
Sees – Bonne Mare – Douai – Antoing
Vezelay – Bonne Mare – Fontaine Guérard
Avalon – Versailles – Bonne Mare – Fontaine Guérard
Bonne Mare – Poitiers – Liguge
Bonne Mare – Marchiennes – Mechelen
Bonne Mare – Maubisson – Troyes
Bonne Mare – Senanque – Aix en Provence
Fontaine Guérard – Bonne Mare – Prouilly
Freibourg – Royaumont – Bonne Mare
Dinan – Bonne Mare – Mortemer
Autun – Bonne Mare – Fontaine Guérard

Appendix 2

Alignments within 100 metres

Brest – Dinan – Chartres – ND Etampes
Sees – Chartres – Belfort
Evreux – Chartres – Puy de Dôme
Brugge W – Beauvais – Chartres
Wervick SW – Chartres – Poitiers S
Bonne Mare – Chartres – Albi – Alet les Bains – Rennes-le-Château
Bruxelles E – Bruxelles C – Chartres
Alencon – Chartres – Preuilly
Chartres – Port Royal – St Dennis
Chartres – Cluny – Chambéry
Mont St Michel – Chartres – Clairvaux
Chartres – Nôtre Dame Reims – Orval
Chartres – La Ferté – Stenay – Virton

Alignments between 100 metres and 250 metres

Chartres – Sacré Coeur, Paris – Soissons
Le Mans – Chartres – Nôtre Dame Reims
Coutances – Chartres – Bern
AntwerpE – Antwerp S – Pontoise W – Chartres
Chartres – Versailles – Laon
Vannes – Chartres – Dourdan – Ruins, Landonvillers
Vannes – Chartres – Metz
Chartres – Senlis – Charlroi
Chartres – Ablis – Chalons sur Marne – Nôtre Dame en Vaux – l'Epine – Kaiserslautern
Lyons St Jean – Lyons – Chartres
Caudebec – Chartres – Bourges
Chartres – Gisors – Les Dunes

Alignments between 250 metres and 1000 metres

Chartres – Autun – Annecy
Colmar – Troyes – Chartres
Sees – Chartres – Sens
Chartres – Dourdan – Metz
Chartres – Melun – Nangis

Chartres – Nangis – Toul – Nancy
Caen – Chartres – Vezelay
St Lo – Chartres – Auxerre – Dijon
Chartres – Nevers – Fréjus
Chartres – Bourges – Nîmes
Dieppe – Chartres – Perpignan
Abbeville – Chartres – Auch
Chartres – Amiens – Ypres NW
Lens E – Chartres – Bayonne
Angers – Chartres – Nôtre Dame, Paris
Chartres – Sens – Langres
Tours – Chartres – Douai
Chartres – St Germain en Laye – Compiegne
Liege E – St Denis – Port Royal – Chartres
Nantes – Chartres – Rethel – Sedan E
Chartres – Tournai – Oudenaarde
Chartres – Etampes – Troyes – Freibourg
Chartres – Sees – Basel
Rennes – Chartres – Melun
Evreux – Chartres – Montlucon
Chartres – Uzes – Arles
Chartres – Orléans – Le Puy
Chartres – Vaison la Romain – Trets – Toulon
Chartres – Ablis – <u>Donnersberg</u>
Chartres – Autun – Annecy
Colmar – Troyes – Chartres
Chartres – Meaux – Francheval
Chartres – Roubaix – Kortijk
Sacré Coeur, Paris – Versailles – Chartres
Savigny – Chartres – Troyes
Chartres – Marchiennes – Antoing
Chartres – Royaumont – <u>St Quentin</u>
St Ouen, Rouen – Chartres – Béziers
Chartres – Maubisson – Vaucelles – Valenciennes
Toulouse E – Chartres – Mortemer
Acey – Fontenay – Chartres
Rennes – Chartres – Trois Fontaines
Le Mans – Chartres – St Remi

Appendix 3

Alignments within 100 metres

Bruxelles C – Mons – St Quentin – Noyon – Senlis
St Quentin – Versailles – Ablis
St Quentin – Nevers – Narbonne
Antoing – St Quentin – Nangis – Albi
St Quentin – Bayeux – St Pol de Leon
St Quentin – Cambrai S – Cambrai N – Menen
Roubaix – St Quentin – Le Puy
Cologne – St Quentin – Vannes
St Quentin – Cambrai S – Cambrai N

Aligments between 100 metres and 250 metres

Amiens – St Quentin – Arlon
Mons – St Quentin – Noyon – Compiègne
Calais – St Quentin – <u>Nôtre Dame Reims</u>
St Quentin – Nôtre Dame, Paris – Poitiers
Mechelen – St Quentin – Sacré Coeur, Paris – Dourdan
Valenciennes – Caudry – St Quentin – St Bertrand de Comminges
St Quentin – Nevers – Narbonne – Elne
Tourcoing – Cambrai – St Quentin – Auxerre
Lille – Vaucelles – St Quentin – Avallon – St Etienne
Douai – St Quentin – Valence – Senanque – Marseille
Ypres NW – Douai – St Quentin – Vienne
St Quentin – Grenoble – Digne
St Quentin – St Lo – Coutances
Cologne – St Quentin – Beauvais
Antwerp E – St Quentin – Nôtre Dame Etampes – Angoulême
Sion – Nôtre Dame en Vaux – Chalons sur Marne – Laon – St Quentin – Calais
Prouilly – St Quentin – Tournai – Waregem
Lens E – St Quentin – Dijon
Calais N – St Quentin – St Remi, Reims

Alignments between 250 metres and 1000 metres

Abbeville – St Quentin – Stenay
St Quentin – Noyon – Compiegne – Senlis – Versailles – Ablis – Tours

Mechelen – Bruxelles W – St Quentin – Nôtre Dame, Paris – Poitiers S
Bruxelles E – St Quentin – Compiegne
Bruxelles W – St Quentin – Nôtre Dame, Paris
Antwerp E – St Quentin – Nôtre Dame Etampes
Valenciennes – Caudry – St Quentin – Meaux – Saarlat St Quentin – Troyes – Fontenay
Roubaix – St Quentin – Auxerre
St Quentin – Nôtre Dame Epernay – Dole – Geneva
Arras – St Quentin – Laon
Cologne – St Quentin – Rennes
Liège NW – St Quentin – Gisors – Evreux
St Quentin – Lisieux – Quimper
St Quentin – Melun – Auch
Valenciennes – St Quentin – Tarbes
Bonn – St Quentin – Mortemer – <u>Bonne Mare</u>
Gent – St Quentin – Bourges
Kaiserslautern – Luxembourg – St Quentin
Bayonne – Bordeaux – St Quentin
Luxembourg – Francheval – St Quentin
Uzes – St Quentin – Cambrai
Sens – St Quentin – Marchiennes – Kortijk
St Quentin – Vezelay – Nîmes
Lyons ND – St Quentin– Douai – Ypres W
Lyons St J – St Quentin – Vaucelles – Douai – Ypres E
Autun – St Quentin – Douai
<u>Chartres </u>– Royaumont – St Quentin
Wervick – Vaucelles – St Quentin
Morimond – l'Epine – St Quentin
Besançon – St Quentin – St Omer
Béthune – St Quentin – Clairvaux
Albi – Vaucelles – St Quentin
Caudebec – Fontenelle – St Quentin
<u>Rennes-le-Château</u> – La Ferté – St Quentin
Mont St Michel – Avranches – St Quentin
La Releque – Caen – St Quentin
Acey – St Quentin – Woestine

Appendix 4

Aligments within 100 metres

Reims – Auxerre – Rodez
Reims– Valence -Carpentras
Valenciennes – Reims – Grenoble E
Bonne Mare – Reims – Ruins, Landonvillers
Antwerp E – Bruxelles S – Reims – Narbonne – Perpignan
Bruxelles C – Reims – Narbonne
Orleans – Reims – Cologne
Mechelen – Reims – Pontigny – St Flour
Reims – Ypres – Ypres N
Reims – Arlon SW – Arlon NE
Quimper – Savigny – Reims
Langres – Reims – Vaucelles
Reims – St Remi – Clairvaux
Ypres SE – Reims – St Remi – Clairvaux
Reims -St Remi – Acey
Douai – Reims ND – St Remi
Geneva – St Remi – Nôtre Dame Reims
Angers – La Ferté – Reims

Alignments between 100 metres and 250 metres

Orval – Reims – Chartes – Le Mans
Reims – Epernay – Albi
Reims – Lyons – Vienne
Caudry – Reims – Clairvaux – Dôle
St Martin , Etampes – Nôtre Dame, Etampes – Reims
Reims – Roubaix – Tourcoing
Boulogne – Reims – l'Epine
Nôtre Dame, Le Havre – Nôtre Dame, Rouen – St Ouen, Rouen – Reims
Reims – Nangis – Poitiers
Reims – St Quentin – Calais
Reims – Beauvais S -Fontenelle – Caudebec
Bruxelles W – Reims – Vezelay
Trier – Reims – Sacré Coeur, Paris
Bruxelles W – Reims – Vezelay
Elne – Reims – Antwerp

Reims – de Vaucelles – Lens E
Cambrai N – Cambrai S – Reims
Antoing – Reims – St Remi

Alignments between 250 metres and 1000 metres

Mons – Reims – Troyes – Nîmes
Reims – Autun – Arles
Gent E – Reims – Avignon
Arras – Reims – Sion
Reims – Gisors – Bayeux
Virton – Stenay – St Remi, Reims – Reims – Notre Dame, Paris – Versailles
Reims – Chalons-sur-Marne – Besancon
Boulogne – Vauclair – Reims – l'Epine – Bern
Oudenaarde – Reims – Aix en Provence
Dieppe E – Reims – Nancy
Béthune – Reims – Chalons sur Marne
Reims – Montpellier – Maguelonne
Le Releque – Evreux – Reims – Kaiserslautern
Reims – Epernay – Auxerre – Rennes-le-Château
Charlroi SW – Reims – Auxerre
Bonn – Sedan – Reims – Melun
Quimper – Savigny – Reims – Donnersberg
Treguier – Senlis – Reims
Woestine – Bethune – Reims – Chalons sur Marne
Luxembourg – Reims – St Denis – St Germain en Laye
Reims – St Germain en Laye – Rennes
Arlon SW – Reims – Meaux
Coutances – Lisieux – Reims
Reims – Fontenay – Cluny
Reims – Merchiennes – Wervick
Morimond – Reims – Vauclair
Lille – Reims – Clairvaux
Kortijk – Tournai – Reims
Vezelay – Reims – Bruxelles W
Reims – Preuilly – Bordeaux
Dinan – Maubisson – Reims
Metz – Reims – Fontaine Guérard
Metz – Reims – Abb Mortemer
Reims – Meaux – Port Royal
Reims – Ablis – Noirmoitier
St Omer – Reims – Nôtre Dame en Vaux
Douai – Reims – Acey
Nevers – Epernay – Reims

Appendix 5

Alignments within 100 metres

Verdun – Troyes – Bordeaux NW
Verdun – Dole – Trets
Verdun – Stenay – Francheval – Bruxelles E
Verdun – Valenciennes – Lille
Metz – Verdun – Bayeux
Verdun – Senlis – Caen
Verdun – l'Epine – Nôtre Dame en Vaux – Chalons sur Marne – Le Mans
Pontoise W – Pontoise E – Verdun
Verdun – Lens E – Béthune
Verdun – Pontigny – Auxerre
Royaumont – Verdun – Ruins, Landonvillers
Verdun – St Remi – Fontaine Guérard

Alignments between 100 metres and 250 metres

Luxembourg – Verdun – Angoulême
Verdun – Nevers – Saarlat – Agen
Arlon SW – Verdun – Toulouse SE
Liege E – Verdun – Valence
Oudenaarde – Verdun – Belfort
Verdun – Epernay – Sacré Coeur, Paris
Le Havre S – Nôtre Dame Rouen – St Ouen, Rouen – Verdun
Metz – Verdun – Gisors
Ruins, Landonvillers – Verdun – Lisieux – St Lo
Donnersberg – Verdun – l'Epine – Nôtre Dame en Vaux – Châlons-sur-Marne – Le Mans
Verdun – Roubaix – Wervick
Colmar – Verdun – Douai
Chartres – Ablis – Verdun
Verdun – Koblenz SW – Koblenz NE
Auch – Trois Fontaines – Verdun
Verdun – Clairvaux – St Flour
Verdun – Ypres SE – Ypres NW

Alignments between 250 metres and 1000 metres

Verdun – Beziers – Elne
Verdun – Citeaux – Vienne – Arles
Verdun – Belley – Grenoble E
Verdun – Tournai – Menen
Verdun – Sedan W – Gent E
Ruins, Landonvillers – Verdun – Coutances
Verdun – Nangis – Nantes
Friebourg – Verdun – Vaucelles – Boulogne
Charlroi NE – Verdun – Sion
Strasbourg – Verdun – Laon
Verdun – Meaux – St Dennis
Verdun – Nôtre Dame Etampes – St Martin, Etampes
Verdun – Douai – Calais N
Metz – Verdun – St Remi, Reims – Bonne Mare
Savigny – St Germain en Laye – Meaux – Verdun
Quimper – Epernay – Verdun
Antwerp W – Mechelen – Verdun
Tournai – Antoing – Verdun
Lillebonne – Beauvais – Verdun
Carpentras – Vaison la Romain – Verdun
Bonn – Verdun – Montlucon
Granville – Evreux – Verdun
Verdun – St Denis – Dinan
Vezelay – Trois Fontaines – Verdun
Caudebec – Compiègne – Verdun
Noyon – Vauclair – Verdun
La Releque – St Malo – Verdun
Verdun – St Remi, Reims – Mortemer
Verdun – Langres – Senanque
Trier – Verdun – Liguge
Geneva – Morimond – Verdun
Fréjus – Morimond – Verdun

Appendix 6

Alignments within 100 metres

Ruins – Antoing – Tournai – Roubaix
Ruins – Tourcoing – Wervick SW – Ypres SE
Ruins – Autun – Toulouse, St Sernin
Ruins – <u>Nôtre Dame, Reims</u> – <u>Bonne Mare</u>
Ruins – Sacré Coeur – Dinan
Ruins – Metz – Sees – Versailles – Quimper
Ruins – Uzes – Nîmes
Sees – Metz – Ruins
Brest – St Malo NW – St Malo NE – Ruins
Caudebec – Fonenelle – Compiegne – Soissons – Ruins
Ruins – Cîteaux – Cluny
Arles – Ruins – Trier

Alignments between 100 metres and 250 metres

Ruins – Beziers – Perpignan
Ruins – Geneva – Annecy
Ruins – <u>Verdun</u> – Lisieux – St Lo
Ruins – Evreux – St Pol de Leon
Ruins – Epernay – Mont St Michel – St Brieuc
Ruins – Metz – Nôtre Dame, Paris
Ruins – Dourdan – <u>Chartres</u> – Vannes
Aix en Provence – Grenoble W – Ruins
Trier – Ruins – Avignon
Granville – Pontoise W – Pontoise E – Maubisson – Ruins
Woestine – Marchiennes – Ruins
Bruxelles W – Bruxelles S – Ruins

Alignments between 250 metres and 1000 metres

Ruins – Nevers – Périgueux SE
Ruins – Nancy – Montpellier
Ruins – St Jean Baptiste, Lyons – Maguelonne
Ruins – Sedan E – Douai – Béthune
Ruins – Cambrai NW – Caudry
Ruins – Soissons – Compiegne

Ruins – St Remi – Gisors – Bayeux
Ruins – Verdun -Senlis – Caen
<u>Donnersberg</u> – Ruins – Troyes
Ruins – Metz – L'Epine – Port Royal
Ruins – <u>Verdun</u> – Coutances
Ruins – St Flour – Rodez
Bonne – Ruins – Valance
Ruins – Meaux – St Denis
Kaiserslautern – Ruins – Orléans
Toul – Ruins – St Bertrand de Comminges
Ruins – Metz – l'Epine
Ruins – Metz – Chalons sur Marne
Ruins – Metz – l'Epine – Nôtre Dame en Vaux
Koblenz SW – Ruins – Albi
Alencon – Chalons – Metz – Ruins
Strasbourg – Ruins – Francheval – Orval
Lillebonne – Soissons – Ruins
Savigny – Metz – Ruins
Royaumont – <u>Verdun</u> – Ruins
Liège NW – Liège SE – Ruins
Ruins – Sedan W – Lens W
Ruins – Sedan W – Lens E
Rennes – Metz – Ruins
Ruins – Preuilly – la Blanche
Ruins – Orval – Lille
Tours – Trois Fontaines – Ruins
Sens – Trois Fontaines – Ruins
Ruins – Clairvaux – Limoges
Ruins – Clairvaux – Vezeley
Ruins – La Ferté – Nôtre Dame, Paris

Appendix 7

Alignments within 100 metres

Donnersberg – Virton – Rethel – <u>Bonne Mare</u>
Donnersberg – Orval – Fontenelle – Caudebec – Lillebonne – Le Havre N
Donnersberg – Arlon – Sedan W
Donnersberg – Rethel – <u>Bonne Mare</u> – Caen – St Lo
Donnersberg – <u>Verdun</u> – l'Epine – Nôtre Dame en Vaux – Chalons-sur-Marne – Le Mans
Donnersberg – Aix en Provence – Marseille
Donnersberg – Bruxelles W – Gent E
Ypres NW – Menen – Donnersberg
Liege NW – Liège SE – Donnersberg
Donnersberg – Pontoise E – Pontoise W

Alignments between 100 metres and 250 metres

Donnersberg – Kaiserslautern – Le Puy – <u>RLC</u>
Donnersberg – Oudenaarde – Waregem
Donnersberg – Antoing – Lille
Donnersberg – Bonn – Cologne
Donnersberg – Metz – Sens
Donnersberg – Belley – Arles
Donnersberg – Strasbourg – Basel
Donnersberg – St Denis – St Germain en Laye
Donnersberg – Pontoise W – Dinan
Donnersberg – Puy de Dôme – Auch
Donnersberg – Belfort – Geneva
Brugge NW – Brugge SE – Gent W – Bruxelles W – Bruxelles C – Bruxelles E – Donnersberg
Calais – Roubaix – Donnersberg
Noirmoitier – Nantes – Donnersberg
Donnersberg – Senlis – St Malo NE – St Malo NW

Alignments between 250 metres and 1000 metres

Donnersberg – <u>Ruins at Landonvillers</u> – Troyes
Donnersberg – Nôtre Dame Lyons – Nar bonne
Donnersberg – Besancon – Perpignan

Donnersberg – Melun – St M, Etampes
Donnersberg – Trier – Abbeville
Donnersberg – Virton – Rethel – <u>Bonne Mare</u> – Caen
Donnersberg – Rethel – Soissons
Donnersberg – Senlis – St Malo S – St Brieuc
Donnersberg – Nôtre Dame, Paris – Rennes
Donnersberg – Vezelay – Bordeaux
Donnersberg – Grenoble E – Chambéry – Senanque
Donnersberg – Strasbourg – Sion
Donnersberg – Laon – Nôtre Dame Rouen
Donnersberg – Gisors – Lisieux
Donnersberg – Treguier – St Pol de Leon
Donnersberg – Amiens – Dieppe
Donnersberg – Kaiserslautern – Acey – Dôle
Donnersberg – Mons SW – St Omer
Donnersberg – Vienne – Elne
Donnersberg – Compiège – Coutances
Donnersberg – Luxembourg – Bayeux
Donnersberg – Evreux – Avranches
Donnersberg – Versailles – Alençon
Donnersberg – Ablis – <u>Chartres</u>
Donnersberg – <u>Nôtre Dame Reims</u> – Savigny – Quimper
Donnersberg – Nancy – Fontenay
Donnersberg – Mons NE – Woestine
Donnersberg – St Remi, – Quimper
Donnersberg – Clairvaux – Angoulême
Donnersberg – Royaumont – St Michel
Donnersberg – St Remi – Savigny
Donnersberg – Lens E – Lens W

Appendix 8

Alignments within 100 metres

RLC – Pontoise E – St Germain en Laye – Beauvais NE
RLC – St Michel, Carcassonne – Troyes
RLC – Alet – Albi – Chartres – Bonne Mare
RLC – Poitiers SE – Poitiers NW
RLC – St Michel, Carcassonne – Châlons-sur-Marne
RLC – St Michel, Carcassonne – Nôtre Dame en Vaux
RLC – Preuilly – Caudry

Alignments between 100 metres and 250 metres

RLC – Lisieux – Le Havre NW
RLC – Castres – Etampes St M – Versailles – Maubisson
RLC – Castres – St Germain en Laye – Pontoise E – Beauvais SW
RLC – Tourcoing – Brugge E
RLC – Alet les Bains – Albi
RLC – Alet les Bains – Nôtre Dame Rouen
RLC – St Michel, Carcassonne – Vezelay
RLC – Marseille – Fréjus
RLC – Soissons – Oudenaarde
RLC – Metz – Trier
RLC – Carcassonne Cité – Liège E
RLC – Carcassonne Cité – Liège W
RLC – Toulouse SE – Toulouse NW
RLC – Noirmoitier – La Blanche
RLC – Castres – Port Royal
RLC – Vaucelles – Cambrai – Marchiennes

Alignments between 250 metres and 1000 metres

RLC – Alet les Bains– Nôtre Dame – Sacré Coeur – St Denis – Woestine
RLC – Meaux – Lille
RLC – Lens E – Ypres SE
RLC – Montlucon – Douai – Menen
RLC – Rodez – Bruxelles W – Antwerp C
RLC – Soissons – Valenciennes
RLC – Auxerre – Epernay – Reims

RLC – Carcassonne OC – Sedan W
RLC – St Etienne – Besançon
RLC – Lyons, St Jean Baptiste – Strasbourg
RLC – Béziers – Nimes
RLC – Béziers – Montpellier
RLC – Limoges – Tours
Elne – RLC – Auch
RLC – Ablis – Gisors
RLC – Avignon – Carpentras
RLC – Le Puy – Kaiserslautern – <u>Donnersberg</u>
RLC – Puy de Dome – Bruxelles C
RLC – Limoges – Sees
RLC – St Malo S – St Malo NW
RLC – Bordeaux SE – Bordeaux NW
RLC – Narbonne – Senanque
RLC – Albi – Mortemer
RLC – Nevers – Vauclair
RLC – Fontenay – Trois Fontaines
RLC – Alet les Bains – Castres – Etampes – Versailles
RLC – Wervick SW – Wervick NE
RLC – Grenoble S – Grenoble N
RLC– Carcassonne – l'Epine
RLC – Alet les Bains – Evreux
RLC – La Ferté – <u>St Quentin</u>

Appendix 9

Relative positions of the Plough, the pointers, Polaris and the pole of the ecliptic in 2500 BC

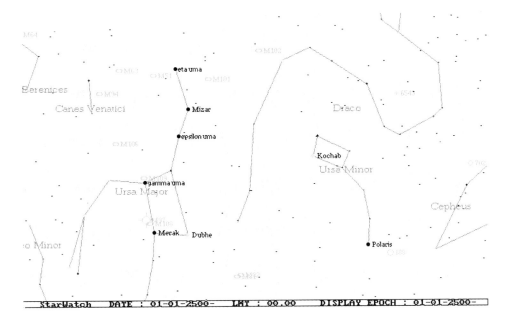

Appendix 10

Relative positions of the Plough, the pointers, Polaris and the pole of the ecliptic in 1500BC

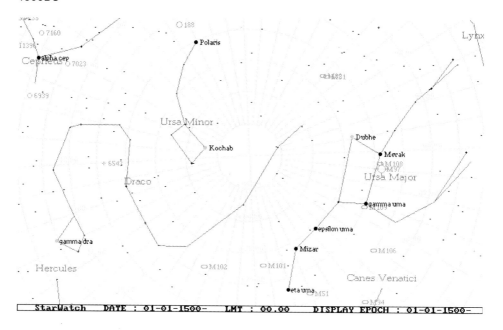

Appendix 11

Relative positions of the Plough, the pointers, Polaris and the pole of the ecliptic in 500BC

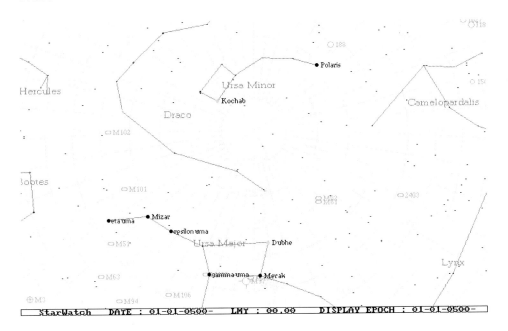

Appendix 12

Relative positions of the Plough, the pointers, Polaris and the pole of the ecliptic in 100AD

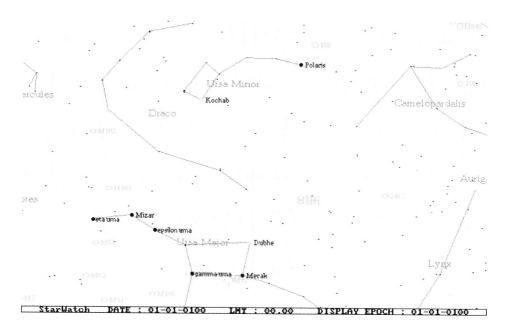

Appendix 13

Relative positions of the Plough, the pointers, Polaris and the pole of the ecliptic in
1100AD

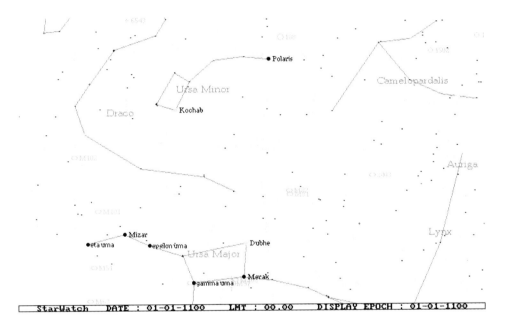

Appendix 14

Relative positions of the Plough, the pointers, Polaris and the pole of the ecliptic in 2000AD

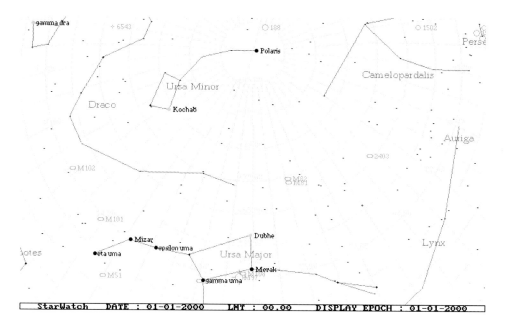

Appendix 15

Relative positions of the Plough, the pointers, Polaris and the pole of the ecliptic as they will be in the year 2500AD

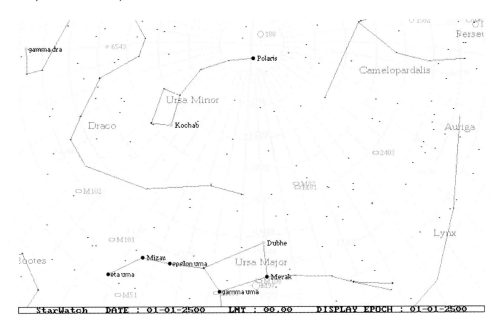

Appendix 16

1 Château at Aguts – Château at Monygay – RLC – Eglise at Serralongue – Al Castell, south of Serralongue

2 Château de Montségur – RLC – Château de Blanchefort – Château at Durban Corbières

3 Eglise at Unac – RLC – Caraguilhes Château, south of Fabrézan

4 Château immediately north west of Roquefixade – RLC – Château de Leucate, overlooking the bay

5 Château de Falgas north of Chalabre – ruins of chapel of St Michel east of Chalabre – RLC – Château Quéribus – Eglise at Espirade de l'Agley – Notre Dame de Salut, north of Perpignan

6 Château farm and Castillane Traouqués south of Montbrun Brocage – Courtade ruins east of le Mas d'Azil – Château at Léran – RLC – Peyrepetuse

7 Château at Montmaur – RLC – Château des Templiers – Ancient Priory/Monastery south of Marcevol and north of Vinca – Fort les Bains at Amelie-les-Bains Palalda

8 Château de Lalberède – RLC – Ermitage de St Antoine de Galamus north of St Paul de Fenouillet

9 Ruined château 'le castela' north of Bonnac – ruins of Château at Lagarde – Château ruins south east of Lagarde – RLC – The 'Palais' at Perpignan

10 Eglise at Lapenne – RLC – Ermitage de St Antoine de Galamus north of St Paul de Fenouillet

11 Château de Terride north of Mirepoix – RLC – Tour de Tremoine south of Maury – Chapelle St Julian

12 Château at Caudeval – RLC – Château Valmy south of Argeles-sur-Mer

13 Bruxelles Château at Montgisard – Château des Courtines south of Castelnaudary – Château at Monthaut – RLC – ruined Château des Maures north west of Candies de Fenouilledes

14 Château at Goudiès – RLC – the Basilique at Elne

15 Château at Castelnau Durban – RLC – Château d'Opoul north of Rivesaltes

16 Château at Puivert – RLC – ruined Château at Auriac east of Arques – Château de Segure north of Tuchan – ruins of Castelmaure south of St Jean de Barrou

17 The ruined Château at Junac – ruins of Château Renaud near Capulet – RLC – Château de Blanchefort – ruined Château at le Lac north of Sigean

18 The ruins of St Touret high in the mountains above Merons les Vals – Château at Quillan – RLC – Eglise at Pouzols Mivervois

19 The ruins of Château d'Able north of Belfort sur Rebenty – RLC – the ancient Abbey of Lagrasse – the fortress town of Pezenas

20 The 'Satuariode' at Nuria – RLC – Eglise ruins at Hautpoul south of Mazemet

21 Château at Nyer – the 'Eglise' at Castres
22 Château at Castelfranc west of Montredon – RLC – Chapelle St Etienne – Thuès-les-Bains
23 Château ruins at Montredon – RLC – ruins, refuge d'entre Valls
24 The Fort at Lafenasse – RLC – Chapelle de la Roque – high in the mountains south of Nyer
25 El Castell north of Planés – RLC – Carcassonne Cathedral
26 The ruined tower at Llagonne – RLC – Carcassonne Cathedral in the old city
27 El Castell south west of Porte Puymorens – RLC – Château de Cazillac north of Bousquet d'Orb
28 The ruined Château at El Castell north east of Llivia – RLC – Château Citou south of Lespinassiere
29 The tower ruins at Querol – RLC – Coustaussa – Château de Miramont south east of Trèbes – vestiges of the Roman camp high in the mountains in the Forêt Dominiale west of St Gervais sur Mare
30 Ruined Château de Donezan at Quérigat – RLC – Château de Fayet – Ancient Abbaye de Sylvanes
31 Château de Lacroix north of Lacroix Falgarde and south of Toulouse – Château de Roquefoulet east of Nailloux – RLC – Château Corbère de Dalt south of the village of Corbère
32 Château at St Rome – RLC – the fortified town of Bouleterère
33 Château at Fourquevaux – RLC – Le Castellas south of Ceret
34 Château at Prouille north east of Fanjeaux – Château des Maures next to the Roman ruins at Boulo – RLC – ruins of the 'Tour de Batere' north west of Arles sur Tech
35 Château ruins on the hill overlooking Auzat from the east – RLC – ruins of St Victor Ermitage high in the mountains, east of Fonjoncouse
36 Goudanes Château at Château Verdun – RLC – Château at Arques
37 Ermitage de St Pierre east of Les Cabannes – RLC – ruins of Château de Termes south west of Lagrasse
38 The ruins in La Meunière south east of Espezel – RLC – Fabrezan
39 The fortress village of le Castelet – RLC – Ruins on the hill at Montlaures north of Narbonne (Oppidum)
40 The Château at Foix – RLC – The ruined Château d'Aguilar ou Viala south east of Tuchan
41 'Le Fort' at Plaque south west of le mas d'Azil – RLC – the ruined Château de Padern
42 Château ruins just north of DUN – the Château at Chalabre – RLC – the ruined Château at Tautavel
43 Château at St Amadou – RLC – Perpignan Cathedral
44 'le Castela' north of Bonnac – RLC – Ruins east of Priory at Serrabonne
45 Château de la Reynerie at Villefranche de Lauragais – Château at Monthaut – RLC – Château at Montalba-le-Château
46 Eglise at Castelnaudary – RLC – Eglise at the fortress town of Arles sur Tech
47 The Monastery at St Papoul – RLC – Tour de Cas; the ruined tower north and on the other side of the valley from Serralongue
48 Château Ferrals east of St Papoul – Château at Bram – RLC – Abbaye St Michel de Cuxa
49 The Château at Magrin south west of St Paul Cap de Joux – the ancient fortress

town of Bram – RLC – Château at Prades – the ruined 'Tour Cabrens' south of Serralongue

50   Château at Montréal – RLC – Château Paracol south of Montitg les Bains

51   'L'Estanque ruins' west of le Pomerade – RLC – ruins of the 'Château Feodal' at Valmanya

52   Château at Villarzel du Razes – RLC – Tower de Goa south east of Sahorre

53   Château at Belloc – Abbaye at Alet-les-Bains – RLC – Château Thorrent west of Sahorre

54   Château at Serres – RLC – ruined tower at Llagonne

55   Cabrespine Villalier – RLC – ruins at Nentilla

56   Chapel Santa Maria de Belloc high in the mountains north of Ure – RLC – Chartreuse de Nonenque east of Versols

57   Château de Gissac south of Lapeyre – RLC – Eglise at Angoustrine

58   Château d'Usson overlooking 'Gorges de l'Aude' – RLC – Caustaussa – Château Belcastel east of Limoux

59   Abbaye at St Hilaire – RLC – le Castell ruins south of Prats-Balaguer

60   Eglise in the fortress town of Caunes Minervois – RLC – ruins south of Angustrine

61   Basilique at Realmont – Château Vennes – Abbaye at Alet-les-Bains – RLC – ruined 'tour' at Bastide

62   Eglise at Gaillac – Eglisein Limoux – RLC – Ancient Monastery at Corbiac, north west of Motitg les Bains – the ruins of Chapelle St Marguerite south of Prats de Mollo la Preste

63   RLC – Abbaye de Rieunette – Château north of Minervois

64   Eglise at la Pomarède – RLC – La Castell (ruins) and the ruined 'tour' together north of Montferrier

65   Château Bellevue la Forêt – Château St Sernin – The ruined 'tour' at Cour tête – RLC – Priory at Serrabonne

66   Château Barthelemy north of Castelnau Durban – the ruined Château at Bastide de Serou – The 'tour' at Fa – RLC

67   Château at Monastruc la Conseillère – Fanjeaux – RLC – Castel Sabordas south of Caudiès de Fenouilledes

68   Cathedral at Toulouse – Château at St Rome – RLC – ruined Château at le Vivier

69   The 'tour' at Fa – RLC – Fort des Salses north of Salses-le-Château

70   Château at Couiza – RLC – ruined 'Tours de Cours' north west of Tourinya

71   Ruins of Château Calames south west of Bedeilhac – ruins of Castel d'Amont at Belesta – RLC

72   Tour de Monorgued east of Saurat – Château north of Montferrier – RLC

73   RLC – ruins of Château at Villerouges Termenes – ruined 'Tour Barberousse' overlooking the harbour at Gruissan

74   RLC – ruins of Château de Dufort south west of Lagrasse – ancient Abbaye de Fontfroid south west of Narbonne

75   RLC – Château de Terral north of Narbonne – Château Anmalas west of Montpellier

76   RLC – le Castellas, the ruined Château east-south-east of Narbonne – Château Celeyran east of Coirsan – 'Fou Gallo Romaine' – the ancient Cathedral of St Pierre de Maguelonne

77   RLC – Eglise at St Thibery – Château de la Mogere east of Montpellier

78   RLC – Abbaye fr Valmagne – Cathedral at Montpellier

79   RLC – Cathedral at Beziers – Château at Castries

80 RLC   Abbaye de Fontcalvy   Roman ruins west of Montpellier
81 RLC – Cathedral at Narbonne – Vestiges du Temple de Venus
82 RLC – Château Cassan north of Pouzolles – Château Cignac west of Montpellier
83 RLC – Château St Martin south of Château Cassan -Château de Vivioures north of Montpellier
84 RLC – Château Villarzel du Razes – Ancient Abbaye de Villelongue – Château de Gua south of Lescout
85 ruins of 'Tour de Lansac' south of Maury – ruins of Castel d'Ultrera which accompanies the Notre Dame de Château Ermitage in the mountains south east of Sorede – ruins of the 'Tour de Carriog'
86 RLC – 'Tr Rnée' on Mont Redon north west of Montpellier – ruined Château de Montlaur north of Castries
87 RLC – Château de Caladroy west of Perpignan – 'Tour' Madeloc in the mountains west of Banyuls sur Mer
88 RLC – The ruins 'Al Castillas' south of Maury – Fort St Elme west of Port Vendres
89 RLC – la Sybille – Chapelle St Sebastian near Fourques
90 RLC – ancient Château north of Argeles sur Mer – Fort Carre overlooking the sea
91 RLC – Château de Roquevidal – Eglise at Montricoux
92 RLC – Abbaye at Alet-les-Bains – Château at le Pit Versailles south of Montolieu – Cathedral at Albi
93 Château Berthier at Pinsiguel south of Toulouse – RLC – Château at Castelnou south west of Perpignan
94 The 'feodal' Château at Lagarde – Château at Festes St André – RLC
95 RLC – Château Cuxous south of Maury Tour de l'Etoile, close to the Fort Carré Château des Templiers on the south coast of Collioures – Fort Béar further down the coast
96 RLC – Chateau du Réart south of Perpignan – Castel Béar east of Banyuls sur Met

N.B. All of these alignments fall within 250 metres of the Château at Rennes-le-Château.

Bibliography

Abelard & St Bernard; A Victor Murray: Manchester University Press

The Age of Constantine the Great; Jacob Burckhardt translated by Moses Hadas; University of California Press; 1983

Analysis des Conciles – Generaux et particuliers; R P Charles Louis Richard; Tome Second; Paris 1772

The Ancient Secret; Flavia Anderson;Thorsons Publishing Group; 1987

L'Anjou de 1109 à 1151; Joseph Chartrou; Les Presses Universitaires de France

Aus der Frühzeit des Weierhofs; von Heiner Baab; Donnersberg J B; 1983

The Ancient Wisdom; Geoffrey Ashe; Macmillan London Limited;1977

Bernard – Saint, Abbot of Clairvaux; A biography (482.c.16)

Les Cahiers de Rennes-le-Château, nos 3,4,5/6; Cl Boumendil, Belisane 1984 -1986

Cathédrales de France; Zoé Oldenburg; Librarie Hachette 1972

The Cathedral Nôtre Dame de Rouen; A M Carmerut; Lanfry

La Cathédrale de Verdun; official history and guide available from the Cathedral

Recent Crusade historiography; James A Brundage; The Catholic Historical Review, Vol XLIX Jan 1964

Cambridge Star Atlas 2000: Wil Trinion; Cambridge University Press

Celtic Gods – Celtic Goddesses; R J Stewart: Blandford 1990

Chartres, Petite Histoire d'une Vieille Cité; André Blondel; Chartres 1906

Chartres Cathedral; Malcolm Miller, Sonia Holliday and Laura Lushington; Pitkin Pictorials; 1985/1992

Châteaux du Valais; André Donnet at Louis Blondel; Martigny, Editions Pillet;1982

Chronologie de l'Histoire de Cîteaux; Frère Marcel LEBEAU

A concise history of the Cistercian Order; A Cistercian Monk: Thomas Richardson & Son, London, The Abbey of Mount St Bernard, Loughborough, 1852

De la Consideration; Saint Bernard, Traduction de Pierre Dalloz suivie d'un essai sur l'architecture de S. Bernard: Les Editions de Cerf, 29 boulevard Latour-Mauberg, Paris; 1986.

The Crusades, Holy War and Canon Law; James A Brundage; Variorum; 1991

Le Dessein de l'Histoire de Reims; M Nicolas Bergier; Reims; 1785

Dictionary of the Bible; edited by James Hastings; T & T Clarke, Edinburgh; 1902

The Dimensions of Paradise; John Michell; Thames & Hudson Ltd, London: 1988

Der Donnersberg; von H Joseph Engels; Franz Steiner Verlag GmbH; Weisbaden; 1976

Der Donnersberg bis zum Frieden von Rijwijk; Der Donnersberg; von Renate Engels; Franz Steiner Verlag GmbH; Weisbaden; 1981

The Devil's Brood – The Angevin family; Alfred Duggan; Transworld Publishers

Encyclopedia Britannica Volume XXVI

The Fall of the Roman Empire; Michael Grant; Macmillan Punlishing Company; 1990

The First Crusade, The Chronicle of Fulcher of Chartres and other source materials; Edited and with an introduction by Edward Peters: University of Philadelphia Press, 1971

From Lutetia to Paris; Philippe Velay; Caisse Nationale des monuments historiques et des sites

From Ritual to Romance; Jessie L Weston; Princeton University Press; reprinted 1993

Die gallo-römischen Villen bei Kurzel in Lothringen;von T Welter und H E Heppe; Dahr Buchder Gesellschaft für Lothringische Geschichte und Allertumskunskunde; Metz; 1906

Gematria, A preliminary investigation of the Cabala; Bligh Bond & Lea: Chameleon Press

Geneset; David Wood & Ian Campbell; Bellevue Books; 1994

GenIsis; David Wood; The Baton Press, Tunbridge Wells: 1985

The Geography; Claudius Ptolemy translated & edited by Edward Luther Stevenson; Dover Publications; 1991

The Gnostic Gospels; Elaine Pagels;Vintage Books, Random House Inc, New York; 1979

The Gnostic Scriptures; Bentley Layton; Doubleday & Co. Inc., Garden City, New York; 1987

Gothic Cathedrals and Sacred Geometry; Alec Tiranti

A guide to Glastonbury's Temple of the Stars; K E Maltwood; 1950

A guide to the Cistercian Abbey of Fontain Guérard; The Salvation Army, Chateau de Radepont, 27380 Fleury sur Andalle, Eure, France.

Histoire du Château de Radepont et du Abbaye de Fontain Guerard; L Fallue; l'Académie de

Rouen; 1850

Histoire de la Basilique la Maitresse de Saint-Quentin; St Quentin

Histoire de la Cité des Carnutes; M Michel-Jean-François Ozeray; Chartres; 1834

Hoistoire de la Guerre Sainte; Guillaume de Tyr (contemporaneous) translated into Franch by Gabriel du Preau in 1573

Histoire de la Ville, Cité et Université de Reims; R P Dom Guillaume Marlot; Reims; 1843

L'Histoire de l'Ordre des Templiers et les Croisades; Gérard Surbanesco:

l'Histoire de Rennes le Château antérieure à 1789; Jean Fourie; Jean Bardou, Esperaza; 1984

Histoire des Comtes de Champagne; Robert Martin le Pelletier

Histoire des Conciles; Charles Joseph Hefele; Letouzey et Ané, Paris; 1912

Histoire des Ducs et des Comtes de Champagne; H D Arbois de Subainville

Histoire de Tonnerre; P Bailly; 1884

Histoire de Tonnerre; A Challe; Auxerre; 1875

Histoire de Verdun; M l'Abbé Clouët; Verdun; 1867

A History of the Crusades, Volume II; Steven Runciman; Cambridge University Press; 1952

The History of the Franks; Gregory of Tours translated by Lewis Thorpe; Penguin Classics; 1974

The History of the Knights Templar; Charles G Addison; Longman, Brown, Green and Longmans; 1842

The History of the Primitive Church; Lebreton, Zeiller, Fliche & Martin, translated by E C Mesenger: Burns Oats & Washbourne.

The Holy Bible; C Goodcliffe & Neale

The Holy Blood and the Holy Grail; Michael Bagient, Richard Leigh & Henry Lincoln: Transworld Publishers Ltd, 1983

The Holy Place; Henry Lincoln; Jonathan Cape, London; 1991

Kaupt ums Königtum 1298 am Hasenbühl bei Göllheim; von Klaus Radenheimer; Donnersberg J B; 1982

Die Kelten auf dem Donnerberg; von Ronald Heynowski; Donnersberg J B; 1979

Der Ludwigsturm auf dem Donnersberg; von Erich Nessel; Donnersberg, Jarbuch; 1981

The Life of Stephen Harding, Abbot of Cîteaux; J D Dalgairns

Les Moines Blancs – Histoire de l'Ordre de Cîteaux; Marcel Pacaut; Fayard

Monastic Republics, Cities and Citadels, Mont St Michel.

The Mysteries of Chartres Cathedral; Louis Charpentier; Robert Laffont/Thorsons; 1972

Les Mystères Templiers; Louis Charpentier; Robert Laffont, Paris; 1967

Mystiques Cisterciens;Robert Thomas; O E I L Paris;1984

Nene Ausgrabungen am Schlackenwall auf dem Donnersberg; Donnersberg J B 1980

The New Atlas of the Universe; Patrick Moore; Michell Beazley

Norton's 2000 Star Atlas and reference handbook; edited by Ian Ridpath; Longman 1989

Nôtre Dame de Paris; Jacques Perrier; Maurice de Sully; 1992

Oeuvres de St Bernard; traduites par M Armand Ravelet précédées de la Vie de Saint Bernard par Le T R P de Ratisbonne: Victor Palmé Paris

Origen and the Life of the Stars; Alan Scott; Clarendon Press, Oxford; 1991

The Origin & Development of the Christian Church in Gaul during the first six centuries of the Christian Era; T Scott Holmes DD: Macmillan and Co Ltd., London, 1911

Parzival; Wolfram von Eschenbach; translated by A.T. Hatto; Penguin books, 1980

The Pelican History of Medieval Europe; Maurice Keen: Penguin Books; 1969

Die Pfalz unter den Römern; Die Götterverehrung; Dr Friedrich Sprater

Places of Power; Paul Devereux; Blandford 1990

Poussin Paintings; Christopher Wright; Harlequin Books Ltd; 1985

The Quest for the Holy Grail; Jessie L Weston; 1913, reprinted by The Bantom Press, Nelson St, Largs, Scotland; 1990

Refuge of the Apocalypse; Elizabeth Van Buren; C W Daniel Co Ltd, Saffron Walden; 1986

The Refutation of all Heresies; Hippolytus – The Ante Nicene Fathers

Reims Cathedral; Maurice Eschapasse

Rennes-le-Château; Lionel and Patricia Fanthorpe; Bellevue Books, 1991

Rheims Cathedral; P Demouy; Editions la Goulette; Reims

Der Ringwall auf dem Dennersberg; von Helmut Häßel; Donnersberg J B; 1978

Das Römerjuliläum zu Bonn au Rhein; Verlag Franz Schmitt Sieburg

Rouen; description historique de l'Eglise de Saint-Ouen

Saint Bernard; Ivan Gobry: La Table Ronde, Paris 1990

The Secret Teachings of all Ages; Manly P Hall; The Philosophical Research Society, Los Angeles; 1988

The Secret Tradition in Arthurian legend; Gareth Knight; The Aquarian Press; 1983

Serpent in the Sky; John Anthony West; Harper & Row; 1989

The Seven Wonders of the Ancient World; Peter Clayton & Martin Price; Routledge 1988

The Sign and the Seal; Graham Hancock; William Heinemann Ltd, London;1992

Stonehenge Decoded; Gerald S Hawkins; Fontana 1970

The Story of the Grail; Chrétien de Troyes translated by R W Linker; University of California Press

The Sword and the Grail; Andrew Sinclair; Crown Publishers Inc., New York; 1992

The Temple of the Stars; Brinsley le Poer Trench; Fontana; 1973

The Times Atlas of the World; Times Books

Un Pauvre Chevalier du Christ, Hugues de Pagan, fondateur de l'order du Temple (1070-1136); R P Dom Marie

Val d'Oise, abbayes cisterciennes no.34; Conseil Général du Val d'Oise;1990

La Vie de Saint Bernard; Monsieur de Villefort, le Duc de Bourgogne: Jean de Nully, Paris;1704

Vie de Saint Bernard, Abbé de Clairvaux; l'Abbé E Vacandard: Paris, 1895

Xanthus, Travels of discovery in Turkey; Enid Slatter; The Rubicon Press; 1994

Index